EMPTY

EMPTY

A MEMOIR

SUSAN BURTON

RANDOM HOUSE

NEW YORK

This memoir reflects the author's life faithfully rendered to the best of her ability.
Some names and identifying details have been changed to protect the privacy of others.

Published in the United States by Random House, an imprint and
division of Penguin Random House LLC, New York.

RANDOM HOUSE and the HOUSE colophon are registered trademarks of
Penguin Random House LLC.

LIBRARY OF CONGRESS CATALOGING-IN-PUBLICATION DATA
Names: Burton, Susan, author.
Title: Empty: a memoir / Susan Burton.
Description: First edition. | New York: Random House, [2020] |
Identifiers: LCCN 2019037475 (print) | LCCN 2019037476 (ebook) |
ISBN 9780812992847 (hardcover) | ISBN 9780679644040 (ebook)
Subjects: LCSH: Burton, Susan—Health. | Eating disorders—Patients—
United States—Biography. | Women journalists—United States—Biography. |
Eating disorders in women—United States. | Eating disorders—
Patients—Family relationships—United States.
Classification: LCC RC552.E18 B868 2020 (print) | LCC RC552.E18 (ebook) |
DDC 616.85/26002 [B]—dc23
LC record available at https://lccn.loc.gov/2019037475
LC ebook record available at https://lccn.loc.gov/2019037476

Printed in the United States of America on acid-free paper

randomhousebooks.com

2 4 6 8 9 7 5 3 1

First Edition

Book design by Debbie Glasserman
Jacket art: Lee Price

FOR MIKE, WHO KNOWS I COULD NEVER QUARANTINE THE PAST

CONTENTS

PROLOGUE

1991

August, a campsite in the Catskills. Dark, after dinner, tents pitched, bear bags hung. Ten freshmen and two upperclassmen in a circle around a fire pit. All of us dirty, after four days on this wilderness orientation trip, most of us bonded. Slips of paper are passed out and we are given the instruction, "Write down what scares you about going to Yale." The slips are so small there is room for maybe one sentence. No names; the exercise is anonymous. I rest my slip on a rock and try not to press too hard with a ballpoint pen. We put our sentences in a baseball hat and then pass the hat around. "You can't get your own fear," a counselor says, and when one boy picks his own slip he returns it to the hat. When the hat comes to me, I reach in, pull out a slip, unfold it, and am startled by the gravity of the words I read; and then I am selfishly anxious because it will be hard to find the right tone for this sentence, hard to deliver it.

   The recitations begin. The girl from North Carolina reads my fear, which is somehow diminished by her mild accent: "I am scared that I will not have good friends." We discuss this fear but the discussion does not touch me, because while this is not a false fear it is a lesser one. But what level of thing is okay to say? Because then it is my turn and I read the fear I drew: "I am scared that I will go crazy."

There is a silence. I think I know whose fear this is. Nathan is pale even after all these days of sun. He wants to have deep talks. He is sensitive and perceptive and I am scared of what he has seen in me. The other day on the trail we ran into another orientation group. There were cries of delight and introductions, but for some reason I just couldn't do it, couldn't go forth and present myself to a whole new pack of freshmen. I climbed to the top of a high rock and started eating gorp very quickly, a lot of gorp. It was the only time on this trip I'd been anything but totally controlled and relentlessly friendly. Later, when I was helping Nathan with a tent, he brought up the encounter. "Yeah, I just couldn't deal," I said. "Yes, I noticed," he said, and looked at me hard, like he'd seen into me, he'd seen everything. And that was it. I'd been nice to Nathan before, but I shut him out then.

One of the counselors speaks first, mentioning the student-run crisis hotline and therapy at the university health service. I can't decide if Nathan is really scared of going crazy or if this is just a part he plays. I know this sounds callous. But when it comes to my own problems, I am reluctant to draw attention. My impulse is not to say.

I keep his slip of paper. I keep everything from this trip, like the sheet where people write nice things about you. On mine it says things like "Beautiful energy" and "You could be named Joy." But months later when I look at the sheet in my dorm room, those seem like descriptions of another girl, one, even then, I'd had to try really hard to be.

You can't get your own fear. But I did get mine, didn't I. I pulled my own fear out of the hat, and I delivered my own sentence.

IT'S BAD RIGHT AWAY. Oh, not the first few nights, of pizza and pitchers and jukeboxes; of *I have found my people* joy in new friends; of smoking bud in the courtyard and zoning out in front of fractal screen savers in the bedroom and talking about our parents' divorces at two A.M. But one morning I just break. I need to do it the way I do it, hovering, shoving, all alone. I leave my room and go across the street to Wall Food and buy a pint of Heath Bar Crunch and then walk down the sidewalk as if someone is tailing me: *must go fast, must go fast, must go fast,* but also be normal. I have no idea where I can go to eat this. It's a beautiful fall Saturday morning, the sky a coastal New England blue; a perfect morning, which I could not inhabit if I tried; a perfect morning, which I am ruining. Have already ruined, because being on the way to doing this is tantamount to having done it. A block down there's a parking lot, almost empty except for a dumpster—*there*—and I go behind the dumpster and eat the pint of ice cream with a spoon I've taken from our room. The spoon belongs to one of my roommates, and it has a thin silver handle with flowers. The ice cream is deep-frozen, and when I drive into it, the spoon's handle bends. When I finish the pint, I throw the carton in the dumpster (so convenient!) and then I look at the bent spoon, and I throw that away, too. Partly because it's bent, but partly because I feel like I've desecrated it. And then as soon as I've tossed these things in the trash, I start walking again as if I have never stopped, as if I had been going in this direction all along. I feel exhausted relief but also disgust, as I continue under this bright sky, because is this where I will be? Crouching behind dumpsters while everyone is boarding buses for the Yale Bowl? Foraging while everyone else is tailgating? But these are still just questions; I haven't yet accepted this as my certain end.

IT'S NOT THE LAST of my roommates' spoons that I'll throw away. Whenever I do it, I wonder if this is a piece from the family's old silverware, a spoon from the parents' first set.

Most of the time I get a plastic spoon with the pint. The guy behind the counter at Wall Food is from Haiti and has a space between his two front teeth. "Do you want a spoon?" he always says, ready to open the drawer beneath his register, where the utensils are kept. Sometimes I pause before answering, as if I have to think about it. Sometimes I start to say no but then change to yes, as if I'm so glad he's suggested it because I would have forgotten. Sometimes I say I need three spoons, as if I am about to go share the ice cream with others, even if it's an improbable time for ice cream, ten-thirty A.M.

What I do here at college scares me more than what I did at home in Boulder. Away from my own kitchen, I thought, the impulse to eat like this would fade. Instead, I've just found other places to do it. Soon I am spending about forty dollars every few days on food. This is money I should not be spending. I have a check from my grandfather for two thousand dollars, and I need it to cover the whole first semester, books, everything.

I thought my life had been reduced to this already, but it hadn't; it has never been like this.

I HAD BINGE-EATING DISORDER, but back then I couldn't have told you that. When I grew up, in the 1980s, binge-eating disorder wasn't on the list of things you could have. I knew anorexia; I knew bulimia. But there were no after-school specials or first-person magazine stories about binge eating, which wasn't recognized as a formal eating disorder diagnosis until 2013. Binge eating is not just overeating. It's eating in a way that feels involuntary and out of control. It's eating tons of food far past the point when you are full—"full," an irrelevant word. A baby word for people who don't know the first thing about this. (That's part of it, too, the anger; the fury at those who are normal, at those who have no fucking idea, at those who can't understand.) Binge eating is eating to the point where you feel sick. It's eating past that point. It's doing it first thing in the morning and then hating yourself and swearing to "be good" and then, hours later, doing it again. And it's eating without purging—eating without vomiting or taking a laxative.

The way it began for me is not unusual. I was anorexic first, and then I started bingeing. Later I went back to anorexia. Many people with eating disorders cycle through more than one of them. For a long time it was easier for me to admit to the anorexia than to the bingeing, which tells you something about both me and the hierarchy of eating disorders. The stigma of binge-eating disorder starts with its inelegant name. "Anorexia" and "bulimia" are both derived from ancient Greek: loss of appetite; ox-like hunger. "Binge-eating disorder" is copy in a magazine ad showing a sad, kneeling woman surrounded by food wrappers. But there is nothing JV about BED. It's not eating disorder–lite. It's also called compulsive eating, a name I like better, because it captures the defining qualities of this illness: urgent, gripping, and hard to kick.

Because BED was only recently recognized as a formal diagnosis, there's less research on it than on anorexia or bulimia. Statistics are also hard to come by, not just for BED but for eating disorders in general, which are less likely to be included in epidemiological studies than illnesses like anxiety, depression, or substance-use disorders, even though their impact can be equally devastating. What does seem clear is that BED is more prevalent than anorexia and bulimia, but just how much more prevalent is hard to say.

Anorexia and bulimia have more recognizable symptoms than BED, which is often overlooked as a diagnosis. Information may not be offered by the patient: Eating disorders are characterized by secrecy. Even after I stopped bingeing, I told no one about it. Not my husband, not a therapist, not anyone. Anorexia was impossible to hide—it was a demand to be seen. But I didn't talk about anorexia, either. I was ashamed that eating disorders had figured so prominently in my past and, as I entered my forties, could not admit, even to myself, that they continued to define my present.

The fact that I was ashamed of my own story was among the reasons I finally decided to tell it. Eating disorders are primarily women's illnesses and exist within a patriarchal culture that diminishes female suffering. But even among women, these illnesses are regarded uneasily. When a woman writes about her eating disorder, she might alert the reader that she knows that this has been said before or that this subject is boring. She might enfold her own experience in theory and history. Both approaches are legitimate: *This is boring* speaks to the risk of romanticizing anorexia in particular. Context can be illuminating. But it can also be a defense against anticipated criticism that an eating disorder story is barely worth telling.

I, too, began this project intending to situate my story in a larger context. I set out to write a book that would intertwine the story of my adolescence with a cultural history of teenage girlhood. But when I wrote the first draft, my eating disorders took over the narrative. They'd once taken over my life and now they were taking over the story I was trying to tell about my life. I was embarrassed; I was paralyzed. For years I kept trying to write the book I'd committed to, the one that was about both the history of adolescence and my own experience of it.

In many ways my adolescence was typical. Prototypical, even. I was an awkward middle-schooler who transformed herself with the help of *Seventeen* magazine. I was a teenage girl in a public high school at the end of the twentieth century, at the edge of the Great Plains. I stood in bleachers at Friday night football games. I read Sylvia Plath and wrote furiously in my journal. I took the SAT and drank wine coolers. I learned to smoke cigarettes on a weekday afternoon in a wood-paneled car. I learned to drive in the middle of the night in the middle of Utah. I learned American history from the Native American to the Vietnam War, which was where the textbook stopped. I signed the notes I passed in class *Love, Susan*.

I tried to be the iconic teenage girl. But I was also a troubled one, and the dark part of my adolescence became its heart. My eating disorder never completely relinquished its claim on me.

For years after my adolescence ended, I remained preoccupied with food. "Preoccupied" is too mild, but it was the word I used in my head. My days were structured around food. If I ate the right thing at the right time, I was fine, but if I didn't, I wasn't, and most of the time I wasn't, because most of the time I didn't. When, on the eve of my forty-first birthday, I made the resolution I'd made on every birthday since I was seventeen—to "fix my eating"—I was suddenly startled by the incantation. I was a grown woman still thinking her teenage thoughts. "Fix my eating" didn't mean "get help" or "recover." To me it meant "eat perfectly."

I called a psychiatrist who specialized in eating disorders. On the phone I stammered out what background I could. "Are you experiencing symptoms now?" she said. "Symptoms" was a word I had never applied. In one way, "symptoms" made my problem seem simpler: Symptoms could be treated. But my problem, as I saw it, was myself. Could selfhood be addressed as a collection of symptoms?

I went to see the psychiatrist. But I found that I could barely get my story out. I'd held this secret so hard. It went against everything in me, to speak it aloud. There was a risk of cheapening it by giving it away. This was something that had happened to me totally alone. It had been the most solitary part of my experience.

The psychiatrist said she could treat me with CBT, cognitive behavioral therapy. She gave me an appointment slot, but I left the office knowing I would cancel. I didn't think I could change my behavior until I understood my story, and I didn't think I could do that with her.

That was the morning I realized that the story of my adolescent eating disorders was the one I needed, and wanted, to tell and that in order to do so I would need to own up to the real secret, which was that these issues had never really gone away. I wanted to insist on my distance from the eating disorders, but the past I was writing about was part of my present.

I have an out-of-print book called *Growing Up Female*. A paperback the pastel colors of a tampon box. The author, a literary critic named Barbara White, observes that authors of coming-of-age stories often present "a weak adolescent self to furnish a happy contrast with the transcendent mature writing self." The mature writing self offers perspective and context the adolescent self cannot. But the transcendent mature writing self would be a false pose for me. "Mature" is a demographic fact; "writing" is implicit; but "transcendent"?

While I wanted to transcend the problems that had shaped my

adolescence and continued to plague me, I wasn't writing this story in order to do that. I was writing this story because any other story about my adolescence felt false. Maybe this is what happens with shame—the buried thing insists that it is the most important. The writer Sarah Manguso captures this feeling in her book *300 Arguments*: "You might as well start by confessing your deepest shame. Anything else would just be exposition." That's what I felt when I wasn't writing about the eating disorders—lots of blah blah, lots of backstory, lots of exposition.

Also in that book, Manguso says, "We hide in plain sight, in our bodies." Writing about my eating disorders was a way of revealing what was hidden but also remaining so. As long as I was still writing, I was still alone with my experience, still in possession of my secret. And that's where I would stay until I got to the end, until I had laid it all out and offered myself up, in plain sight, both as I am now and as I was then.

ANOTHER SPARKLING FALL DAY in New Haven. Another day I wreck. Another day I'm walking out of Commons after lunch, licking a soft-serve ice cream as I cross Beinecke Plaza. Beinecke, the rare-books library made of thin marble that lets in just the right amount of light. One of the Beinecke sons was in my father's class; everyone called him "Books"—Books Beinecke, J. Press, my father, the Fence Club, heeling the *Daily,* Kingman Brewster, no women here then; and I often feel adrift, so much at Yale is about tradition, and it's crazy that it's 1991 and we are *still* among the first generation of women here. But this train of thought does not spark meaningful consideration of elitism, feminism, or power; I cannot examine anything of substance, because I am so ground down by what I am doing, ground down by finishing the ice-cream cone and walking up Broadway to David's Cookies, where I buy two muffins, raisin bran and blueberry, and then scuttle with them, like the twitching creature I am, to Machine City, the dirty-but-sterile fluorescent-lit space beneath the library. And I have French in fifteen minutes, but

I'm going to eat the muffins instead of going to class even though we have a quiz today and if I don't go I will get a zero. And I open the bag, and I eat the muffins, reading *The Yale Herald* while I'm doing it. And then I finish and there's a sag of nothingness and then panic because I need to remain in the hand-to-mouth, automated place, so I get up and go to the vending machines and buy a candy bar. It drops into a trough and I stick my hand into a slot to get it. This gesture is unfamiliar; I have never bought much from vending machines. In fact, this is the first candy bar I have ever bought in my life and it is a milestone for me, me of Boulder and soy milk and oat bran and pesticide-free. I hold the candy bar curiously, turning it upside down to see if there is nutritional information on the wrapper, then take it back to my table. But my pleasure is diminishing: I eat the candy bar like medicine, like a nurse is standing over me and making sure I finish. As soon as I do, I feel sick. And now that I've stopped eating, self-loathing flows in: the tank filling with premium hate, until the nozzle handle clicks. And even though technically I could still make it to French, now I know for sure I won't go, because instead I am going to solve everything. I am going to stay in the library and write in my journal and fix this, once and for all, examine the origins of this issue and make resolutions for however long it takes.

I sit in Machine City until the smoking bothers me. Then I pick up my things and move to a wood-paneled room upstairs. I get out my journal and in the soft afternoon light have started to write when I see Philippe from French. He whispers, "Suzanne, where were you?" and I shrug and whisper, "I just couldn't deal," and he whispers, "We didn't take the quiz," and then I am overjoyed, not only because I don't have a zero but because clearly I was meant to use this time to fix everything.

And for the next ten minutes I am buoyed up, living in this hour I will never forget, the hour in which I will put this behind me. This is over, *finis, jamais, ne rien;* never, never, never again.

This is all part of the pattern. After each episode I scrawl, berating myself, but after a couple of pages the nutty stream gives way. I distance myself from the experience. I begin to think rationally. I calm and resolve to begin again. I write determinedly positive sentences. But today when I get to the rational-thinking stage, I can't look brightly ahead. Because—I mean, come on. The reality is that I have spent *two whole years* making resolutions to quit ("quit," that is the word I always use) and I am still doing this.

And meanwhile I am wasting time, so much time.

But it's okay. Because today is really, really it. And if I change today, everything, this afternoon, last night, the past two years, everything, has been worth it. So I write a typeface-neat resolution and sign it. I devise a schedule for the following day. I open my backpack and take out *Hedda Gabler.* I read the introduction by the critic who puts the play in context and record in my notebook a hopeful quote from a letter of Ibsen's. "I am greatly occupied with the preparations for my new work. Sit tight at my desk the whole day. Go out only towards evening. I dream and remember and write."

And the next day I do that. I do everything right.

And by the day after that I am back to doing everything wrong again.

TWO WHOLE YEARS. I'M not poking fun at my young self with her distorted sense of time. Two years (and it would be still more) is a significant amount of one's adolescence, and it saddens me to see this number, not least because here I am, almost thirty years on, still *examining the origins of this issue,* still trying to *fix my eating.*

PART 1

1

DIET

CULTURAL HISTORIES OF EATING disorders start with the saints. Personal histories start with first diets.

"Diet" is a strange word, one that describes both a deviation from the norm and the norm itself: the foods that make up a day, a week, a lifetime.

From the beginning, my diet was a big part of my story, even the one others told about me. "All babies like rice cereal," my mother will say. "But you didn't."

In the high chair, I would tighten my lips and turn away.

When I was two, I started preschool. At the first parent–teacher conference, they told my mother, "Susan never eats snack."

The information didn't surprise her. I refused so many foods that she'd come up with novel ways to get them into me. In the morning I would sit at the kitchen table and she would crack an egg into a sippy cup and mix in cranberry juice. When she set the cup before me, I'd peer down the hole at the thick drink. Beside the cup would be a colored vitamin, its surface rough like construction paper. My mother would be emptying the dishwasher, the radio going. Occasionally the voice of my father, the news director of a local station, would come through the speaker: *This is W-O-O-D WOOD Radio, and I'm Bob Burton.* I was so small that the white Tulip chair was big around me, like a throne. I'd sneak the vitamin under the seat cushion—grainy beneath there, with crumbs and small tan-foam flecks—and ignore the drink.

Recalling encounters with foods I disliked as a small child raises an old alarm in me. A sip of a soda at the zoo one afternoon, the prickling shock of the bubbles. It would be more than a decade before I would try something fizzy again. Melba toast at a white-tablecloth restaurant in Chicago. The next day, I vomited. The bright yellow worm of mustard on a hot dog at a public beach. The jagged chopped nuts on a hot fudge sundae, even though I'd asked for it plain. In any choice about food, I always preferred plain.

I went through primary school never eating a salad or a single bite of fruit. And it wasn't just healthy foods I disliked. It was basic kid things like sugar cereal and potato chips. I couldn't tolerate flavors in drinks. The only ones I liked were milk and water. No Coke, no apple cider, no orange juice. No Kool-Aid, no Capri Sun, no etc., etc., etc.

I was always steeling myself for things like sleepovers and school trips where you went overnight to nature camp—not because I dreaded being away from home, but because of what food might be served to me elsewhere.

But as embarrassing as it was to overhear someone alerting the mother of the birthday girl that "Susan doesn't like pizza" or to go up to a vendor and order a "Plain sno-cone; yes, just the ice," I never wavered, even when I knew my behavior had been registered as rude or strange. I never once even pretended to take a bite of red licorice or a sip of the shamrock shake. I could never, would never, let these things in.

The term "picky eater" didn't apply to me. Picky eaters had to be reminded to pay attention to their plates. But I never forgot about food, in the way you never forget about anything you fear. A picky eater was indifferent, but I was vigilant. I stayed away from food self-protectively, the same way, as a small child playing on the floor, I had steered clear of the round red tins my mother used to poison ants.

I was scared of feeling sick. I was scared of not liking tastes. I was scared of something getting in me that I could never get out. I was scared of something happening to my body that would make me not me.

2
PUBERTY

GOT MY FIRST PERIOD when I was ten. I was sitting on a beanbag in the reading corner at school. I was wearing madras Bermuda shorts and my legs were spread a little bit. My friend Vickie kept looking away, like she was embarrassed for me, and suddenly I felt frightened, because I knew what she was trying not to see.

In sex ed when we were nine, they had told us that at ten we could start. Since the moment I learned this information, it had been ticking inside me. Now the timer had gone off, and my years of being good and normal had come to an end.

I had always known I would get my period first. Not just first in my class or first among my friends. I would be the first girl in my generation, the first girl in the pool of girls eligible to begin.

There was no real reason I knew this. It was just a fact that I owned. I knew it the same way I knew my parents would get divorced. Someday I would be a child with the name of only one parent beside hers on the class list.

Burton, Susan 3330 Hawkins Rd. SE, Ada 49301 555-7409 Nancy

I could see this line of text as clearly as if the sheet had already been handed out.

Later that afternoon, at home in my bedroom, I showed my mother my underwear. My bedroom had a Laura Ashley wallpaper border of garden roses and the pink-and-white four-poster that had been my mother's when she was a little girl in Connecticut. My mother said menstruating early was "in our family." Then she went to the bathroom for a pad. I stood there in the alcove, waiting. It was like being sick: feeling helpless, stalled, hearing the regular sounds of everyone moving in the house around you.

My mother returned and showed me how to stick the pad into my underwear. There was no belt, like in *Are You There God? It's Me, Margaret.* I had never understood that book, in which the girl yearns for her period instead of dreading it.

Of course, Margaret was twelve. I was ten. It was against nature to get it that soon; I wasn't equipped to deal with it yet.

The madras shorts were in a heap on the floor. My mother picked them up and took them to the bathroom. I heard the thunk of the drain being closed and then the gushing tap. Beside the open window, I fastened a new pair of shorts. The ruffled blind was up, but the neighbors across couldn't see in. Our suburban street was wide, the lawns wooded. My mother told me that where we lived had once been a forest. A forest: That was a place you lived in a fairy tale or a fantasy series.

It was September 1984, and we were a family in Michigan.

WE LIVED NEAR GRAND Rapids, a small city in the western part of the state. Out in our rural suburb, there were farms, roller-coaster hills, and rivers. Families water-skied out of the backyards of their mock Tudors. Most people had a history in this region, but not my parents, and my early, defining relationship to my environment was a feeling of being *not from here,* even though I had never lived in any other place.

My parents had grown up in the Northeast and met while they were both in college. They married in 1969, a year after they graduated, my father from Yale and my mother from Smith. My father was building a career in radio news, and a relative on my mother's side owned WOOD. My parents moved to Grand Rapids and settled into a routine. My father rose for work each morning at three-thirty. My mother got up with him to make his breakfast and lay out his clothes and his shoes, which she polished, cross-legged on the floor before his closet. My father did not want my mother to work. My mother did want to work, but she did not know any way to be around a man but acquiescent. So she joined the Smith Club and the Junior League. And she worked as a kind of stringer for my father, scouring the newspapers for leads.

She had always longed to be a mother, and when she got pregnant with me, she immersed herself in the literature of child development. She drank a quart of milk a day, like the doctor told her to. Her water broke in the grocery-store checkout aisle, plastic jugs of Country Fresh in her cart.

I was a fretful baby. My mother told the doctor, "She never stops crying," and he dismissed her: "All babies cry." But it was true. As a baby I cried at all times except when bunched up in a corduroy pouch my mother strapped to her chest. Then one morning when I was five months old, she set me on the changing table, unpinned my diaper, and saw a purple bulge beneath the skin. She was scared but relieved: Here was an explanation. I had been born with an inguinal hernia. My intestines slipped through my abdominal wall, and the carrier comforted me because it pushed the protrusion back into place.

When I consider the story of my infancy now, it seems noteworthy that what soothed me was not nursing but being held in the pouch. It's possible that I did not form an association with food as comfort in the usual way.

After surgery, I stopped crying, but I did not become bubbly or easy. I was wary and shy. When someone cooed at me or tried to play peekaboo, I'd burrow my face into my mother's shoulder rather than make eye contact. I've understood myself to be shy since pre-school, a quiet girl on the edge of the classroom in orthopedic white shoes. Shyness was like being pigeon-toed: a certain way I was bent.

But I was one of the shy people whose impulse to hide coexisted with a desire to be seen. As I grew older, I moved from the sidelines to the center. I was a blond, bossy older sister who sang solos and won blue ribbons. My name was on the swim record board at the country club, and my photograph was on the wall at the community theater. I won the spelling bee. I won the math contest. I read all fifty titles on the Battle of the Books list. I was kind of famous. Other girls wanted to be my friend.

Reaching puberty complicated all this. My achievements were still noted, but so, increasingly, was my awkwardness.

People tried to be polite, but they saw. "Susan, a mosquito bite on your forehead is bleeding," a girl said to me one afternoon at play rehearsal. It was a huge pimple I'd picked.

But mostly it was my mother saying things. Standing before the fish tank in my room, gently suggesting that I start using deodorant. Handing me a bottle of rubbing alcohol at the bathroom counter: "For your skin." Coming in with a pile of folded laundry, wonder-ing if I wanted to go to the department store to shop for bras.

"I don't want a bra," I told her.

"Why not?"

"Bras for little girls are tacky," I said.

I couldn't imagine myself in a bra: I still wore day-of-the-week underpants. I'd always been drawn to things for little girls and un-easy about anything suggestive of sexual maturity. I liked one-pieces, not bikinis; Madame Alexander dolls, not Barbies; *Annie,* not *Grease.* Social maturity also provoked anxiety: While a girl on my swim team already knew what kind of car she was going to get when she turned sixteen, I had a recurring nightmare about steering our sta-tion wagon home all by myself. I could not make an imaginative leap into adolescent girlhood, much less an actual one.

"Sweetie," my mother said, "you need to start wearing some-thing. If you don't want a bra, then undershirts."

"Undershirts," I said.

I was close to my mother. The deepest comfort I knew was still her, the mother who had snuggled me close in that pouch. But increasingly there was a kind of relief I needed that she couldn't provide; no one could. I didn't feel like myself in this new body.

It's often assumed that precocious development makes a girl sexy. That it exposes her to male interest for which she is not ready. If this was happening to me, I didn't notice. I didn't feel attractive. I was not "blossoming"; I was coarsening. I was oily, erupting. When I got my period I was in sixth grade, the highest one at my small Montessori school. I'd always loved my school, which I'd attended since age two, but now I was embarrassed I was still there. I'd walk past classrooms where preschoolers worked at tiny desks, uncomfortably aware of the maxi-pad in my underpants.

I was no longer the person I'd been my whole life, a little girl. I was actually little, always the shortest girl in the class. And thin. That was one thing puberty wasn't changing. I had curves now, but I was lean. Being thin was important in our family: "Oh, I'm so glad I have thin grandchildren," my grandmother had said once, clapping her hands in the dressing room where my sister, Betsy, and I were trying on back-to-school clothes.

I'm so glad I have thin grandchildren. It became a family joke. But I always felt a little guilty when we made fun of my grandmother, because it was a sentiment we all shared. While my parents knew better than to say things like "I'm so glad you're thin" to their daughters, they both watched their weight. My mother drank a soda called Tab, which had one calorie. My father was a triathlete who espoused the diet in a bestseller called *Fit or Fat?*

It interested me that my grandmother had described Betsy as thin. I took this to mean that my little sister was officially no longer chunky. For years my parents had called Betsy "the round-pounder." She was an adorable, big-eyed preschooler, with a piping voice and high–low tastes in food: Her favorites were hot dogs and liver pâté. She was almost five years younger than I was, but the distance didn't prevent the inevitable sibling comparisons. Among the earliest ways we were differentiated: Betsy is sunny and Susan is shy. Betsy has brown hair and Susan is blond. Betsy says yes to food and Susan says no.

I guess you could say that I was glad I was thin. But being thin was more like an internal mandate. At the pool, I looked at other girls' bodies. Some I was glad weren't mine; others I envied. Heidi Vos had thin knee backs. I wanted those knee backs. When I saw Heidi, I couldn't resist craning to see my own for comparison. But my bones were set wider. I thought Heidi's knee backs might be impossible for me to get.

Heidi also had such skinny legs that the leg holes of her swimsuit were loose. I wanted my swimsuit baggy like that. I wanted the leg holes to gape. So I went on a diet. This was the summer I was nine. I didn't substitute things like celery for regular food, because I didn't like things like celery. I just ate less. I remember one night at dinner. A small breeze shifting the curtains, sprinklers ticking on the front lawn. Me at one end of our long table, my father at the other, my mother reaching over to cut Betsy's steak. Before me was my own untouched plate of flank steak and corn. I stuck my fork into the steak, but I had told myself not to eat it, and after only a few minutes of deliberate avoidance, the meat became absurd. It was a cut-up sponge—why would I ingest it?

At the end of dinner, I felt such pleasure, the first spark of something I would come to know intimately later. The power of renunciation, of waiting out a meal. Of rising from a table still empty.

I did this for a week. I stopped the morning I caught my reflection in the window of a shop. My legs were the right width: I'd done what I needed to do to get what I wanted. My mother seemed to notice at the same time. "You don't look like yourself," she said. "You're too thin." Her assessment gratified me, even though she was wrong: I was more myself with less.

After that week, I went back to the way I usually ate, which at that point in my childhood meant average amounts of an unusually limited number of things. While I didn't deliberately try to lose weight again until several years later, now I knew that I could. I was a natural. Already I perceived food as a threat. But now I had another reason to stay away from it. If you ate too much of it, it would make you fat.

ONE NIGHT AT THE end of sixth grade, I slept over at my friend Carrie's house. I had my period. At bedtime my pad was already soaked with blood. I'd packed one more but I had to save it for the morning. Standing beside one of Carrie's twin beds, I watched her change into her nightgown. When she took off her shirt, I ached, because she was still perfect: She had the flat chest of the boys I liked on swim team. I couldn't even remember how it felt to have a chest like that.

Carrie pulled on a frilled nightgown and climbed into her stiff sheets. "Aren't you going to take off your bathrobe?" she asked.

"I like to sleep with it on," I told her. The bathrobe was an extra barrier. I thought it might help.

In the morning there were some spots of blood on the duvet. I licked my finger and tried to erase them, but they didn't come off.

Still in our nightclothes, Carrie and her sister and her sister's friend and I went out into the backyard. It was a cool spring morning. The sister's friend, Noel, was talking about a short story I'd written. Noel knew about the story because it had just won a prize in our local newspaper's annual contest. The story was called "Bellamys," and it was about three friends and a project on the meaning of last names. Bellamy means "good friend," and the last line of my story was "We sat by each other, because that's what you do when you're Bellamys."

Now Noel said, "I think the last line should have been, 'We sat by each other, *and that's what we'll do for the rest of the year,* because that's what you do when you're Bellamys.'" I didn't think this was a good suggestion, but I nodded my assent. I had always been a little in awe of Noel. She had freckles and a flat face like Sissy Spacek. She lived in a brick mansion on a boulevard. At Christmastime, her parents hung a banner across the house that said her name. But mainly I didn't say anything because I was so worried. I sat on the picnic table and tried not to let others see the back of me, which I had been too scared to examine yet.

Later, upstairs in Carrie's room, when I finally took off my seersucker bathrobe, I saw a circle of blood the size of a pizza. It was impossible they hadn't seen.

When I got home, I handed my mother the balled-up robe in the basement at the washing machine. She shook it out. My mother was almost mad at me then. "I mean, except after childbirth, I've never seen anything like this," she said. I was mute, helpless. There had never been so much shame.

"Did you get anything on the sheets?" my mother asked.

"No," I lied.

"I don't see how that could be possible," my mother said.

I DIDN'T KNOW THEN that my breasts, which seemed so big, would never get any bigger; that I was one inch away from my adult height of five feet; that Carrie, when we found each other on Facebook years later, would be a new size, the size of a mother, and even though by that time I was a mother myself, I would remain the size of a sixth-grade kid; that I would take a perverse pleasure in my smallness; and that there would be some months when I'd run too much and eat too little and miss my period, and that I would view this as a relief. While part of me knew it was wrong to feel this way, so wrong, another part would shrug and say, Well, obviously.

3

IN OUR FAMILY

THE PRIZE FOR MY story "Bellamys" was seventy-five dollars, and on the day the check came in the mail, I showed it to my father.

"That is really something, Dee Doo," he said, using the name Betsy had given me as a young child.

"Thanks, Daddy," I said. He was in his chair at the kitchen table, and I was standing beside him. It was after work and he was sipping beer from a frosted mug. He laid the check on the table, smoothing it with his freckled hand. His freckles always reminded me that he had grown up under another sun, with another family. My mother's family was our orientation. My father was an only child, and both his parents were dead.

"You're a published writer and this is your first check. That's more than I can say, right, Nance?"

He turned to see my mother, who was at the counter shaking his peanuts into a bowl. "Every writer has a manuscript in a drawer," my mother said. "Or inside fifty boxes in the attic."

My father hooted. He was happy. He didn't always like it when she joked back. But tonight his mood was light.

I knew the boxes my mother was talking about. They were dark-green manuscript boxes, and when you lifted the lid the top sheet said:

STRANGLE HOLD
By Robert Burton

I had raised the title page to see how the first chapter opened but had never gone farther. I knew the novel's premise, though: A president-elect does something wrong in between the election and the inauguration. When I was in first grade, my father had quit his job at WOOD in order to write it. As a child I never really thought about the fact that *Strangle Hold* hadn't been published. To me *Strangle Hold* was something that existed in the world, something I planned to read one day when I was old enough. Writing a book: There was nothing you could do that was higher. And my father had done this. My father had written a book.

On any list of hobbies, I always put reading first, and my parents would have, as well. Every Sunday we went to a bookstore instead of to church. Spring break we'd come back from the beach with tan bodies but pale faces; we bent our heads toward our books instead of tilting them up to the sun. At dinner we brought our books to the table and read them even on special nights like birthdays, when in other families there might have been rules that you had to talk.

When a space in the shopping plaza on 28th Street became available, my parents spent an evening brainstorming bookstore names. The name my father liked best was one my mother came up with, The Bookie. I don't think that opening a bookstore was a venture they seriously considered for more than one night, but it is an evening about which I still feel tender. It tells a story about who they were as a couple as well as who we were as a family. Our family romance was books.

My mother came to the kitchen table with my father's peanuts. "Thanks, Pephant," my father said. Pephant was his name for my mother, and hers for him was Gawayne, though I never heard her say the endearment aloud: I knew it only from the title pages she inscribed for him. I read "Gawayne" as "Gowanee," like a Native American name, like one of the counties in Michigan—Lenawee, Keweenaw, Washtenaw—I saw spelled out when the TV flashed tornado warnings. I didn't know until I was much older that Gawayne was King Arthur's most mercurial knight, the one who tries to do the right thing but is beset by black moods that derail him.

My father was loving, cuddly, funny. One of my earliest memories is of dancing with him in the living room to Bunny Berigan, "I Can't Get Started": I would dance to the same song with him at my wedding. He orchestrated a suite of tickles and performed it nightly: chin chuckie, knee fraddle, pit tickle, fudd duddle. His humor included both dad jokes and more subversive material, like a personalized coffee mug with an acronym so profane no one would spell it out for me.

Some of the things he did in his black moods were hard to explain to others. I didn't share these stories back then, and for the most part I still don't. When I do, I'm almost inevitably asked, "Why did your father do that?" and I stammer, "Well, I mean . . . It was just the way he was." (Once a person nodded and said, "We have the same father"—a sentence of profound fellowship.)

For example, one day a few months before the evening I'm describing, my father had locked us out of the house. He was in his study, and we were in the driveway, and he wouldn't let us in. Why had he locked us out? It wasn't a question I asked or needed an answer to. This was just the kind of thing my father did. "What are you going to do?" I'd asked my mother. She had just returned to the car after pounding on the front door. From the passenger seat, I had seen her press the bell and clap the knocker, as if my father couldn't hear her entreaties. He could, but he was ignoring them. "I don't know," my mother said, and got out of the car again. She crossed the lawn, then rounded the corner of the house. When I lost sight of her, a faint whirring began at the edges of my consciousness, like the lowest setting of a fan. My father could be cruel to my mother, shaming or insulting her, and I imagined her walking the length of the back patio past the wall of glass and my father following along, yelling, like a basketball coach hollering at a player from the sidelines of a court. Soon my mother came out the gate on the opposite side, picking over the ground in flats. The lawn was covered with layers of heavy, wet, dirty brown leaves. "He locked the back door, too," my mother said, panting a little, sliding into the driver's seat. I imagined her jiggling that stiff knob. On the other side, the suncatcher—oven-baked crystals, suction-cupped to the glass—would have swayed.

My mother put the keys in the ignition. We would drive elsewhere, wait this out. As we backed down the driveway, I got nervous. I felt as if we were leaving my father alone in the house with a bomb. Once we were gone, there would be nothing to stop him from exploding it. I didn't want to leave him. I wanted to keep him safe.

Locking us out of the house was a psychological game, but his rage had more concrete manifestations: a dinner table, overturned; school photos, ripped apart in a fit. When my father raged, I was frightened. But the person I was always most frightened for was him. I wonder if I already saw his traits in myself. My father could be out of control, but he was also highly disciplined. For me, as, I think, for him, the discipline was penance.

My father today would not immolate or lash out; he has transformed. And my mother wouldn't knock on that door; she'd walk right out of it. Both my parents transformed with age, showing me that midlife might be defined by metamorphosis. But my childhood was defined by apprehension, and I grew guarded in response. As an adolescent, I both envied the stable homes of peers and believed what I had was superior: not a neutral, dull mom and dad, but vital, beautiful, intelligent parents who struggled. Even as an adult, I am sometimes annoyed at those who emerged from calm homes and find myself clinging to an old attitude: *I know things you don't, that you will never know; this is my thing you will never have.* But what confers power also creates distance: *You wouldn't understand.*

———

"VERY IMPRESSIVE, SUSAN M," my father said, handing me the check.

M was for Mason, my middle name, the same as my father's.

My mother took a wooden salad bowl from the cupboard. It was early summer, and on the table were huge blue hydrangeas she'd picked from a bed in our yard. Outside the picture window, our sprinklers arced. I could see the individual strands of water rising and falling. I'd been wearing glasses for one month, though I'd known I needed them for years, ever since I'd tried on another girl's at school. When I put them on it was as if the blurry windshield through which I'd always viewed the world had been wiped clear. I should have said something to my parents. But I never mentioned such things: that when I breathed deep, I felt a pinch that might be a heart attack, that my frequent bloody noses suggested leukemia. I was always worried that there was something wrong with my body, but I didn't want anyone to know about it other than me.

I took the check from my father. "Mom's going to deposit it for me," I said.

Then my father reached for the check again. "Nance, before you deposit it, let me make a copy," he said, and the next evening when he got home from work he came into my room and put three photocopies on my desk. (He was now a computer systems analyst at a large local company. My mother was now working, too, teaching at our Montessori school.)

"For your archives," he said.

I'd been saving things for my archives for as long as I could remember. "Archives" was my father's word. He had a master's degree in library science, as well as voluminous archives of his own in our attic. My father had been proud of me for winning a prize in the writing contest, but I had expected that. The photocopies moved me more. He'd preserved the check for me out of a conviction that such things mattered and an understanding that they mattered to me as much as they did to him.

MY FATHER HAD GONE to Andover, a boarding school in Massachusetts, and I'd known my whole life that I would go to Andover, too. Andover was so fixed in my future that as a little girl I'd turned my dollhouse into a dormitory. Once a friend said to me, "I don't think I could leave my family like that." To me, going to Andover was part of being in our family.

But because our Montessori school ended at sixth grade and Andover didn't start until ninth, in seventh grade I moved to the local public school, Forest Hills Central Middle.

Without realizing it, I ostracized myself immediately. I joined Science Olympiad and entered the spelling bee. I was voted Student of the Month the very first month of the school year. On the morning fall-quarter report cards were distributed, my homeroom teacher was so impressed by my grades that he read them aloud: "Five A's and two A-pluses." A few days later, I got a hate note in my locker. *You think your so great but your not.*

Not only did I do the wrong things, I looked the wrong way, too. My clothes weren't anything like what other people wore. I had graduated from children's apparel straight to my parents' preppy store. Girls at Central Middle wore tight jeans and puffy white sneakers they bought at Woodland Mall. Central Middle: a redundant name, befitting a school that favored uniformity. My old school had honored weirdness and achievement, and this new culture was foreign to me.

One afternoon I was in my room making a list of "names in the news" for current events. *Margaret Thatcher, Muammar Gaddafi, Tip O'Neill.* Midway through this exercise I had the impulse to make my own list of names, and I opened a notepad. *Lynn Mazza, Brandi Bauer.* Lynn and Brandi were also new to Central Middle, but, unlike me, they'd been snatched up by the perfect group of popular girls. *Discovered* was how I thought of it, like a starlet at a lunch counter or a model in a mall. *Lynn Mazza, Brandi Bauer,* and, I added now, *Susan English.*

Not my actual name, Susan Burton, but Susan English. I stared down at it, a little surprised this had come out of my pen. It wasn't like I had anything against the name Burton; after all, Burton *was* English. But perhaps a girl with such a reductive last name was herself less specific, reduced to her essence. She was all my problematic details, stripped away. *Susan English*. She came to me unbidden. She was the first iteration of the girl I would invent, of all the girls I would invent. She was the prototype, the earliest model.

She appeared to me in a vision: standing above the seat of her ten-speed, pedaling with a group of friends. She was graceful and sunny. I was the type of child with a grave expression who was sometimes asked by concerned grown-ups, "What's wrong?" But nobody would ever ask Susan English what was wrong. Cresting the hill on her bike, Susan English was light, relieved, unburdened.

Up until now I'd mainly imagined my actual self into other situations. Getting discovered by a talent scout. A boy I had a crush on coming to watch my play. Those were the fantasies of a child; Susan English was my first adolescent fantasy. Rather than a fantasy about an encounter I would have, it was a fantasy of a different me.

I DID HAVE ONE close friend at Central Middle, a girl named Kelly. One weekend afternoon, on a beanbag in her sister's bedroom, I read my first issue of *Seventeen*. I recognized myself as the age the magazine described, and there was pleasure in that demographic affinity. (Despite the magazine's name, its target age group was, and had always been, younger.) The same principle had informed my love of the Girl Scout handbook and the Kids' Choice awards at the public library. The difference was I had felt secure in those spaces. I did not yet feel as if I belonged in adolescent girlhood, and *Seventeen* gave me a place to explore it outside of Central Middle, to assimilate in private, in a zone uncompromised by reality.

Immediately I got a subscription. Each month, on the day the magazine arrived in the mail, I'd sit on one of the twirly chairs in our family room and read the entire issue from start to finish, including every word of every ad. Clairol Pazazz, Bonne Bell, Gunne Sax. I read even the information from the Audit Bureau of Circulations, which allowed me to imagine the editors in their offices at 850 Third Avenue, New York, N.Y., 10022. I was especially curious about the editor who wrote the quizzes. I assumed she had the same specialized training as the designers of standardized tests.

Though a few years later, in my mid-teens, when I picked up *Seventeen* again, I instantly hated myself for not being thin, I did not consciously respond to size in seventh grade. (That year, food preoccupied me in the same way it always had, not to a degree that was unusual or new. I was scared of it and careful with it, but there was no permutation or emerging pathology.) What spoke to me then was the emphasis on the bodily changes that still made me foreign to myself. I loved the ads for menstrual products. My favorites had a testimonial style: "My breasts are so sore it hurts to wear a bra." But while I was taken with the magazine's focus on insults to the body, I rejected its suggestions for the management of them. That would have been practical. My engagement with the magazine was more fantastical. It was a world I imagined myself inside.

In my thirties, when I went to a library to look at the old issues again, I realized that in every ad showing a pink bedroom—and many did—I had always assumed it was the girl's same room since childhood. That the girl in the ad had grown up with both her mother and her father, her past connected to her present in her same whole-life house. It was not the story the ads were trying to tell. It was the wish I had pressed on them.

4

SUNDAY MORNING

THE SUMMER AFTER I finished seventh grade, my mother went away for six weeks, to a Montessori training program in New York. With her gone, the house felt messy. My sheets were never tight. I did the things she'd taught me before she left: carried the wicker basket down the basement stairs and, in that underground cool, poured detergent to a line in a cup; pulled the tab on a tin of cat food, dumped the slimy puck into the bowl. Upstairs in the kitchen, I made our dinners and my father's breakfasts. On his way to work, my father would drop Betsy and me at swim team, and after practice we'd spend the day at the club.

Three years earlier, at nine, I'd been fixated on Heidi with her thin knee backs. This summer, size was just one part of what concerned me. Now, at twelve, my interest was in identity, and I turned my attention to Kate. To me, Kate was the perfect teenage girl. She was fifteen, with a nut-brown tan and a bikini that tied with strings. Across the lane lines in the morning, I'd stare at her profile. Her beauty was the structural kind actually enhanced by a bathing cap.

Her body was ideal, too: flat-stomached, like nothing ever went inside. One day I stood behind her at the snack bar. She ordered, then leaned against the brick wall to wait for her fries. I couldn't help it, I looked over. Her legs were tan and smooth until a few inches above her knees, where there was very fine white-blond hair.

I had the same white-blond hair on my legs, except it extended down to my ankles. Shaving scared me. Once, when I was younger, a babysitter had run my palm along her shin, which prickled. "That's from shaving," she'd said. Shaving became linked in my mind with consequences: with hair that would grow back coarse or in a different color. My father used the phrase "mutilating your body" to describe his position on ear piercing and tattoos. Shaving seemed to fall into the same category. It was disfiguring, impure. The natural state was always better. This philosophy applied to makeup, too, but more to shaving, because it was severe. Not shaving comforted me; I still had all my original hair. It was a point of hygienic pride, the same as never having had a cavity. Also, I liked the way my hair looked on my body, blond against tan skin.

But one day the hair on my legs got noticed. I was on a lounge chair near the locker room. The door opened and a group of older girls emerged. "Oh, my God," one said, "she doesn't even shave!"

I stared hard into the pages of my book. Had I been previously assessed?

I got rid of the hair as soon as I got home. In the shower, I bent down over my shin with one of my mother's pink plastic disposable razors. I razed a timid stripe, then looked: Hair clogged the blades. It worked! More confident now, I pressed harder and bled.

"What happened there?" someone said the next morning as we waited in line behind the blocks at practice.

"I did that shaving," I said, rolling my eyes. I loved saying that, and I loved walking around the pool with smooth legs. Because people had noticed the presence of the hair, I assumed they noticed its absence. *Oh, yeah, Susan Burton—she shaves.* Yet I felt uneasy, like

I was asking for trouble by getting rid of something that didn't really need to be gone.

EIGHTH GRADE STARTED, AND it was a little better than seventh. I still had my big round glasses, my braces, and my A-pluses. But I was not as stiff and frightened, and I had new clothes, enviable ones, like a turtleneck hip-length Benetton sweater available only in Italy (my aunt had brought it back). I'd turned from a weird nerd into a cute nerd, and that protected me.

But if school was easier, home was not. My father started coming home late. His absence made me nervous but also, guiltily, glad. Eating with just my mother and my sister was more relaxed.

One night I was watching TV in the family room when I heard the garage door trundle open and my father's car pull in. I turned to the back hall and saw him standing there in his khaki trench coat. He bent to remove his galoshes. It was November, the rain downing leaves.

My mother appeared from the kitchen. "Where were you?" she said.

My father straightened. "I was at work, *Nancy*." There was ridicule in the way he said her name.

Later my mother came into my room to say good night. She sat on the edge of my bed. I had my electric blanket turned up to HI.

"Turn it down to five or you'll be hot in the night," she said.

I let her do it, even though when she left I would turn it up again and later wake sweating.

"Mom?" I said.

"Mm-hmm," she said.

"Do you think Dad is having an affair?"

My mother looked startled. She swept a hand over the blanket— pale blue, worn almost to coils. Then she answered me straight out. "I don't know."

I was shocked less by the idea that my fear might be true than by the fact that my mother hadn't tried to assuage it.

———

ONE SATURDAY SOON AFTER, my friend Kelly came for a sleepover. We watched her VHS tape of *Nadia,* a TV movie about the Olympic gymnast Nadia Comaneci, which we'd watched one million times previously. Then we went to bed in sleeping bags on the floor of my room. This was my favorite part of any sleepover, the closeness of secrets in the dark. At slumber parties I always chose truth instead of dare. Yet there was a limit to what I would offer. I was always guarding something: a crime or a passion. (The content was youthful, but the feeling was potent.) I didn't disclose what went on at home, either, but that was different. Those stories weren't shameful, but they were private and by definition could not be shared.

In the morning I woke to the sound of my parents fighting. The light was pale through the balloon blinds. Across the landing, I heard my mother's murmur, my father's rebuke. My father had the sonorous voice of a public figure. In regular conversation, he sounded like the newscaster he had been; angry, he sounded like an actor playing someone mean.

I had my eyes open: It was better to be vigilant. Kelly didn't seem like she was breathing deeply enough to be asleep. I found that I hardly cared what she thought. I was somewhere else, transported. My parents' fights existed on a plane of the biggest things, like the fact that I had been born as me and not as someone else; of God and my grandfather and presidents. My parents' fights were part of the story of who I was in the world and who they were and who their parents had been. Kelly was nothing compared to any of that.

"You're disgusting," I heard my father say to my mother. "You disgust me."

A door opened and closed. My father's running pants made a swishing sound as he descended the stairs. I wondered if my father had called my mother disgusting because she was fat. She wasn't really fat, but she said that she was. She said that no matter what she did she would never have a flat stomach. My eyes were drawn to it when she brought that up, the tiniest convex curve under a corduroy skirt.

I checked Kelly again. I felt bad for her. Several years earlier I had slept over at the home of a girl whose parents later divorced. I had put my bag in her room and then come downstairs. At the foot of the stairs was a room that had no furniture in it except a mattress on the floor. The sheets did not look crisp. They looked like sheets I would imagine for someone in college, or a person who was sick. Next to the mattress was a juice glass and a *Sports Illustrated.* "My dad sleeps in there because he snores," my friend said behind me. Then she closed the door. But it was too late; I had seen it. In that room I had seen what could happen to a family. I had seen what I knew was someday going to happen to mine.

You're disgusting. You disgust me. The words were unsettling in their cruelty but in their mystery, too. What disgusted my father? Was it something about my mother's personality—her shyness or hesitance? Some character weakness you could point to? Or the other possibility: My father was disgusted by my mother's body, and he had told her so.

I was accustomed to my father's contradictions, but this insult threw me. I'd always thought that brains mattered more to him than bodies.

THAT FALL IT WAS finally time to do my Andover application. I wrote an essay and asked teachers for recommendations. A parent had to write an essay, too—respond to a question like, *Why do you think your child belongs at Phillips Academy?* The first sentence of my father's answer was, *Quite simply, Susan is smart!*

My father had always sent a clear message about the kind of women he respected: the smart kind. When I wanted to be an actress, he pressed upon me the model of Jodie Foster; when I got a little older and wanted to write, he gave me essays by Susan Sontag. Even today I still think of these two women in connection with my father, as ones he wanted me to like. And I did like them, even before I understood what made them great. They seemed similar to me. Jodie Foster was blond and not super-girly; Susan Sontag had my same name.

My father did call me his "blond bombshell," but his usage was innocent. I thought the term was original, something he'd made up for me—a little girl with a shining pelt of hair in a tank suit. I never thought of it as belonging to a voluptuous pinup, as referring to something platinum, fake.

IN DECEMBER MY MOTHER went away again for Montessori training, this time for a long weekend. She arranged for Betsy to stay with a friend. It would just be my father and me.

On Friday I had an acting class at the theater downtown. Afterward, I walked across the street to meet my father at a new vertical mall. He was in the food court, and he rose when he saw me, as he always did when a woman approached the table. But I was frightened when I sat down. With my father were two people, a woman and a teenage girl. And there was something wrong, the light above us yellow. It was as if there had been a mistake, the wrong bulbs installed, heat lamps meant for fast food.

"Susan, this is Debbie," my father said. It was the only time I ever heard my father introduce someone without giving a last name.

Debbie was nothing like my mother. She wore long press-on nails and was orange-brown, as if from tanning cream. My father said the daughter's name and then, approvingly, "She does Junior Achievement." When he said this, something spun in me, starting out slow and gathering speed. My father was saying things he didn't believe. Junior Achievement was a program for future business leaders, advertised on TV. It was vocational. It was not something our snobby family esteemed.

Debbie and my father knew each other, he explained, from Toastmasters, a public-speaking club at their company that was sort of like debate. So maybe, I thought, Debbie might be a little smart— she had made a speech that impressed my father, or she was witty in big groups. But there in the food court, I couldn't tell whether Debbie was smart or not, mainly because I hardly took in what was said. I had been prepared for the fact of the other woman—what I had not known was that with her my father would become someone else.

My father and I drove home along I-96. It was not quite dark. The billboards showed Klingman's, a furniture store, and Arne's Funland, a water park. Years earlier there had been a billboard of my father: BOB BURTON THE NOSE FOR NEWS. As a young child, I thought it was perfectly natural that my father's face would be on a billboard. Meeting Debbie hadn't lowered him in my estimation, torn him down from heights. I didn't hate him. I was scared for him. I had seen him altered. I allowed myself to look at him: He was the same as ever in the driver's seat. His groomed fingernails tapped the steering wheel. He held out one hand, and then the other, and mouthed words, as if weighing options or practicing a speech. When the car slowed, he put his wrist to his mouth and sucked it. This was his suite of motions, a private sequence I had observed from the passenger seat my whole life.

I looked out the window as we curved off the ramp and crossed the bridge over the Thornapple River. After the bridge we were almost home, climbing the hill past the Episcopal church where I had been baptized; past the cemetery where one of the carpool mothers had once pulled over so that I could throw up; past the house of the girl who had achieved immortality as a soap opera star; and finally to our street, its pebbly crunch beneath our wheels, and our house, a gray two-story on a high lawn. Looking out the car window at this picture was as familiar as writing my name.

I thought I knew why my father had introduced me to Debbie: He was proud of me. Later my mother would round out my understanding of the encounter. She'd asked my father not to see Debbie that weekend, and he'd not only seen her but flaunted their meeting. My mother believed I'd been used as a pawn.

But some part of me still insists on my interpretation. As we pulled into our driveway, the garage unfolding to receive us, I felt secure in my father's love. The meeting had been a way of explaining himself to Debbie. *This is who I love; this is who I am.*

I SPENT MOST OF the next day downtown at the theater. A friend's mother drove me home in the late afternoon, and as we approached our house, I saw that our mailbox had been knocked over. Our mailbox! Our yellow mailbox, the last line of the poem that we gave daily as directions: "Halfway down the street, on your right, the house with the yellow front door and the yellow mailbox."

The post that held the mailbox in the ground was bent, as if somebody had driven into it.

"What happened?" said my friend's mother. I didn't know.

When I reached the front door, I found that it was unlocked. The light was on in the foyer, the candle fixture blazing in the gray afternoon. In the living room, the ornate cabinet was open to the stereo. On the marble-topped coffee table was a Linda Ronstadt record and a brown drink. I didn't even know my parents owned alcohol like this. I had never seen my father drink anything but beer.

He called soon after it got dark. I was at the kitchen phone, which was attached to gingham wallpaper.

"I'm at work," my father said. "I'm going to be here longer. I'm sorry, baby."

"What time do you think you're going to be home?"

"Probably late," he said.

I stayed up as long as I could. Before I went to bed, I called his office, even though I knew he wasn't there. The phone rang and rang. I waited for someone, annoyed or furious, to pick it up. I stayed on the line until I elicited the phone company's angry buzz.

From my bed I heard rustling trees and shuffling, like animals in the chimneys. I slept little, waking frequently, looking at the clock. At six I stepped out to the landing. No one was in my parents' room. On my way down the stairs, I peeked down the hall to our kitchen, as if my father might have materialized there. The fact of his absence finally settled in me when I saw he had not.

I stood watching an English muffin toast. I had never woken in our house so warm. My parents always turned the thermostat down to sixty before bed. Having the same air in the house contributed to the sense that though it was morning, the day wasn't new. I was living an experience that stood outside ordinary time.

In the family room, I turned on the TV: *Rocky and Bullwinkle,* that same muted-color early-morning cartoon of my whole life, the shrill "Watch me pull a rabbit out of my hat!" and my sense that the whole show was a trick. It was a cartoon, but it was really for grownups. There was too much I didn't understand.

When the sky lightened, I went back to the kitchen and picked up the phone. I knew that by dialing the long-distance number I was switching from bystander to participant.

Someone had to go find my mother. She was at a camp in upstate New York. I'd called a pay phone in a main building.

"Mom?" I said. "Dad didn't come home last night."

To me his absence was the critical piece of information, the one to relay first. That was the line he had crossed. Debbie was something he had done to my mother. Leaving me alone was something he had done to me.

Soon after I hung up with my mother, I heard the rumble of the garage.

When my father came in, I was reading on the couch in the family room. I glanced up, then went back to my book. I was acutely conscious of how I looked to him. My cheeks burned; my eyes stared at nothing on the page. My father stood in the door and neither of us moved.

He had showered; I imagined him in a different bathroom somewhere. Other bathrooms were always humid. There were hairs on the bars of soap. When I showered at a friend's house, I never felt really clean. I had to come home and take my real shower, start the day all over again at two P.M.

"Where were you?" I asked, and my father didn't answer. "I was scared," I said.

He sat down beside me on the couch. He looked at the cover of the book I was reading and then out the wall of windows at the leaf-strewn lawn.

"What happened to the mailbox?" I said.

I thought that my father had knocked the mailbox down. Not by accident; that he had deliberately destroyed it.

"Roy Koops ran into it with his Bronco," my father said.

"Mr. Koops?"

My father nodded. "Mr. Koops," he said.

Roy Koops was our next-door neighbor. He owned a car dealership. It had been years since he had been a presence in our lives, anything but a name. Already he seemed like someone from another time, from a life my family had had in history. In that era, I was a child playing Matchbox cars with Roy Koops's son, Glenn. Once, there had been a blizzard and the snowbanks were taller than we were. Another time Glenn got a staple in his finger and we were allowed to have ice cream. Now I wondered if the Koops family was also in a bad situation. Mr. Koops was a drunk driver or—like another father in our town—stealing money from his own store. Maybe every family's trajectory was like this: The golden moments happened when the parents were young and the children were in preschool. Then life rolled forward through all the years and you started having problems; Roy Koops, too. (None of my imaginings about the Koops family were true.)

"I'm sorry, baby," my father said then.

I wasn't going to say okay, wasn't going to forgive. I pulled my legs up toward my chest, tugged my flannel nightgown over my knees.

My father was wearing his weekend clothes: wide-wale corduroys, a button-down shirt, a Shetland sweater. My whole life, a hug from someone wearing such a sweater—a really woolly kind called a Shaggy Dog—would be the definition of masculine comfort.

And my father did reach out to me at that moment, put a tentative hand on my shin.

"Do you shave your legs?" he asked.

The question startled me. "Sometimes," I said.

My leg was dry, pale from winter. I hadn't shaved since those summer days at the pool. My father's question hung there. Was he critical or curious? *Quite simply, Susan is smart!* I was not a daughter who defied him by mutilating her body, not a vapid, tacky, makeup type.

Even in that moment I was sure my father regretted the question. It just was so unlike anything he had ever said.

I believed I knew his train of thought. His hand on my leg, noticing the hair. His hand had just been on her shin; it had unthinking expectations of legs. My brain forced me to visualize that then, Debbie and my father together; only when I did, the picture was twisted, wrong, my imagination could not be controlled, it was like my father's hand became mine, and I was forced to feel the leg, too, the other woman's leg, her awful, silky, mannequin skin.

5
GOING WEST

OVER THE NEXT FEW months, our life as a family in Michigan ended. My mother filed for divorce and decided she and Betsy and I would move to Boulder, Colorado, which was where her sister, Marcie, lived. She flew out and interviewed for Montessori teaching jobs. A FOR SALE sign went up in front of our house; a day later, a banner said SOLD. My father bought a new house in a neighborhood nearer to downtown.

I got my acceptance to Andover. They sent you a certificate with the school seal, like you had already graduated, like getting in was the hardest part. But I knew that wasn't the case; my father said Andover was harder even than Yale. I called him at work, told him first. "Congratulations," he said. But when my mother came home, she sighed. I wasn't going to go—because of money and because she thought that boarding school, on top of everything, was too much change.

"I'm sorry, sweetie," my mother said. "I know it's a disappointment."

"It's really fine, Mom," I told her.

And I meant it. It was really fine. In fact, I was glad I wasn't going to Andover, both for the reason my mother had identified as well as for others I didn't think she would understand.

Usually in a coming-of-age story, boarding school is the thing that holds promise. Going to the elite place is the transformative opportunity. Not going to boarding school is the thing that promised change to me. I would get to be like everyone else, in a big, national, we're-the-kids-in-America way. By going to public high school, I would be entering not the hallowed halls but the fluorescent-lit ones. To me they burned more brightly. I had never seen a single mention of boarding school in any issue of *Seventeen*.

In Boulder, I would attend Burbank Junior High for ninth grade and Fairview High School thereafter. Everything about Fairview High School seemed to epitomize the American high school experience, beginning with its name. Its football team would soon be ranked among the top twenty in the nation, and a junior named Holly had just won the *Seventeen* cover-model contest.

I had the issue upstairs in my room. Next to Holly's face on the cover was the single word BEAUTIFUL. Holly had auburn hair and tiny freckles, and she wore makeup such as Hours Longer Lipstick in Ripe Plum. In Colorado she shopped at department stores with unfamiliar names like Joslins. At a makeup counter at one of these stores, she had pushed her cover-model application across the glass.

I had always assumed that I would spend my high school years in old New England buildings, hunched beneath a library light. But now I myself would be part of true teen life. I would stand at that makeup counter just like Holly.

I might even buy makeup. Just before eighth grade ended, I got contacts. Then in early summer, the orthodontist removed the braces on my top teeth. Glasses gone, braces off: It was like scaffolding being dismantled. I spent a certain amount of time before mirrors, evaluating the progress.

One evening, out doing errands with my father, I told him I needed something at the pharmacy. When he pulled into the lot I said, "You should just stay in the car," and then went by myself to buy menstrual pads.

When I left, carrying the pads in a bag, two boys followed me out. I tensed, preparing for them to holler, "Are you on the rag?" then double over in hilarity, snorting.

From behind me, one of the boys said, "Do you go to East?" naming the local school.

I knew the menacing way teasing started, and this wasn't it.

I turned to face them. My heart was flicking, frightened but light. "I don't go to East."

The boys took me in, my white-blond hair and my lean, tan body. I was wearing one of my favorite outfits, a mint-green-and-white Benetton top and matching cotton bottoms the length of shorty pajamas.

"What's your name?" the boy said.

"Susan," I said.

"Susan what?" he said.

I almost told him. But then I wondered if he would try to find me. The boys would come by my father's new house, and he would get angry, and I would have to explain. At least I assumed he would be angry. Really, I had no idea how my father would react to a boy pursuing me. It hadn't been a possibility yet. Also, I still had the unforthcoming reflexes of childhood. These boys were my age, but they were also strangers. Your last name was like your Social Security number—something that could be used against you, something you needed to protect.

"Susan what?" he said again.

I mattered to the boy; there was something he saw in me. It was a thrill to attract interest: a spring inside.

My father was waiting in the car. I looked over to him and back at the boy. "Susan English," I said.

WE LEFT FOR COLORADO the week my parents' divorce became final. I wasn't sure if the timing was a coincidence or something legal.

My mother drove, and the trip took three days. The first day, we wound south through the smokestacks of the industrial Midwest, and on the second, we crossed Kansas, a windy, sunny, flat state, the highway a stripe down the middle.

In the car I felt nervous, anticipatory. In my lap I had a spiral notebook, and in a bag at my feet I had a brand-new clock radio called the P'jammer. I wanted to plug it in as soon as we arrived. I'd coveted this clock radio, which was a white cube with pastel dials and a teal snooze button, since seeing it advertised in *Seventeen*. I imagined it in the bedroom of a typical teenage girl: a girl who bopped around to music as she dressed for school; a girl who came home, flicked the P'jammer's pink dial, and flopped ecstatically on her bed. It was the radio of a popular, carefree girl—the girl I would be when we arrived in Colorado, I was sure of it.

The sureness had something to do with a sense of possibility and something to do with size. I weighed a couple of pounds less than usual—just barely under my normal number. But this minor variation changed how I felt. In fact, the loss sparked the exact sensations I craved: light, relieved, unburdened. It had never before occurred to me that I could achieve this state with an alteration to my body.

I'd lost the weight while performing in a play at the children's theater. Every day the stage manager went to pick up McDonald's for lunch and we ate it in the dressing room. I didn't like any of the food at McDonald's except the hot fudge sundaes. So that was what I ordered every day, a hot fudge sundae without nuts. The hot fudge sundae was small. When you ate it, you could hardly feel it in you. It was like eating snow. For the whole rest of the day after consuming it, I felt lively and completely at ease.

On the car trip, I would have stuck to hot fudge sundaes if I could. But my mother wouldn't stop at McDonald's. She'd packed turkey sandwiches in a cooler and sleeves of Pepperidge Farm butterfly crackers that Betsy and I passed between the seats. We played MASH in a hot-pink spiral notebook. I looked out the window at the prairie. Every August we drove from Michigan to my grandparents' summer house in the Adirondacks. But that trip was all about going backward: back East, back to the shingled house in the meadow in which generations of my family had slept. Now the landscape was new, shorn of features instead of thick with them. Now we were going forward, outbound instead of on a return trip.

When, in college, I took a class on "the writing of history" and was assigned an autobiographical essay, there was no question what I would write. It was the story of this journey across the American frontier, the story of how I went West to seek my fortune as "a normal teenager."

ALL THROUGH THE COUNTRY, my mother played NPR. I had my Walkman for when I wanted to listen to my tapes. It was too exposing to broadcast them. When I let my mother hear my songs, it was like having a light shined into my essence. She had access to me for the duration. When the song ended I would recover my privacy, but it would be too late, she would have already seen. Days earlier, driving on the far side of Grand Rapids, I had played her a Bon Jovi song. I was trying to like their album *Slippery When Wet*, but the only song I responded to was "Never Say Goodbye," the ballad. Cueing the track in the deck, I told my mother that this was my favorite song. When it finished she said, "Well, I don't think it's hard to figure out why you like that song, what it means to you. You're saying goodbye to our life here. And this song is about how hard it is to let go."

I wanted to close my eyes or crank open the window, hide from the moment by blacking it out or blowing it away. She'd seen directly into what I couldn't say. I was losing the life I'd known, and this loss was so big that I couldn't face it head-on.

During the last weeks we'd lived in our house, I'd been uneasy and panged. I wanted to explain to the house that we wouldn't be there anymore. But how would the house understand? One afternoon I'd lain on my stomach on the family room floor, the sun warming my back, for no reason other than I wanted to make contact with the house, to show that I loved it and to feel it against me.

I regretted playing that song for my mother. It was mine. It was private. The things that meant the most to me were always the things I held tightest but also the things I longed to share. If I did share something meaningful, I would minimize it so that the other person wouldn't grasp its importance, and then I'd feel a sense of self-betrayal, as well as regret that I'd ruined my chance for connection.

Or for insight. Even in the car that afternoon, I had to admit that my mother had said something smart about the Bon Jovi song. If I had never played it for her, I would never have heard her articulate something I felt but had not named. *You're saying goodbye to our life here. And this song is about how hard it is to let go.*

ON THE THIRD DAY, the mountains appeared before us on the highway. "Look!" said my mother, and then got annoyed when I told her that they looked like mountains in a movie, fake. But I didn't want the mountains to seem like a backdrop on a set. It made me scared I would never be at home in this state.

When we reached Boulder, I already knew the streets. I had spent months on the rug in the family room in Michigan with the map beneath my palms. I imagined friends I would visit on Hardscrabble Drive and Powderhorn Lane. I looked for the ways subdivisions connected, the routes you would take so you wouldn't have to ride your bike on major streets.

We drove up Foothills Parkway toward our new house, which I had seen in photographs my mother had taken the weekend she found it. There were only a handful, in an envelope from a one-hour chain, and I had shuffled through them again and again. I stared at those pictures so much that years later, when I went back to Boulder and rode a rented bike to my old neighborhood and stood over the crossbar, regarding my house and its triangular planes, the first thing I thought of was the photographs, not my life inside. The house imprinted itself on me not in the time we lived there but in the time I'd spent imagining myself into a future under those eaves.

ON THAT FIRST DAY, we stepped out onto the driveway, stiff from the car. My uncle Robert let us into the house. Robert looked like he belonged here, with his mix of preppy and cowboy: an Oxford shirt tucked into Levi's, a belt with an elaborate silver buckle. Beside him, my mother still looked like the country-club mother she'd been just three days earlier. A Pierre Deux quilted purse over her shoulder, small gold hoop earrings, Pappagallo flats.

Robert and my mother's sister, Marcie, had met twenty years earlier as students at the University of Colorado and had lived in Boulder ever since. To me they were glamorous: younger, freer versions of my parents; world travelers who performed athletic feats. From my earliest childhood, I'd been aware of Marcie as not just my aunt but my mother's sister. They were linked by their physical resemblance—chestnut hair, compact build—as well as by something unnameable. Like many *Annie* fans, I often imagined what would happen if I were orphaned. I felt secure in knowing that the closest person in the world to my mother would take me in.

Robert and Marcie were philanthropists. They ran his family's foundation, which funded causes like the environment and reproductive rights. I knew that Robert had helped my mother pay for this house. She didn't have enough money to buy anything herself.

We stood under the cathedral ceiling on carpet. The house felt hot and close. Aside from the day the movers had unloaded our van, it had been shut up for weeks. High-altitude sun streamed in from a huge window, and Robert cranked it open. He started telling my mother practical things: the box in the garage that controlled the sprinkler system, the handyman we could call to fix the broken doorbell.

I wanted Robert to leave, so I could poke around. On the basis of the pictures, I'd looked forward to this house, but now that we were here, I felt uneasy.

As soon as he was gone, I went upstairs, carrying the P'jammer. In my new bedroom, I went straight for the closets, which had the kind of doors that folded like accordions. I'd been excited about these doors. But when I tried them, they felt flimsy, and I closed them without putting anything inside.

Squatting, I plugged the P'jammer into the back wall. Then I spun the ridged dial until I found a familiar song, Suzanne Vega's "Luka." I stayed very still and listened all the way through, conscious that this soft, warbling tune was the inaugural song of my new bedroom.

When the song finished, the DJ came on. "This is 97.3 KBCO . . ."

The radio stations started with K instead of W. I had moved out of W into K! W was the real system and K was the secondary one, for people who lived far away.

Then, though it had been hot and bright, my room darkened. I stood and went to the window. Clouds raced through the sky like a special effect. I didn't know then that it would happen every summer day, a brief storm rolling in from the mountains. On the deck of the house in back of us, two girls sat on lounge chairs. As drops began to fall, one screeched and put a magazine over her head. They ran inside through sliding glass doors. I stayed at the window, watching, until I felt my mother in the doorway and turned around.

I can't see her there in the doorway on that first day without flashing ahead to her in that same spot three years later: me sitting on my bed, slinging cruel words, a talent of mine by then; she, drunk, slamming the door so hard that the frame came out of the wall. Our later selves would have been impossible for us to predict: her drinking, my anger; and the way I ate. What I would have given at that future point, bloated and crazed, to be the girl whose lunch on a hot summer day had been a cup of snow.

On that first day, she merely nodded at the radio. "You already found your station."

She was pressing on the music, my private thing.

"No, I didn't," I told her.

I felt nervous, as if I might be punished. We were new to this, sullenness and defiance.

My mother looked at me and ran a hand down her side, smoothing her cotton skirt. She had not changed from the car. We always wore skirts on car trips. In service-station bathrooms, it was important to lift up. You didn't want your clothing to touch the floor.

"I wonder if we should move your bed," my mother said. "It might be better by the window."

"I don't care," I said. It was an iron twin that had been Betsy's. My new room was too small for my old bed from Michigan.

"I think it would look pretty—" my mother started.

"I hate that bed," I said. And then I told her, "This is the ugliest house I've ever seen."

My mother withdrew slightly. Then she just looked sad. "Sweetie, it was the best I could do."

She could not cry; my mother could not cry!

I turned my back to her and stared out the window at the neighbors' wet deck. I hadn't meant it. I wanted to take it back. The only thing wrong with the house was that it wasn't mine.

Night came. In Michigan the summer nights were thick with the scents of trees and flowers, and the air was soft through the screen. Here in Colorado the night carried the flat sounds of cars and of children I didn't know. I got in bed early, before I was tired, and couldn't sleep.

I went downstairs to the kitchen, where my mother was unwrapping china. Balls of newspaper filled a garbage bag. "I can't sleep," I told her, and she came upstairs. "Could you rub my back?" I said. It was rare that I asked her to comfort me, and I wonder now if she appreciated this unexpected invitation.

When she left, I closed my eyes. Then I opened them again, reached over to the P'jammer, and pressed the pink button that said SLEEP. I lay in the narrow bed beneath the open window. Music from a K station played. I had a low feeling then, that I might never use the P'jammer the way I'd envisioned. I wanted to be that light girl, that dancing teen, but there was a real possibility that I couldn't. I needed the radio not to raise me up but to drown things out. In Michigan I had sometimes pressed the SLEEP button so that I wouldn't hear my father raging. Now I was drowning out nothing. That's what you needed to muffle most, all that was missing.

PART 2

6

THE MIND-BODY PROBLEM

KNEW NOBODY WOULD EVER love me for my body," my mother said. "They would have to love me for my mind."

It was a June morning, and I was sitting on the edge of my mother's unmade bed while she tidied up. Her room was king-size, its dimensions conspicuous because she was the only one here. The master suite had a dressing area with double sinks beneath a long mirror; a walk-in closet the size of a nursery; and a windowed bathroom. My mother was showered, her hair blow-dried and fluffy. I was still in the tank suit I'd put on for swim practice, almost dry now, except for the crotch and the piping. I was fifteen and I would be a high school junior in the fall. We'd lived in Boulder for two years.

When my mother said that someone would have to love her for her mind, she paused, holding the water glass she'd just lifted from her nightstand. I nodded but did not know what to say. If I spoke I might mess this up, and I wanted her to continue.

Instead, my mother resumed moving around the room, pouring the water from the glass into the sink, recorking the china jar in which she kept cotton balls, tossing a pair of canvas hiking shorts into the laundry basket. I watched her, considering her body.

My mother was slim and small-boned. But my eye was drawn that morning to what she'd often named as her flaws. She claimed she had thick calves, and she was self-conscious about her stomach. I was self-conscious about my stomach, too. All of the women in my family were focused on stomachs.

When I was nine, I'd flown out to Colorado to visit Marcie. One afternoon we visited a clothing store to buy my mother a gift. "She's not fat, but she has a little pot belly," Marcie told the saleswoman, arcing the air in front of her own stomach with her hand.

Then she looked at me to confirm. "Right?"

"Mm-hmm," I said.

Instantly my loyalty surged toward my mother, a thousand miles away in our lush, perfumed Michigan backyard. She would be wearing an eyelet shirt; she would be bending over pale-blue flowers the size of crystal balls. I desperately wanted her then, wanted her to look through the world and see me. I felt unsafe with her sister; I felt like I was going to cry. It wasn't fair for Marcie to say bad things about my mother and then force me to agree.

The reach of that small insult: It found in me those years when my mother and I were still conjoined. The years when I knew her body in the way only a young child does, standing next to her in the master bedroom's avocado-green tiled shower, watching her from a bench in a changing room at the club. I knew even her insides; that small stomach gurgled. I'd lain my head there at night while she read. Hers was the female body I learned first, and in a million complex ways, it will be forever connected to mine.

If you were trying to find flaws in my mother's looks, you had to try hard. My mother had the kind of beauty that happens only once in the family tree—the idealization of the phenotype. The fact that she didn't feel herself to be beautiful just made her more so. Men were drawn to her. Days after we'd moved to Boulder, the tennis pro giving me a lesson had asked her out on a date. More recently, walking together on University Hill, we'd neared two college boys.

When they passed, my mother said, "You know, I was wondering why those boys were looking at me, but then I realized they were looking at you." I was pretty sure she wasn't right.

Before the mirror, my mother cupped her hands beneath her hair. She paused a second, evaluating, then picked up a hairbrush. She ran the brush through, set it back on the counter, then cupped her hands beneath her hair again. The evaluation in the mirror was tinged with disappointment, whether about her looks or something else.

I knew nobody would ever love me for my body. They would have to love me for my mind. This was the kind of disarming intimacy I was drawn to. But while the admission itself was bold, there had been hesitation in my mother's delivery. The tumbler in her hand was a reinforcement, like an object gripped to disguise a quiver.

Another mother might have approached the conversation differently, as a lesson: "Your mind matters more than your body." But if your body mattered to you more than your brain told you it should— why deny that? Why not acknowledge that feeling and try to understand why you felt it?

My mother switched off the bulbs over the mirror. She was done in her room now. I stood, turned the lights back on: "I'm just going to borrow some earrings."

From her china dish, I took a pair of silver triangles set with tiny opalescent stones. I leaned in to my mother's mirror, inserted the earrings, stood back. Picked up her brush, ran it through my hair, which was flat around my face because I had not blow-dried or even combed it after swim team. I didn't look good with flat hair. It made my nose seem wide. *I knew nobody would ever love me for my body. They would have to love me for my mind.* At least my mother had total confidence in one of the two things. I didn't know if I could rely on either.

MY MOTHER SAID THAT when you moved to a new place, it took a year to get used to it and another year to feel like you'd always been there.

Boulder was familiar to me now: The mountains no longer looked like a Hollywood backdrop. But I did not feel settled, maybe because I was so mercurial myself.

In Michigan, I had been such a good girl, but in ninth grade in Boulder, I'd reinvented myself as a bad one, someone who ditched and cheated and shoulder-tapped. My new personality was a radical transformation, yet it was also not a lie. I was pretending at being a bad girl, but I found her in me. It was a systems test, a deployment exercise: These weapons were in the stockpile. How did they function in the theater?

Meanwhile, I hid the parts of myself I didn't want anyone to see, mainly shyness and smartness. Instead, I was disruptive, obnoxious. *Her conduct and effort are lousy and she is lucky to get a D in my class* was the type of sentence on my midyear report. But I could not keep up the act. By the end of second semester I'd retreated, become studious, watchful. The year had been tumultuous and destabilizing yet worthwhile: It freed me up, saved me from a fate as an obedient girl who started every paragraph with a topic sentence. But it also limited me in profound ways I wouldn't recognize until much later on. Now I knew how to create and maintain a false self, and this would become my default mode. You'd think I would have learned not to hide my essence, but instead what I'd learned was how.

Sophomore year I wanted goodness. This would always be my pattern—purity, control, following excess.

In the fall I decided that I'd watch for a while before I decided who to be. We'd moved from Burbank Junior High to Fairview High School, and now, among more than one thousand students, I could hide. This year I'd be an observer, the way I'd been taught in Montessori, hands crossed behind me as I stood beside another student's tiny desk. It was a comfortable position for me, the way a former ballerina might fall naturally into first. But in retrospect I see this stance as wobbly, unstable—hanging back until I decided which self to invent or pose to adopt.

My closest friend was named Lisa Tanner. Lisa was "loud"—the word we used to describe both somebody's persona and their decibel level. Her parents were divorced, too. She listened hard and remembered my stories as well as her own. But her social circle was wider than mine: She drank, and I didn't, which put me on the wrong side of the biggest dividing line of all. I was scared of alcohol: of the taste of it, of what it would do to my head. But some nights, sitting in my room writing papers about Emerson and Thoreau, contemplating the big questions, who to be and how to live, I would imagine Lisa out in the moonlit dark at a party and wonder: Wasn't her way of living better, more vital?

Over winter break I caught a stomach virus, and though it lasted only twenty-four hours, I lost two pounds. This was the kind of information the women in my family shared, and at Christmas dinner, I mentioned it. "It's just water weight," Marcie said. "You'll gain it back." But I didn't. And, as it had the summer we'd moved here, the small subtraction mattered. The way I felt in clothes was different. I liked moving through a day with a little air inside pants that had once clung. Some critical roundness had been shaved off my hips, and I was pleased by my reflection in the little gold-framed mirror leaning against my bedroom wall.

I knew nobody would ever love me for my body. It had never occurred to me that someone would be drawn to my body, except to admire its size. I tried to look pretty and thin. That was the most important thing about a body—thin.

There was a girl on my swim team, Leigh Custer, who had broad thighs but a flat stomach. Her body was a logic problem. Leigh had more fat on her than I did. But was she thinner than I was, because her stomach did not stick out? My stomach puffed out after anything, even one sip of water. I would watch Leigh when she raised herself up out of the pool and crossed the deck for a kickboard. She really was not tensing her abdomen. I wondered what that would be like, to move through the world without holding anything in.

My fixation on Leigh's stomach resembled the one I'd had years earlier on Heidi's knee backs. The difference was that at nine, that fixation hadn't heralded a permanent shift. At fifteen, it did. This was the summer when my preoccupation with thinness became a pathology.

EACH MORNING AT SIX I'd have a granola bar, then ride my bike to swim team. Afterward I'd come home and toast half a bagel to the perfect caramel color. Sometimes I'd also have a piece of cheese, because protein was important. Then I would stop. I'd wait longer than usual before eating again and eat a smaller amount than usual when I did. I wanted more. But I liked the feeling of less inside—light, relieved, unburdened—and I wanted *that* more. I wanted the reward for denying my desire more than I wanted to sate it.

After my bagel I'd drag a wicker chair across the backyard. I'd squeeze lemon juice over my hair, set a glass of ice water in the dry grass, and open a book. When I got too hot, I'd come inside and shower.

Some days I'd go down to the basement, where it was cool. Shelves in one corner held my mother's books and papers from college. Handling a volume of Trollope that cost $1.25 was a way to encounter her as an undergraduate. I would raise the cover page of an essay on the top of a stack and fear I'd never be able to write papers as sophisticated as the ones my mother had produced. How had she acquired that knowledge? It made me nervous, all that I lacked.

Another shelf held the work she'd done to earn her teaching certificate, including a beautifully written personal essay set during her pregnancy with me. She'd spent those weeks at the bedside of her mother, B.J. B.J.'s blouse had caught on fire at the kitchen stove at our family's summer home in the Adirondacks. She was in a hospital on a respirator, and her prognosis was poor. She might never know her grandchild. But the story ended happily: The day I was born was the day B.J. was able to breathe on her own again for the first time.

I was moved by the grace of these events. In one day, my life had begun and my grandmother's had been renewed, with my mother as the conduit. And just as precious as the story itself was the perspective of its teller. I both wanted to be close to my mother and was shy of that, and reading her writing was a safe way of drawing near.

I would go upstairs from the basement to her bedroom and look for things to borrow. While there, I would pick up the books on her nightstand. Certain titles float to the top when I place myself back there: *The Mind–Body Problem,* by Rebecca Goldstein, and Mary Gaitskill's *Two Girls, Fat and Thin.* They weren't both on the nightstand the summer I was fifteen. The Gaitskill wasn't published until I was a senior. But the two books are stacked together in my head. Examining the novels beside my mother's bed felt more invasive than my investigations in the basement. The books from college were ancient history; her contemporary syllabus was a diary. The jackets were bleached by backyard sun. They showed water-glass rings, like colorless circles made by somebody pressing hard with an invisible-ink pen. I would turn the books over, read the backs: "Ms. Gaitskill writes with such authority, such radar-perfect detail . . ."; Goldstein "turns everything, from logical positivism to orgasms, into the stuff of comedy."

Orgasms. It made me uncomfortable when there was sex in books I borrowed from my mother. I would pretend she was a nun reading these descriptions. She was someone who didn't feel anything. She was a reader who observed scenes rather than inhabiting them.

It didn't work.

My eyes on this page, where my mother's eyes had also been. It was like melding with her, sitting on her lap as I read.

ONLY A FEW MONTHS earlier, I actually had been pressed back into a moment of physical intimacy with my mother. One Saturday, I'd walked timidly over the dry grass of the backyard to the wicker chair in which she was reading and said, "Could you show me how to put a tampon in?"

She shaded her eyes, squinted up at me.

"What have you been doing at swim practice?" A look crossed her face. "Never mind," she said.

Inside the house, she took the tampon out of the plastic. She showed how you fanned the bottom by pulling the string. She put her finger in the cotton. Then she gave me a fresh one and left.

But I couldn't insert it and I asked her to come back in. We were in her bathroom, which was cool and clean. The casement window was open, its metal joint hyperextended.

"Can you just do it for me?" I asked.

"No," my mother said.

I sat on the toilet seat, looking down at the water, not at myself. I had never masturbated or even examined my genitals. The alarm of early puberty still ruled me. I was not going to touch myself; I could not risk what I might discover.

Again I tried to push the tampon up, but it didn't work. Clearly this was something I wouldn't be able to do. This was an intrinsic limitation, a birth defect.

"Someday a man is going to put his penis in your vagina, and it's going to be a lot bigger than this tampon," my mother said.

My mother's crudeness alarmed me. Now there was a surge, and with it I shoved the tampon in.

"Okay, I did it," I told her.

"Okay," she said, and immediately left the bathroom.

I stood and pulled up my shorts. The tampon was in wrong, I could tell. The pamphlet said you weren't supposed to feel it inside you. I unfolded the instruction sheet and studied the anatomical illustration of the vaginal canal. There was a curve that didn't make sense. It didn't match what I had in my head, a tube that went straight up. But the designers of these tampons were female doctors; it said so on the box.

For the rest of the afternoon I worried not about the tampon but about the penis and the way it would rip its way in. Again I was certain that it wouldn't work on me, that I had a different body, with something wrong.

I liked the idea of sex. I understood it as a way to get as close to someone as you possibly could. The act was the thing that made me uncertain. And I wonder now if what bothered me when I read my mother's books was not the thought of her desire but unease about my own.

LEARNING TO USE A tampon so late was a consequence of menstruating so early. There is no way I would have been ready for a tampon at ten.

These days, early puberty is so common it's an "epidemic" about which many articles are written, but in the 1980s it was unusual to get your period at ten. I'd gotten mine early because my mother had. *It's in our family.* Our oft-used phrase conferred a sense of continuity and identity. But the impulse to narrow everything to inheritance can obscure other influences.

When I was seven months old, my mother saw an article in *The Wall Street Journal* about cattle deaths in Michigan. In a freak industrial accident, fire retardant had been mixed with cattle feed. For months, residents—including my mother, pregnant with, then breastfeeding, me—had consumed the contaminated milk and meat. My mother called my father at the radio station. Nobody local had this news yet. The *Journal* was first with the story, one that is still being reckoned with today, in large part because of its health consequences, which include cancers, thyroid problems, congenital hernias, and early puberty. Girls exposed to the fire retardant in utero or in breast milk were significantly more likely to menstruate early.

I didn't know about this until I was diagnosed with a thyroid problem in college. In those days we all talked about how our exposure to images of "perfect" bodies had distorted our perceptions of our own. This story was about another kind of exposure—not visual but chemical. I'd considered how I'd acted in response to my environment but never how my environment had acted on me. The milk story offered a new explanation for my accelerated development yet fit inside an existing one, too, about what a mother transmits to her daughter. Through the mother passes the world.

"LOOK," I WHISPERED.

It was July, and my mother and I were in the library near my grandparents' house in the Adirondacks. I was in the children's section, performing one of my annual rituals, searching for due-date cards that showed both my name and hers. On one side, *Nancy Jordan* in unfamiliar child's cursive and a rubber-stamped date like 24 JUL 1954; on the other, my own careful script, *Susan Burton,* 4 AUG 1981.

We left the library with our books in our arms. Across the street was the white church where my parents had been married.

We wound through Keene Valley back to the house, a glorious sky overhead. This was the High Peaks region, so named because it was home to the tallest mountains in New York, but they looked mild to me after Colorado. Soft, friendly, starter mountains. We drove over the old wooden bridge across the river, then down the long dirt driveway through the meadow. As we passed the stone wall and approached the house, I could see my grandfather in his chair through the large windows, and, by the time we'd parked and started down the walk, he'd appeared at the back door.

"Dear, I was watching you as you came down the drive," he said to my mother through the screen.

Of course you were, I thought. Inside, I slipped away as my grandfather continued, "You don't know the first thing about driving on dirt, Nancy."

Seeing my mother here was the closest I got to seeing her life as a child. None of the personalities had changed. My grandfather watched and criticized all the time, and my mother deferred and accommodated. And then there was Marcie, pushing back, resisting, occasionally making fun of him. Their aspects had been fixed since childhood. Marcie had been the one who rebelled and threw parties and, when it was time for college, got as far from her parents as she could. She was confident and candid. My mother was always trying to please. This was the story my family told about itself, and as a teenager I accepted it. Only as an adult did it occur to me that this characterization of my mother was itself a means of keeping her down and insisting she was less. Her defining qualities of independence and strength were nowhere in this portrait.

The story of Grack—our name for my grandfather—was that his parents had sent him to a military boarding school at the age of eight. "He always felt unwanted," my mother or Marcie would say. Grack was controlling in a way that masked a desperate protectiveness. He was also an alcoholic whose drinking had been enabled by professional aimlessness and inherited wealth. He spent a lot of time at home, and he had a lot of time to drink.

Most nights at dinner, Grack would say something outrageous. B.J. would mutter in response, and Grack would turn to her and bellow, "What's that, woman?"

B.J. would dismiss him. There was something hard and practical about B.J. As a grandmother, she wasn't permissive or doting. In my twenties, after Grack died, she would gain a new freedom, and I would grow close to her. But when I was a child, she needed to look out for herself.

If my mother's personality can be traced back to her father, the way she is about food begins with B.J. The way *all* the women in my family are about food begins with B.J. Today my mother and aunt and my sister and I are at home in one another's kitchens, where we know we will find the best olive oil, the plain sheep's milk yogurt, dark sea-salted chocolate, a dense miche. We are good at food—but also vigilant about it.

B.J. was good at food before being good at food was a thing. She owned the first model Cuisinart ever made and had been subscribing to *Gourmet* since the second issue. She ground her own cornmeal, picked blueberries, baked bread from starter, prepared beef bourguignon and chocolate mousse. She was not a jolly, pillowy cook. She was small and elegant. A magnet on the refrigerator said SEXY SENIOR CITIZEN.

As a child, B.J. had been told by her mother that she was too fat. A framed photograph on a bedroom bureau showed B.J. at maybe seven, wearing a blue party dress. I wouldn't have called her chubby. She stared down at her cupped hands, in which she held a shiny apple. Even as a little girl that apple kind of freaked me out, and by the time I was an adolescent I did really wonder about it. Why was there food in the picture, and why the most obscenely symbolic food of all? Was B.J. looking at it like she wanted to eat it but had to resist?

The kitchen at Keene was a space both fraught and transcendent. Devil's food cake and a library book: That was bliss, as was a ham sandwich—Grack's ham, we called it—on the toasted cornmeal bread that B.J. baked. I remember the comfort of sitting on the floor as a very young child, running my fingers against the fine rubber treads of a stool as if over a zither, my grandmother standing above me, cooking. Cooking at the stove where her blouse had burst into flames.

AT THE END OF the visit, we celebrated Grack's seventieth birthday with a party on the flagstone terrace. From the kitchen, B.J. and my mother and Marcie brought out Triscuits from the Brisker and homemade gougères. I held the video camera, once jerking it around to capture myself, thin and tan, in my sailor dress. The next morning we sat around the dining room table and I recorded our breakfast. We were recapping the party, eviscerating certain guests. "This video can never be shown outside the family!" B.J. said, teary from laughter. Later she wrote it in careful ballpoint on the tape's label: FAMILY VIEWING ONLY. Behind the camera, I came out with zingers. "She's like her father," Marcie noted. I was silent when she said it. But, oh, my pride! My father was known for his wit. In that moment I understood my resemblance to him gave me power at this table. All of them with their brown hair and brown eyes and then me, light and fierce and unpredictable, a threat like him. They'd thought they were rid of my father, but he was here, in me. I would always have that. I would always be connected to him.

But I was also Susan—their Susan, my mother's Susan. At the table I was in the chair to the left of my grandfather, as I'd been my whole life. He thought he could get me to try things. "Just a bite," he said now, over my plate with Canadian bacon.

"No, thank you," I said. *No, thank you,* I'd been saying all vacation. Refusal in general was nothing new. But I was eating less than usual, and while I don't think Grack noticed, I wonder if Marcie did. I remember her eyes on me that morning and my self-consciousness about the toast I'd left on my plate. This *was* new: I was doing something with food that I didn't want anyone to see.

"It's from Oscar's," Grack said, naming the shop that made the ham.

"No, thank you," I said.

I wrote in a letter to Lisa Tanner, *My grandparents try to make you eat so much meat.*

WHEN I WAS IN my thirties and B.J. in her nineties, I sat beside her as she was dying. We were in her bedroom in Florida. On the bureau were photographs of my own children. B.J. had grown too sick to eat much or even to get out of bed. "Oh," she said to me, "how I wish I had enough energy to get on the scale. I would love to know how much I weigh." She knew there were not many days of her life left, but she wanted the number. Wanted a record of it. Wanted the sensation of stepping on the scale shrunken and triumphant. I did not think that was sad or pathetic or swear not to be the same way. I understood. At the same time she was saying this, I was next to her in a slipper chair, a cookbook open in my lap and a stack of them on the floor. The margins of the cookbooks were marked in her careful hand, and I was looking at all her notes and for all the things she'd made—especially the cornmeal bread. This was not the sweet cornbread that Northerners know, nor cast-iron-pan cornbread from the South. This was a dense loaf of coarse cornmeal, good for sand-wiches and toast. (Later, a shop I lived near would sell a version called broa de milho. "You're the only one who ever buys this," the girl in the apron behind the counter noted one day. Soon, they stopped making it.) "Is this the recipe?" I kept asking. "This one?"

When, in the evening, a nurse arrived, B.J. asked her to move a small table. "Could you lift that?" B.J. said. "I don't want my small granddaughter to do it." I felt pleased that my smallness had been noted. I actually was particularly thin then. I felt spectral, transpar-ent, and closer to my feelings in a way that made these days easier to bear. In fact, being thin was one of the reasons I had been able to pop up, hop on a flight, and get straight down here. I was empty and limber and able. If I had been fat beside B.J., I would have been distracted and hating myself and unable to fully inhabit these hours, the last we would ever spend together.

That's who I was then: a thirty-eight-year-old woman who still believed in the talisman of her adolescence. I still believed that thin-ness strengthened, protected, made me receptive. I did not see it as dangerous or restrictive. I truly did not believe it was possible to be the person I wanted to be, or to feel the things I wanted to feel, with-out it.

Oh, I'm so glad I have thin grandchildren!

THE MIND-BODY PROBLEM. TWO *Girls, Fat and Thin.* Probably these titles from my mother's nightstand remained in my head because these remained my issues. When I finally read the books, as an adult, I found that they weren't what I'd imagined. From their titles, I took them to be about the complex relationship between your body and your brain and your personality; about love and female friendship and competition. But *Two Girls, Fat and Thin* was about voyeurism and brutality and the journalist–subject relationship. *The Mind–Body Problem* wasn't an exploration of my mother's dichotomy: *I knew nobody would ever love me for my body. They would have to love me for my mind.* Instead, it was about mind–body in an abstract, knotty, philosophical way: *What is the world? What am I?* There was a brief, innocuous reference to "dieting." There was a lot more attention devoted to physical pleasure than to self-disgust.

I wondered if my mother had picked up the books expecting them to be about something else, too. You could be smart enough to have the confidence someone would fall in love with you for your mind and still have a mind–body problem.

7

THE WALK

Y FATHER HAD LOVED my mother for her mind. "Your mother is the smartest woman I've ever met," he once told me. Because he said that word, "met," in my head he knew this the instant they met, knew it as he stood in her parents' Connecticut living room holding a flute of my extravagant grandfather's champagne. It was New Year's Eve, the world turning from 1967 to 1968.

Down in the basement in Boulder, I sometimes wondered if I would come across the letters my father had written to my mother during the year between their graduation and their marriage. I'd once seen the packet of them in our attic in Michigan. They were on yellow legal paper. My father's handwriting had been younger, looser, but it was recognizably his. Though I had never read the letters, their existence comforted me. That they'd been written, and saved, was proof that theirs had once been a love story. I didn't know who they had gone to after the divorce, to her or to him.

———

A FEW WEEKS AFTER that trip to the Adirondacks, Betsy and I went to visit our father in Michigan. He had remarried. His new wife, Donna, was also divorced, and she had three daughters. She and my father had met at a 1950s-themed bar that had once been a crumbling Art Deco theater where we saw Shirley Temple movies on Saturday afternoons. That my father had met his new wife in this familiar place both reassured me and made me sad.

My father and Donna were building a house, but because it was not yet finished, we stayed in Donna's summer cottage, which was on a lake in a rural town. The roads were two-lane with four-way stops. The land had corn or was just empty. It was a popular place for radio and television stations to erect their towers. My father would name which station transmitted from which tower when we drove past. On one road there was a WOOD tower. Looking out the window, I'd imagine the time when this structure had been electric with his voice.

Since the divorce, I'd seen my father regularly. On my fifteenth birthday, he'd flown out to Colorado, picked me up from school, and taken me to lunch at the Elephant Bar. Fans shaped like palm leaves wafted overhead, and my father gave me a stack of books: Susan Sontag, Lawrence Ferlinghetti, and an anthology called *The Best of Maledicta: The International Journal of Verbal Aggression*. That book, full of serious consideration of offensive language, was inscribed: *I wish someone had given me a book like this when I was fifteen.* Afterward, we walked up to a Native American jewelry store on the pedestrian mall. I wanted a Zuni fetish: a little animal carved of stone that protected its owner. I chose a bear made of argite. My father picked out earrings for Donna.

My mother and Marcie were curious about Donna. Usually they were the ones telling me about our family, but now I had access to a part of the story they did not. The power this gave me was exciting, but I didn't know how to wield it. "She's blond and really tall," I would say, but they already knew this from photographs. They had questions about the house my father and Donna were building. I knew the questions were connected to things I did not fully understand, like child support. While my mother's family paid for the big things, in a daily way we existed on her schoolteacher salary, and between paychecks she had nothing. I was aware of my privilege, but it was a particular kind, an enormous safety net but no cushion.

Donna had worked her way through high school and college. She thought my parents had been profligate and that I had been indulged. At Christmas, my present from her and my father was one paperback. "Your plane ticket here was your real present," she told me. I didn't consider this visit a present. Besides, I knew from having looked at my parents' divorce agreement that the Christmas trip was a legal requirement.

As an adult, I would come to respect and admire Donna and to be moved by and grateful for her devotion to my father. But as an adolescent, I held myself apart from her.

My father was used to being waited on, but Donna required that he actually do a few things for himself. So now my father would rise from the table and bring his plate to the counter. He performed this task dutifully, as if carrying out a sentence. While I was impressed with Donna's retraining, I believed it was only because my father had lost everything—lost us—that he submitted.

Donna also tried to get me to perform basic household tasks. She wanted me to rub down the Plexiglas door with a hard rubber squeegee after I showered, so that the drips wouldn't leave marks. I ignored this request. Each time I went into the bathroom, I simultaneously enjoyed seeing the shower door covered in dried white droplets and felt bad that I was not giving Donna the one thing she wanted from me in this cottage she had paid for and cared about. But the impulse to resist her was strong.

DURING THE WEEK, WHEN my father and Donna were at work, Betsy and I spent the days with two of her daughters. Laura was a year younger than I was, and Erin was a year younger than Betsy. Laura was studious; Erin, energetic and feisty. The eldest sister, Jessica, was in college, and sometimes she came by in the evenings. She was independent and admirably fierce. "She wouldn't talk to her father for a year after the divorce," my father had once told me. That information got to me, perhaps because it introduced the possibility of a feeling I hadn't yet allowed myself to have toward him—anger. Sometimes, thinking of the punishment Jessica had inflicted on her father, I wanted to say, "See? See how lucky you are that you have me."

But there was no template for me to lash out at my father. And I was so conscious of his losses. My mother had us, her parents, her sister. My father was here, alone, in this new life. As always, I worried about him. Holidays, I bought him fetishes from the Native American jewelry shop. I gave my father a small jade frog. Whenever he said he had been on an airplane, I imagined the frog in the dark of a suit pocket. Also keeping him alive was a crystal I instructed him to hang on his rearview mirror. He drank in the car, tall silver cans of beer he bought at gas stations. One evening he'd locked his keys inside. "Shit," he said; "Motherfucking shit shit shit." It was after we'd seen the movie *Parenthood*. A sheriff was across the street, but we couldn't get him involved. There were too many beer cans. Later it was strange to remember that I'd thought of my father as the one with a drinking problem; that would become my mother's issue. Soon she would become the one to protect, the parent most in need of a guardian fetish.

EACH MORNING I'D PULL a lounge chair to the edge of the lake and read. When I got hot I'd swim out to the little floating dock and push myself up, the scouring-pad covering rough beneath my palms. Lying there, I would think about the boy I liked, whose name was Cord; I would imagine encountering him in the new school year. Before diving back in I'd stand for a moment, feeling my body taut in my suit, wishing that Cord—that anyone—was here to see me.

At the beginning of the summer I'd eaten less primarily to access a feeling—*light, relieved, unburdened*. But something had shifted. I liked the way I looked in that bathing suit, a high-cut one-piece. I liked the way I looked in my electric-blue miniskirt, and I liked the way others looked at me in it. I still sought the free feeling. But size was no longer just a side project.

A few times the four of us girls cut through a field to a roadside ice-cream shack. On those days, the kid-size vanilla soft-serve would be my lunch, and on the walk home I would be conscious of working it off.

Donna's dinners I picked at. I would eat only the celery and carrots she placed on a plate in the middle and the bread. "I thought bread made you gain weight," Donna said one night. The Atkins diet was years away from being revitalized. This was the era of carbo-loading and daily bread in six to eleven servings.

"No, it doesn't," I said.

But Donna knew what I was doing; she had seen this.

"One summer Jessica ate so many carrot sticks that she turned orange," Donna said casually another night. I did pause then.

One evening we went to our old country club for dinner. When I opened the leather-bound menu, I saw many bad options and didn't know what to pick. At the last second I ordered fettuccine Alfredo because it didn't have meat. As soon as it came, I saw it was a mistake. This would be fattening. I would take only a few bites. But cream was so heavy. It sank to the bottom in me. When I weighed myself in the morning, there was another half pound.

The scale I used was off the master bedroom. My parents' bedroom had been breezy, with billowing curtains my mother had sewn. In here there was a low-lit humidity. I tried not to see the bed my father and Donna slept in. I feared accidental discoveries: lubricant on a nightstand. But the scale was an imperative. It was this way in Boulder, too. I resented my mother's boyfriend, Bruce, for a number of reasons, not least of which was that I had to put off breakfast when he was in her bed. I needed to use my mother's scale, the most accurate one, before I had food and water in me. The scale delayed everything from getting started. I couldn't even take a shower, because of the weight of water in my hair.

I'd always taken the scale seriously. Even as a younger girl, I'd never liked weighing myself with clothes on or after eating. But until this summer, weighing myself had basically been a check-in. *Any unusual activity? Nope. Fine, then.* Now I was gratified by the number on the scale instead of used to it. I would stay on an extra second. It had never occurred to me I could get down into this range. These numbers had never been my territory.

I'M NOT GOING TO say the exact numbers here, or anywhere. Offering such data can be harmful to those who are vulnerable to eating disorders. But leaving out my weight is not just a question of sensitivity. I want to deemphasize the numbers because other things were more central to my experience. It's not that the numbers didn't matter at all; they did. They mattered way too much. But other things mattered more. The behavior mattered more. So did the feelings— the actual bodily sensations as well as the emotional states. The feeling provoked by the number—euphoria or disgust—was more important than the number itself. I think of a curriculum night at my sons' progressive school. The math teacher said our second-graders weren't just going to learn multiplication tables but also "talk about how numbers make us feel." Other parents shot glances, but I was instantly interested: *how numbers make us feel.*

There are other ways to describe size besides mass. That summer in Michigan I was five feet tall—my adult height. I can't say what cup size I was, because I just bought the bras stamped CALVIN KLEIN on the elastic. They were like cotton underpants for your breasts. My wrists were narrow and adorned with stacks of Southwestern silver bracelets, and when I raised my arms, hands clasped behind my back in a stretch, I revealed a swimmer's triceps.

The secret I've kept for my whole life is not about the numbers. It's about what I did. It's not about the number the needle landed on that summer but about where that number led.

ONE NIGHT AFTER DINNER, my father and I stayed at the table after everyone was through. He was talking about tarot cards. This would be an unexpected topic if you had only my mother's short-hand character sketch of him. She said that he was a 1950s person and she was a 1960s person, even though they were almost exactly the same age, and that mismatch explained the problems of their marriage. She was being facetious but also totally serious, in the way that baby boomers were about the '60s being the decade that changed everything.

When my mother met my father in college, he had long curly hair and lived in a cottage on the beach. Now he voted for Republicans and got his hair cut every two weeks. Though my mother was scrupulous about not bad-mouthing my father, she saw his conservatism as fair game. But I understood how somebody might want to stiffen. All during fourth grade, I had cheated in math, and in fifth grade I had changed my handwriting, begun printing very carefully in all caps, like an architect, to represent my new, virtuous foundation in the world.

My father's contradictions didn't confound me. This was just who he was. When I was a child, every morning he had done the push-ups where you exploded off the floor and clapped in the air, like a Marine, then gone downstairs to his study and worked on a novel, like an artist. These days, in the mornings he put on a suit and drove to his corporate job and in the evenings came home and tried to interest me in the I Ching.

I was conscious of the table being cleared around me. I was conscious that I did not even offer to help. But I felt like I deserved to sit with my father. I was visiting. This was our time together. Also, I didn't want to observe Donna scraping the food off my still-full plate in the kitchen.

Almost every night, Betsy and Laura and Erin and I walked the dirt road that ringed the lake. This evening my father and Donna wanted to come, too, and we all went into the back hall and put on our sneakers.

Outside, the air hummed with crickets. A boat ruffled the lake, and Erin, my younger stepsister, observed, "He should have his lights on." When we reached the main road, my father said, "Let's go back," and I pivoted toward the cottage.

"I want to keep going," Erin said to her mother.

"Let's go back," my father said firmly to Donna.

"But I want to keep going," Erin said.

This was a mistake; she hadn't known my father long enough. Or maybe it was on purpose. She was as fierce as her eldest sister. She would punish her mother for making her live with someone else's dad.

"All right," my father said. He approached the blacktop and evaluated it as if it were the starting line of one of his races. "You want to walk?" he asked Erin. "No problem. We'll walk all night."

"Bob." Donna's voice had an edge; my mother would have been softer—if not immediately pleading, then willing to. I believed I knew better than both of my father's wives. I believed there was nothing you could do.

"The girl said she wants to walk." My father shrugged. "We'll see just how far she can go. Right, Erin?"

Erin fiddled with the zipper on her windbreaker. My father clapped his hands. "Let's walk."

Donna swore, put an arm around each of her daughters, and started down the road. My father let them get a little ahead before we began walking, too.

We walked on the shoulder, which sloped. My father was on the outside. He also took this position on sidewalks. It was manners, so the woman wouldn't get dirty. Out here it was also safety, so we wouldn't get hit. The cars were infrequent, and they drove carelessly, straddling the yellow line as they crested the hills. At the first sound of an engine, my father would herd us into the ditch below the shoulder. When pickups got too close, he would shout, "Fuck you!"

I wasn't scared. On the edge of that road I felt restored. This was an electric unease I knew. It was more normal to have my father acting this way than to have him doing the things Donna wanted him to do, like make his own toast. It touched the original things in me, the essential place that lit when my father raged.

All the relief was in returning to old versions. This rupture had restored the proper order. Wasn't everyone more comfortable like this? There was a rightness to it, families in the night. If we had to divide, it would go this way. If there was a war, or an emergency, or the apocalypse: He would choose us, and she would choose them. It was so simple. I felt tender to Donna then, sensitive to her bond with her daughters.

Of course, my notion was a fantasy: You never split neatly into your original units again. But the knowledge was firm in me that night. This was a law of the universe, the same as the mitosis we'd studied in science.

It neared midnight. The world was empty and pretty. We walked a loop my father had often traced while training for marathons, and he pointed out landmarks. When we returned to the cottage, my father turned on the light in the back hall and Betsy and I took off our shoes. Then we went into the bedroom where our stepsisters were already sleeping, and he went into the bedroom with Donna.

In the morning I weighed less than ever. There was a thrill in me when I saw the number on the scale. Oh, the power of lightness! I loved the walk then, love it still in memory. I stayed out late, got thinner. We were ourselves that night, our real family. We were two small girls next to our father on the road. We were outside under a huge starry sky, walking past the radio tower that had channeled his voice. We were back in our original frequency, close enough to receive his signal.

8

STOMACHS

WHEN I RETURNED TO Boulder, my body was different. A summer metamorphosis was a familiar plotline in the YA novels I'd once read. Often the teenage-girl character transformed by growing breasts or by getting her period, something that advanced her maturity. I felt I'd moved forward, too, even though I'd turned back the clock: I was no longer menstruating. But if you'd glimpsed me on the street then, you would not have been startled or necessarily thought, *That girl needs to eat.* You might have thought, as I did then, *That girl looks pretty.* I was in the dangerous early stage of anorexia: The world responds to thinness, and the girl subsists on its compliments.

My great-uncle Dick came out West from New York. He was B.J.'s brother. He worked as a designer for the telephone company. He was gay and he lived in Greenwich Village. He was refined and kind. My mother had gone down to Santa Fe to meet Dick, and the day they returned to Boulder I came back from a bike ride and found them in the kitchen. "Why, she's beautiful!" Dick said. "She's so thin that she could be a model. Don't you think?" I was thrilled. Dick was from New York. He knew.

But my mother's lips tightened when Dick said it. She didn't think I needed encouragement. When we went up to Aspen, Marcie got involved. "You're too thin," she said, then took me to Paradise Bakery for frozen yogurt. Outside, we sat on a bench. I looked up at Ajax, the ski mountain, which in the summer was as green as a golf course. Marcie watched me eat.

I thought she and my mother were jealous.

My mother told me I would have to go to a group at the Boulder Women's Center unless I gained five pounds. I imagined a circle of chairs filled with ballet girls who would scorn me. The thought of this group made me nervous. I would have to lose more weight if she decided to send me.

My warped ideas about anorexia were based on a handful of cultural touchstones. The first was Karen Carpenter. At age ten I'd read about her in *People*. Paging through the magazine at a friend's house, I came across a story about the singer who'd grown so bony that her heart had stopped. I felt like I did when reading about a movie star's drug addiction. I was scared of the information but greedy for it. Karen Carpenter's skull face and the assertion that she had once loved tacos and chili. I did think she was a little fat in the "before" photographs. She had gone to the hospital for "force-feeding," but her wrecked, shriveled body couldn't handle it.

The mix of what I felt: disgusted, enthralled, superior.

Across the room, my friend was watching television. I closed the magazine. I felt like something had happened that she did not know about. I'd had an encounter outside with someone scary, a burglar, and run back in. I felt transported and secretive.

I USED TO THINK my anorexia was idiosyncratic. That it grew out of my early fear of ingesting anything. Or that it was unconscious, even: My mother's contaminated milk had primed my body against future incursions. But fear of poisoning can be a symptom of an eating disorder. I was typical in this way and so many others. One of scores of girls lingering over celebrity eating-disorder stories in magazines. There was nothing special about what I did.

THE NIGHT BEFORE THE first day of junior year, I sat down at my dressing table, opened a notebook, and made a list.

> THIS YEAR
> more confident, happier
> friendlier, outgoing, mature
> appear as smart but cool/fun
> "friends w/ everyone" but good friends group
> be known as environment conscious

The goals were nobler than the ones I'd had two years earlier when I'd moved to Boulder. Wanting to be popular and to hide my smartness had involved secrecy and posturing. Reinventing myself as the girl on this list would require transparency and generosity.

I tore the page out of the book and crossed the room to my cedar chest. I placed the list inside with everything else I'd saved. In addition to the artifacts from Michigan were mementos from my new life here: notes passed in class with Lisa; my NASTAR ski membership card for 1987–88; an all-about-me in basic French. *Je m'appelle Susan Burton. J'adore faire les courses. J'aime téléphoner.*

Downstairs, my mother was making dinner, pasta with peppers. The meal was mostly peppers: my mother's preference. She would go to restaurants and say things like, "I'll have the pasta with chicken and vegetables, without the pasta."

I sat at the table and my mother brought me a bowl with a giant pile of sautéed peppers and a few squiggles of fusilli. She sat beside me, put a napkin in her lap, took a sip of wine. I felt mature and close to her: I was eating her food. My mother wouldn't have perceived my dinner as a problem but as progress—finally I was trying something new. The problem was eating nothing. Eating just vegetables: To her, that was normal.

But I had never eaten so many vegetables at once, and I had diarrhea in the middle of the night. When I awoke in the morning, my stomach was finally the way I'd always wanted it, collapsed in. Even without lying on the ground, I could pass the test that proved you were thin: place a ruler like a bridge across your hip bones.

All the things my stomach was that morning: It was a bowl, the shaded part of the mountain on the ski-resort map. It was the math word "concave." It was better than Leigh Custer's from swim team. Hers was the untouched block of plaster; mine had been carved. Mine was scooped out like a melon, down to the rind.

It would be a celebration on the scale; it would be a tingling win.

In my bathroom, I took off my pajamas and wrapped myself in a towel. Through my mother's bedroom door, I heard the fuzz of the shower. I waited a few minutes for her to be done. When I went into the master suite she was in her closet, choosing clothes. *Morning Edition* was playing through a clock radio. I entered her bathroom, hung my towel on the bar across the shower door, and stood naked on the scale. This was the white scale from Target. I could go through all the scales we'd ever had. The one with the big round dial my grandparents had sent. The first digital scale we owned, where the LED readout was raised on a stick.

Now here I was on a pebbly white surface at the beginning of a new year, lighter than I'd ever been. "Lighter": everything in that word, air and joy and wonder. The beginning of anorexia is like heroin before it wrecks you. It's a sensation akin to bliss. (But the rest of anorexia is like heroin, too, in its downward trajectory, and I want to shut myself in the bathroom with the fifteen-year-old me and warn her of the peril: organ failure, cognitive impairment, the highest mortality rate of any psychiatric illness—is anything I'm saying getting through? I want to tell her that even if she escapes that jeopardy and finds a way to be, say, a "functioning" anorexic, she will lose and waste so much. I am her living proof. A silence. I know enough about her to see that I have made her uneasy. But I also know that she is expert at shutting out, at turning away, and that this is what she will do. She will stare back down at the needle on the dial, and that is it, our meeting over: My chance to rewrite my own story is through.)

I stepped off the scale and wrapped myself in my towel. It was amazing, to shrink.

I came out of the bathroom and saw wet marks on the carpet where my mother's feet had been. I wondered if I would make footprints if I was wet or if I was now too light. I loved this idea. I had become a sprite, like Ariel; a fairy, like Tinker Bell. A creature that sparkled and left no trace.

My mother emerged from her walk-in closet. She was also wrapped in a towel, and her short hair was pressed against her head. She wouldn't dip under at the swimming pool, but I thought she looked pretty with wet hair, punk rock.

I knew my mother was going to be mad at me, but I couldn't not show off. I wanted her to know. I wanted her to see.

"I'm so thin," I told her, "that my stomach actually goes in."

But as soon as I saw the look she got, I decided not to open my towel.

My mother screwed up her mouth and tried to make her own towel tighter around her. But in her agitation it fell open, and I saw her stomach, that hard, small stomach. *She's not fat, but she has a little pot belly.* My eye was colder at fifteen than it had been at nine. Now I judged that my mother did have extra flesh. That stomach, but also a heaviness in her thighs, which touched. Mine had a space between them. Her bottom, which bulged out over her leg. I could see all this now that I was someone with the minimum.

"This makes me too upset to talk to you about, Susan," my mother said. "You are deranged. You are too thin." She pushed a wet lock of hair from her forehead. "Your perception is totally distorted. If you looked like I do, you'd probably think you were obese."

"Obese." We said that word in our family, long before it was a national crisis.

"No, I wouldn't," I said.

But I couldn't imagine her stomach on me. It was not a size I would ever expand to fit. Oh, it was impossible. I would have to take to my bed.

My mother could exist like that and I couldn't. I realized that with a start then. You hear these words about mothers and their teenage daughters: separation, differentiation. These are processes. They happen over years. But that was the moment I tore off from her, right then. We were still standing across from each other in her dressing room in our towels, but I was elsewhere now, judgmental, released. She could be like that and I couldn't. I wouldn't. I would never, ever, be like she was then.

Her frustration with me had likely crested. Probably from her perspective, we'd been having this conversation for weeks. For years, even. From the beginning, when I'd been the child who would not eat.

"I don't want to hear any more about this," my mother said.

I left and took a shower, looking down at my stomach.

In my room, I dressed in an Indian print T-shirt. The shirt was large. I belted it at my hips and then poufed the fabric out over the belt. This was how we all did it. Nobody tucked in. There was a horror of the natural waist.

Tops had to be big, but bottoms could be tight. I had tiny moss-green Bermudas. They were not skintight, but they fit. They were from the children's department and they were for a girl of ten. "I fit into size ten," I'd said to my mother the day I tried them on at the store.

"You are deranged, Susan," my mother had said. "Deranged"—that word she kept choosing. "I think you should ask yourself why you're trying so hard to be a child again."

It startled me when she said that. I felt a little nervous. I turned to the rack, with its small crystal-plastic hangers. It was a thing that sounded like it could be true. And I didn't want it to be true: It was weird to go backward.

What was true was that many nights I dreamed myself back into my old house. The house on the hill in which I'd been the child of two parents. But while I would have given anything to step inside my old house, I didn't want to be a little girl in it. I wanted to be me in it now.

While I understood that my mother was talking about something both psychological and physical, it was easier to dismiss her argument if I focused on the concrete part. I didn't want the body of a child: duh! But I did want the body of a preteen. That was the body I wanted to occupy, the one in transition. I wanted the form of a mannequin in the juniors' section. I wanted what I'd been cheated out of by early puberty. I wanted to be lithe, clear-skinned. I wanted no extra. I wanted dryness and ease. I wanted to be a girl in *Seventeen* in tight but not too tight stonewashed jeans, lying on her stomach and writing in her journal. I didn't want no curves at all; I just wanted little ones.

I wanted that body because it was a bridge between childhood and adolescence, and I remained caught between them. At fifteen, I was still trying to figure out how to be a teenage girl. First I'd tried with appearance: clothes, shaving, makeup. Then personality: bad girl, good one. Now I was trying again with my body, and this third time was the charm. In my high-cut tank suit, I looked exactly the way I wanted to. I had this tiny little waist and modest breasts and perfect-width hips. At the pool I felt older, bold, confident. I didn't want to discourage male attention. I wanted to be admired in that bathing suit. "Admired." That's the word I would have used, not "desired," and the language indicates to me now that I both wanted to be sexualized and didn't. For me at fifteen, anorexia was an illness of ambivalence.

In my room, I applied lip gloss with a wand. My mother's assumption was false: I didn't want to be a child. It was the first morning of my junior year, and in this body I was finally the person I wanted to be. I felt I'd crossed through years of awkwardness into grace.

But her comment bothered me. *Ask yourself why you're trying so hard to be a child again.* It was the first moment I wondered if there was something wrong about what I was doing and wrong with me that I was doing it.

9

ARTIFACTS

HAVE TO START THE fall of junior year in retrospect rather than in real time. Because for a few years that followed, fall of junior year was the halcyon period of my memory. My nostalgia for this season began the instant it ended and continued into college. I longed to return to that fall. I longed to get back to the girl I had been then. That glorious period! What about it was so good? It was my body; it was my mind; it was my crush on Cord. And, most important, it was the last moment before I started binge eating. Fall of junior year was the golden past for which I yearned.

I yearned for the first football game of the year, Friday, September 8, 1989, when it rained and my friend Sara Lewis French-braided my hair and a yearbook photographer took our picture, arms-slung-around-shoulders, on the twenty-yard line. I yearned for Cord behind me in the hall, calling "Sooo-san" in his musical-theater baritone, asking if I wanted a ride home. I yearned to sit in the passenger seat of his black pickup, my hair windblown, him singing along to "Hotel California." I wanted to be in the magic-crush stage where daily he made gestures with significance, like drawing a heart on my leg in ballpoint pen. I wanted to make a list of all such moments. I wanted to go to the Channel 9 health fair in the gym third period and get weighed and measured and answer survey questions about how I dealt with stress. (*Take walks. Talk to friends.*) I wanted to get back to a way I'd felt inside. Airy, flexible, disciplined. Idealistic, confident of my intelligence. And happy. A dull, Pollyanna word, but what a shame, because, oh, to be *happy*! It felt so good. And people noticed this! It was true that more people wanted to be around you when you weren't obnoxious or remote. I was wanted. Later, I wanted *that* again. I wanted Lisa Tanner to pick me up for school on the first morning she had her license. I wanted to swerve up Boulder Canyon in the dark with the smell of pine and Camels. I wanted—well, no, actually, I never wanted to drink a wine cooler again, but I wanted alcohol to be new. I wanted to speed down Arapahoe Avenue on Friday night in a car packed with girls. I wanted Squeeze's "Tempted" to come on and all of us to scream-sing the lyric *A foot without a sock.* I wanted stories to happen when we raced around the town. I wanted a policeman to shine his flashlight into the back seat and say, "Girls, get the beer out from under the Ouija board." I wanted to start retelling that story even as we sped away from the squad car. I wanted those doo-doo-doo-doo-doo-doo-doo-doo-doo notes of New Order's "Ceremony" to come on like the opening sequence laid under our credits. Because of course our lives were cinematic! In memory that fall it is always the magic hour, always the best light to film in. Even at night it is the magic hour. Even during third period it is! I wanted to leave school during third period with a friend and not do anything but drive around and slow down when we got to speed bumps and maybe get gas, which cost so little the price was expressed in cents per gallon. I wanted to twist the knob at my locker, open that dented red door again, then sit on the floor with another girl and feel the fortune of my life, of these friends.

I wanted to be me again. I was sure I'd been her that fall I was fifteen. For a long time I remembered this girl as my best version. And even though eventually I recognized this as irrational, and disturbing—partly because some of what I liked about that girl was what she had *weighed*—it didn't change the way I felt about being that girl. I remembered it as feeling pretty ideal.

That fall I felt as though I had unlocked access to the world and to other people. I loved each day as it was happening. There was almost nothing I wanted to change. That should have been a sign that I was in the midst of something unsustainable, but I didn't know that then. It was a first, like so many things in adolescence.

THE FALL PLAY WAS called *David and Lisa*. It was a high-school staple about two students at a school for troubled teenagers. Cord played David. I played a minor character called Girl. It was okay. The main parts always went to seniors.

Cord was a senior, and I'd met him a year earlier in another school play. Almost immediately, he'd appeared in one of my dreams. In the dream it was an overcast day and we were standing beside the hood of a car. Cord moved close and embraced me from behind, and I leaned into him with a languor that felt exquisitely right. I woke up in my little iron bed and understood something I hadn't before: I liked him.

Cord was tall, with dark curls, and he seemed urbane and con-nected. Rumor had it that he'd dated Amanda Peterson, the star of a teen movie called *Can't Buy Me Love*. She lived an hour away in Greeley, but they both had the kind of beauty that emits its own signal. People that attractive just find each other, even if located miles apart along the Front Range. Cord's beauty was sculptural but also feminine. Sometimes seeing him walk down the hall with his Girbaud jeans low around his thin hips provoked in me a shiver that was new.

A year earlier, I'd been timid, but that had changed. I felt some-thing for Cord, and it seemed important to do more than shyly stare. There was a cassette of my mother's I'd listened to all summer in the backyard, pressing the rubber REWIND button of my yellow Walk-man again and again. The girl singer making what might have been sappy words subversive by delivering them as if she were the ruler of an authoritarian state: *Don't you want somebody to love, don't you need somebody to love.* Yes.

One afternoon at rehearsal I was lying on my back, holding a script over my face, half-learning lines and half-talking to a boy named Davis. He had tiny dreads and a demanding intelligence. I liked talking to him because he wouldn't let you get away with anything sloppy. He challenged you, made you think.

Because I was lying on the floor, people would pretend to step on me. "Whoops, sorry, Susan," they would say.

Then I felt a weight atop me. What was Davis doing? But when I moved the script away from my face, I saw that it was Cord. He was mounting me.

"Oh, baby," he said, and then rode me as if we were having sex.

The first sensation was resistance. Everything contracted. But an instant later my body adjusted. Instinct kicked in, and I surrendered to him. We were acting, but this was someplace I had been. I thought maybe I would be okay at sex then.

I felt relieved that Cord was unaware of my inexperience. When it came to sex, I didn't even know the slang. One time on a ride home, he'd been talking about 69 and I'd had to pretend.

"Cord," somebody was saying. "Cord!"

Everyone was looking at us. He was needed in the scene.

Instantly he was on his feet. I raised myself on my elbows. I regretted not the act but the dissolution of the moment.

"Uh, what were you doing?" Davis asked Cord.

"Nothing," Cord said.

After Cord resumed his role, Davis's attention shifted to me. He regarded me critically, as if I had become less to him. I felt debased for an instant but then tough, because anyone would have gone along with it. Or I didn't know: Maybe anyone wouldn't have. I scraped a fingernail along the tight weave of the industrial carpet. But it didn't matter about anyone—about brainy, principled Davis, about the room of nerdy, gaping thespians—because I would have gone along with it again. It was the opposite of last year. I would say yes to everything. I would take it all in.

TWO DECADES LATER, SORTING through the heaps of paper I'd once saved in my cedar chest, I came across a description of that afternoon.

> And he totally started breathing and moving like we were fucking &
> it was like we were both totally in the same world by ourselves to-
> gether . . . he like jumped up and Davis was like, "Uh, what were
> you doing?" and he was like "Nothing," all embarrassed, and it was
> so cute & so cool.

I had a cedar chest because this one had belonged to my mother. I didn't realize cedar chests had any association with teenage girl-hood until seeing ads for them in *Seventeen*. In one ad I still recall, a girl sat on the floor next to her open Lane cedar chest, perusing a yearbook. The implication was that even before you finished your adolescence, you should be preparing to look back on it. While I was a saver by nature, I was different from the girl in the ad. She saved selectively. Inside her chest were discrete objects—pressed flowers, heirloom lace. Mine held sheaves. When it came to personal ar-chives, I was a completist. I preserved not just mementos of the heightened moments but of the mundane and disturbing ones. I didn't have a rosy scrapbooking impulse. I just didn't want to lose access to the world I'd inhabited or the person I'd been.

This book is its own artifact: that of a middle-aged woman look-ing back on her teenage self. What I write about who I was then reveals just as much, if not more, about who I am now.

By the time I was a junior in high school, I'd already reinvented myself a few times. Those inventions didn't stop when high school ended. Instead of inventing the girl I wanted to be, I invented the story of the one I'd been. Because these representations were tied to where I was in my life at the time, they changed along with me. In college, for example, I had an actual list of high school stories I told aloud to my roommates. These were true tales of wild suburban nights. I identified them with titles like "Jamie Goes to Jail in Jefferson County" and drew flowers by the ones I considered "greatest hits." Because a lot of students at Yale had been nerds in high school, my party-hardy stories became a way I identified myself in contrast to the people around me, most of whom seemed to be flourishing while I floundered. I used my high school stories to prove to my roommates, and to myself, that I had once been someone better, someone else. In my stories I was a blond, carefree girl who popped out of sunroofs. I worked in some bad stuff. But only acceptably bad stuff, not the things that scared me. For instance, "'I Was Just Trying to Keep Warm': The Wade Biehn Story" told of a hookup in a line outside an all-ages dance club. The story made me seem lacking in judgment but desired, and reckless, and cool. I left out anything I considered shameful. I left out the binge eating.

While the story I am telling today about my adolescence is different than the one I told to my college roommates, it is still not the full story; how could it be? I am selecting and culling, making choices about this reflection of me. I also know there are things I can't see. It might be years before I can make out, or admit to, the pose I'm adopting or recognize my current biases. Not until thirty years from now when I'm looking back at this book, feeling tender toward the middle-aged woman who wrote it but also conscious of the way her struggle distorted this invention.

CORD AND I WERE growing close. It was the daily rehearsals for the fall play and the rides home. He alternated among three cars: a small black pickup, a gray Oldsmobile, and a white Oldsmobile. In Cord's hands, an Oldsmobile was not staid but louche. In that plush interior we talked about everything: acting, activism, art, my parents, New York City, California, Buddhism, dreams, night, the moon, synchronicity, sex, fun drugs, people we knew.

I was myself with him. Sometimes I feigned knowledge I didn't have (69), but overall I did not pretend. And while I was aware that he had a gift for making people feel seen, I hoped there was more than that going on between us.

One day he turned to me and said, "I feel like I've known you forever."

It was dusk, and we were going north on 55th Street.

"I know," I said. Rarely had I felt like this, so warm and electric. "I can tell you anything."

"Well, that, too," he said. And then for a second I was embarrassed: Anytime there was an opening, I took it. I gave too much away. "But how we can just sit here and zone and not say anything and nobody feels like they have to make conversation. That's so cool."

"Zone" was a word that seemed to belong to him. It sounded right in his voice, which was assured but also stagy. By it I felt strummed. At parties I would hear his voice before seeing him, and then the gorgeous boy himself would materialize, curly-headed, suede jacketed, in front of a china cabinet in a foyer, next to an empty pool, through a gate on a bridle path. He would seek me out, come talk. One time, after a weeknight soccer game, I was standing in a McDonald's parking lot with two friends when Cord approached and embraced me from behind. "Did you have fun tonight?" he said. I stayed still for a moment. I didn't move or answer. I was living inside the dream I'd had the year before: Cord was hugging me backward, and we were near the hood of a car. That was the defining sensation of that fall, one of dreams coming true.

I didn't eat at the McDonald's. It was weird to me that we always went there. Maybe in the rest of the country it was a less enlightened time, where people didn't find fast food horrifying, but this was 1989 and we were in Boulder. Herbal tea was our town's primary product. A popular bumper sticker was I EAT TOFU AND I VOTE. Still, the intractable popularity of McDonald's. We even had a McDonald's in our school.

Later, at home, I was so happy. It had been the best night, even before Cord. The glacier air that came when the sun dropped behind the mountains; friends reaching down arms from the bleachers. This was how people spent their lives. They went to places where other people would be and talked to them. I would do this now, too. It was another one of my resolutions for the year, to accept every invitation.

My mother and my sister were asleep. I was just standing in the kitchen. Normally I wouldn't have eaten anything at this hour, but I was hungry and happy and thin. Still in my mind was the fact that I was supposed to be gaining weight so that I wouldn't have to go to an eating-disorders group. In the freezer we kept blondies. They were called Rachel's Husband's Butterscotch Brownies, and they were better cold. I stood at the counter and ate a blondie slowly. It was a pleasure, the night still in me, something sweet in my mouth. But later I would look back on that blondie as a portent. I had broken a rule of life, standing at the counter, eating late. This was something that had never before occurred to me to do, but for years that followed, not eating at night would become a primary goal. I learned from magazines that I shared this goal with many women. How did we all come up with it independently, the kitchen counter, the sweets? And why, later, was it so hard for me to remember that the blondie had been an experience of bliss? It was not representative of the behavior that followed; it was distinct from it. I'd eaten not to numb feeling but to deepen it. I didn't want to leave the night yet, and that blondie kept me inside the dream.

THAT FALL I FILLED a page-a-week calendar with a record of my doings. Sometimes I noted events in advance of their occurrence—a half day, an audition—but usually I filled in retroactively with shorthand. This was not for planning but for posterity.

Tuesday, October 3. MY B-DAY! 16! Acting test due. Ride to school w/ Johanna. Go to Taco Bell w/ Lisa & Meredith 4th. Go to McDonald's, drive around w/ Lisa after school. David & Lisa 4–7. Ride home w/ Cord. Go to soccer game w/ Meredith.

Years ago, after I first unearthed this calendar, I wondered what else might emerge if each morning I picked up the book and tried to remember all I could about the corresponding slot in 1989. It was an impulse to go carefully over the season when I had started to fray, as carefully as if I were sequencing a gene and could identify the day that held the mutation.

10

NOVEMBER 3–5, 1989

LISA TANNER TOLD ME that Alexander Martin liked me. "He saw you on fall-preview night and asked about you," she said.

The fall-preview night had been in the gym. All the sports teams were there, and the choirs, and our play. I'd stood in the center and read something. Also that night, the huge San Francisco earthquake happened. "I know people there," Cord had said, his hands fluttering. After that I left with him and we drove home in the dark. Even tense, he had a languid, sloppy way at the wheel. That had been the part of the night I remembered, but now I saw myself from Alexander's perspective in the bleachers. I had worn my favorite shirt. It was a hand-me-down from Marcie, an oversize blue-and-black top with a band at the bottom. I thought it read as *moon in the night*. On my feet had been my new shiny black oxfords. They were like Doc Martens, except they were Esprit. They were made for suburban girls like me who were scared of the Sex Pistols and heroin.

My crush on Cord was profound and immutable. But Alexander started calling me, and I welcomed his interest. I'd noticed him, too. He was a senior. He was in National Honor Society, and he played baseball. His dark hair was clipped close. And he was well-liked—friendly and kind. The year before, his girlfriend had been Becca Robertson. They were one of the school's serious couples. She was smart and a little wild, and I thought for sure they'd had sex. Like me, Becca Robertson was on swim team. After practice each morning, we all went to the shower room and twisted under the spigots with our suits on. Most of us wore two, or even three, ripped-up, saggy suits to practice, because of the drag created by the additional material. Sometimes in the showers, people would remove or pull down one of the extra suits, but a layer always remained, like an undershirt. Becca Robertson was the only girl who stripped down to skin. The water fell on her flat chest as she made little half-turns. What she did was bold, almost defiant. The flatness of her chest was part of it. She was flaunting its deviation from the norm. I wondered if part of the reason Alexander liked me was because Becca and I had the same kind of breasts.

One Friday night Alexander and I went to a football game, and when it was over we descended with everyone onto the field. The field seemed bigger when you were on it. I felt the slightly shifted perspective of a dream. Midway across, Alexander picked me up and carried me—and then he kissed me. My first kiss.

For a second I was sad that it had happened like this, in motion, but at the same time I was relieved that he assumed casualness was appropriate, that I had done this before.

SWEET SIXTEEN AND NEVER *been kissed:* My friends said this, meanly, about another friend of ours, but I wasn't sure if they knew it about me.

I could have escaped that curse. Only weeks earlier, when I was still fifteen, a boy on the tennis team had tried to kiss me. But I'd refused. It had been instinctual. An alarm in my brain had gone off when the boy, Marc, leaned in. It seemed to be affixed to the same lobe that rejected foods: Here was another thing I just wasn't going to put into my mouth.

What had changed by the time Alexander came around? Partly I just liked Alexander better. Marc was blond and shy; Alexander was popular and dark. I was drawn to him. But I had changed, too. And my God, the speed at which this happened!

I'd spent the summer denying desire. Now the leaves were turning, and I was letting things in.

"YOU'RE SO SKINNY," ALEXANDER said a few nights after the football game. We were making out in the back seat of a car, and Lisa Tanner and her boyfriend were making out in the front. Alexander's hand was beneath my sweater. "How much do you weigh?" he said.

I said the number.

"And I bet you think that's fat," Lisa said.

"I mean . . ." I said, and they all laughed.

I actually didn't think of that number as fat. But I *felt* fat. I was gaining weight.

This was a liminal stage, one that lasted about four weeks. During this time I ate in a way that was both distinct from the past and predictive of the future. For example: Over Columbus Day weekend, my father had come to town. With him in restaurants I ate more than I wanted to, often food I didn't care for, and when he dropped me off at home, I'd go into the kitchen and open the cupboard. That weekend there was a fat little plastic bag of royal chocolate trail mix from our organic grocery store. I'd dig my hand into the bag and sprinkle the trail mix into my mouth, even though I'd never liked it before, with its bird-food seeds and limp coconut chips. The trail mix was connected in my mind to those meals I hadn't enjoyed. I was trying to replace them, or compensate for them, but the trail mix wasn't what I wanted, either. (What did I want? One might say that I wasn't getting what I wanted from my father, and I ate to compensate. While I couldn't have identified a reason for my behavior, even that weekend I could have named the feeling that drove me to the cupboard. *Want something else. Something more. Want more.*)

By the end of my father's visit, the bag was empty.

I'd been eating more in general. Not a ton: basically just the regular amounts I used to eat before the anorexia. But the weight returned staggeringly quickly, and by the first weekend in November I'd gained back all I'd lost that summer.

November 3–5, 1989. These are the slots in the calendar that I'd walk myself up to again and again. I thought of it as the weekend I lost power. The wall was breached, and the base station flooded. Something in me went dark, and for years I wasn't the same again.

November 3 was a half day, a Friday, and Alexander and I went to lunch at Pizza Hut. It was not a restaurant I would have chosen, but having a boyfriend was so new to me: I would do what he wanted.

While we waited for our pizza, Alexander talked about California, which was where he wanted to go to college. "And then med school," he said.

Our pizza came in a cast-iron dish, and I held out my plate for a slice. It was a thick pan pizza with green peppers, mushrooms, onions, and cheese. With pizza, my guideline for slices was two. Sometimes I'd eat three, but I never felt good about myself after three. Today I ate four slices. Eating in this uncontrolled way made me feel frantic, but across from Alexander, I acted like I was cool and uninhibited. On the way out of the restaurant, I took three red-and-white-swirled mints from a dish. We got into Alexander's MG and I strapped myself into the cracked leather passenger seat.

At Alexander's house, we went down to his room in the basement and laid on the bed. So far I didn't really like kissing. Or was it just that I didn't like Alexander? Days earlier, in the back seat of that car, Alexander had put his tongue in my mouth. I didn't think it was the way you were supposed to do it, because also in his mouth he had cinnamon gum. But then we'd moved close, our pelvises pushing against each other, and suddenly that was what I wanted more of. I'd wished we could just press there and not have the tongue and the gum.

Today when Alexander kissed me, I felt nothing but the food

inside me. Beneath him on the bed, I tried harder, sticking my own tongue into his mouth. He paused for an instant, removed his lips from mine, smiled. I closed my eyes in embarrassment.

Food in me I didn't want; a tongue in me I didn't want. I didn't know why I was allowing all of this in. I was acting against what I had always understood to be my instincts—or maybe for the first time I was acting in accordance with them. I'd grown so used to denying what I wanted, who I was, and how I felt that I no longer knew what my instincts were. I'd reached a moment in my adolescence when the brakes I'd put on everything wore out, and the car barreled forward without my consent.

When we heard feet overhead, we sat up. "I think my dad's here," Alexander said. Upstairs in the kitchen, Alexander introduced me to his father, and then Alexander and I went out on his motorcycle. I wore a big white helmet and held his waist. It was sunny and bumpy, and I felt closer to Alexander when we got off the bike.

At home I unpacked my swim bag—sweatpants, hair dryer, wet bathing suit wrapped in a towel—and my book bag. We'd received our first-quarter report cards that day. I had all A's: French 4, AP History, Acting, Analytic Geometry, Chemistry, Shakespeare. I went down to the kitchen and hung the report card on the refrigerator myself.

I stayed in the kitchen. Stood at the counter. The delay had nothing to do with hunger. Later I could recognize the patterns. Even if I couldn't change them, or preferred to ignore them, I could identify them. But this hadn't cemented into habit yet. This was the day, the original day, and whatever the thing was that made me open the cupboard, I cannot exactly say.

Years later I learned that binge eating is often initiated by anorexia. When you are famished and food is introduced, you feast. The body demands and you compensate. So what I did that day was driven as much by biology as psychology. And the weight I'd gained over the preceding weeks—that was biology, too. Anorexia had slowed my metabolism, and now my body held on to fat, defending against starvation.

I pulled things out and started eating them. Blue-corn chips from the tall cupboard, marble-fudge ice cream from the freezer. Leftover chicken breast and low-fat, low-sodium smoked Lorraine. I was eating fast but not frantically. I tried to act casual, as if I were being observed. I pretended that I was a snacky, chatty teenage girl licking her fingers and talking on the phone. And I was on the phone for a lot of the time, sitting on the stool by the window. A snacky, chatty teenage girl: That was a type, right? An exuberant, carefree girl with appetites. But if I could convince the imaginary observer that this was who I was, I could not convince myself. I did not feel carefree at all. I felt like I was doing something I was going to regret. I was eating beyond what was comfortable, yet I did not stop.

I was acting for someone, but who was that person, and what did I really want them to see—the bouncy performance or the terror underneath? I had no idea what was happening to me. Was it like the trail-mix incident? I wasn't satisfied by the pizza I'd eaten earlier, even though I'd eaten plenty of it. Was it Alexander? I'd wanted something from him and hadn't gotten it. I'd wanted the flood when our pelvises pressed; instead, I'd just had the intrusive tongue.

I decided I really had to stop. I grabbed a handful of blue-corn chips, shut the cupboard decisively, and stuffed the chips in my mouth. Then I opened the freezer, dumped just a tiny bit more of the marble-fudge ice cream into my bowl. That would be my dessert for the blue-corn chips, and now I really would be done. But then I scooped just a little more.

I took a shower, looking down at my stomach, hating myself.

The night started with a pre-party at Lisa Tanner's. In the kitchen there was a grocery-store sheet cake decorated with a mug of beer. We were eating just the frosting. I ate tons. Then someone handed me a cup of real beer from the keg in Lisa's bathtub. I'd never had beer before. I'd been sure I wouldn't like it. But now I didn't care. I drank it easily. A valve had been opened. It didn't matter anymore what I let in, because I was already wrecked. *I'm already ruined, so now fuck it:* This logic would define the years that followed, and I employed it from that very first night. To feel wrecked, you didn't need accumulated badness. One mess-up was all it took.

We left for a party at 61st and Valmont, which was empty land owned by somebody's father. I was sitting on the hood of a car and Alexander was kissing me. Maybe I just needed alcohol to make out with him, because I liked how it felt now, warm and rhythmic. Then I heard Cord's voice and wriggled free. I picked up the cup of beer at my feet and said to Alexander, "Let's go be social."

"Okay." Alexander seemed puzzled. He picked up his own beer but then stayed by the car, and I felt his eyes on me as I walked over to Cord.

"During *David and Lisa,*" Cord said, "when I saw you at parties, you were never drinking. Now you're always drinking." It was not a scold, just an observation, but it made me uneasy, because I didn't want Cord to know I was a beginner. It didn't occur to me that he might have been drawn to me precisely because of the independence or innocence not drinking suggested.

Drinking had the velocity of everything that fall. I'd zipped from never doing it to always doing it in no time at all. Tonight was no exception. Soon I found myself crouched in a shallow gulch, peeing with two friends. I told them, "I want to ditch Alexander," and then I did, escaping from the party in a car with glow-in-the-dark stars stuck to the ceiling.

When I woke up Saturday morning I felt guilty about everything, especially about eating. But then that afternoon I did it again, another urgent, hateful circuit in my kitchen. When evening came, I was too full to buy anything at the drive-through with my friends. Everyone else ordered. I was quiet in the back seat. I felt tired. My knees were pressing against my jeans. I realized with a start that my jeans could get holes in the knees. Was this how it happened, by gaining weight? The girl beside me, Clara, ordered a Frosty, and I passed her the cup of soft ice cream. I wondered if she'd eaten dinner or if this was dinner. What had she done all day to keep her stomach free of food?

I watched Clara spoon the Frosty into her mouth until it was all gone.

For a long time, I returned to that image. It represented a kind of reverse-savings goal. I wanted the coffers depleted. There should always be room for a Frosty, especially if you were going out at night. I craved the feeling of being empty, of harboring only nerves and air. Then, in my thirties, a friend who cut out dairy, sugar, and caffeine told me that dairy was the best elimination because it made her feel "light." *Light.* This level had never occurred to me. I had spent years trying for empty. The red line, the tank down to zero, the challenge and pleasure of ignoring the insistent message to refuel. Would my whole life have been different if I'd conceived of merely being light? (It would be another decade before I'd understand that the question I should've been asking was, "Would my whole life have been different if I'd allowed myself to feel full?")

We went from the drive-through straight to Lisa's. She was having another party. The sheet cake had sat on the kitchen table since the night before and was pretty stale, but I ate hunks of it over my palm.

In later years the eating would have prevented me from enjoying the party, probably would have kept me from going at all. But parties were radiant to me then. It was still so new to me not to feel out of place at them.

Cord was in the foyer. "Hey, baby. What did you do today?" he said.

"I worked on Darlene," I told him.

Darlene, the prostitute in Lanford Wilson's *Balm in Gilead,* was my monologue for acting class. Our drama teacher, Rita, was bewitching and imposing, and her opinions mattered. One of the finest feelings I'd had all fall had come after I'd performed a monologue from *Spoon River Anthology*. Rita had written on her response card the highest praise she gave: *I got chills.* About the same monologue,

Cord had written, *Full of passion and fire.* His praise mattered in a different way than hers. A warm feeling, hot water and honey, had spread through me then.

Rita had made another significant remark, one that Cord had reported: "Rita told me she can see the connection between us." Rita had a sixth sense and was also a straight shooter—a combination that I often feared but, in this case, had exulted in.

"Do you want to do it for me?" Cord said. "I want to see."

I moved to the front door so that we could go outside, but Cord put his hand on my arm and said, "Let's go downstairs."

In me, a shift. A whirring, preliminary feeling: the album turning on a record player before the needle touched the grooves. *Let's go downstairs.* It was happening, it was happening, it was about to happen here. Was this because of Alexander? On the hood of that car at 61st and Valmont, had I suddenly seemed desirable? If so, thank God for Alexander. It was mean to think that, but I did.

I walked downstairs in front of Cord, and, in the narrow hallway, I tripped over an ironing board.

"Baby," Cord said, reaching for my hand. He pulled me from the floor and into a bedroom. He closed the door, and we stood before each other. His head was tilted, and he smelled of suede and, faintly, cologne. He was in his characteristic state, tense and sensual. His gaze was warm and penetrating.

"Remember that feeling, of losing control," Cord said, then stroked the back of my hand.

My heart was insane, like after interval training in swim team. He wanted me to remember how it felt to *lose control.*

"Remember that feeling," Cord said again, "and use it in class on Monday."

Then he released my hand, sat on a futon, and waited for me to perform for him.

Something drained in me, everything collecting in a still, low pool.

But I wasn't devastated. I still felt the charge of having been selected by Cord, of having been pulled away by him. I was still down in the basement with him, and he was still my audience, for the monologue and for the night and for the fall of my junior year.

"God, did we ever have some *times* together. The whole . . . gang of us. God. We used . . . to really have some . . . times together."

I stood very still and wistful-yet-resigned when I hit the last line, and Cord clapped his hands and said, "You got it, doll."

Cord would get so into it that it made it okay for me to be so into it. Maybe it's even why he seemed to like me more than other people did. With most everyone else, I held something back. But acting wasn't any good unless you gave yourself over to it. It wasn't any good unless it was true. To others I might have seemed guarded or fake but not to him.

In a school play in ninth grade, I'd learned how to leave myself and become a different person. Doing this in real life might have shown me how to do it onstage. In character, I was another person in another world and nothing else. This required both focus and abandon. I see it now as a version of what bingeing would become: a way to temporarily shut everything out and exist in an altered reality defined by the loosening of restraint. But bingeing deadened feeling and was incompatible with human connection; acting was a way of accessing them both.

As soon as we went back upstairs to the party, my friend Johanna came over and whispered, "When you went downstairs with Cord, Alexander kissed Mila."

"He did?" I said. I could see Mila sitting on the kitchen counter and Alexander nearby with a red plastic cup.

Johanna nodded. Then she tilted her head toward Cord.

I shook my head and mouthed "no."

"No?" she said.

"No," I said.

"So what did happen?" she whispered.

"I'll tell you later," I said.

But it didn't matter. The news of Alexander kissing Mila produced in me a leap, confirming I was a player in the action rather than an observer of it.

Then Lisa Tanner was yelling, "The neighbor called the cops, everybody out. Cops are coming, everybody out." Lisa was the perfect person to have a party, because she liked to go wild but she also liked to be in charge. She could just snap right into bossiness. I was proud of her then, watching her herd everybody.

A few minutes later, though the condo was nearly empty, there was still a light, electric, party feel. Cord and his whole group of friends were still there. They stayed because directives didn't apply to them. They were like royalty or government officials: above the law.

We were all huddled together on the floor.

"You have that dazed make-out look, Susan," Cord's friend Liam said.

"Me?" Oh, I was so pleased. "No, I don't. I didn't get on anyone."

"'Get on,'" Liam said. "All of you Burbank girls say that. 'Get on.'"

I was so happy to be identified as one of the Burbank girls. I felt as bound to Boulder then as if I'd never been new.

"What else are we supposed to say?" Johanna said.

"Get *with*," someone said.

"That's what Southern Hills girls say," Liam said. "Get *together* with," he suggested, and then:

"Susan!" My friend Beth put her hands on my shoulders. "Susan! It's time to go to Pogo's."

I loved being snatched away, squired in a motorcade to the next event. I slid into a back seat and we gunned out of the subdivision.

We were a few minutes early for Pogo's, a dance club that opened at midnight. We walked to a Dairy Queen to wait. On the way there, Beth's friend Ella ran into the street to say hi to some girls in a car. When the light turned green, she held on to the car and jogged with it across the intersection, and a policewoman who'd been watching followed us into the Dairy Queen.

She came straight to me and began speaking. I was so frightened, I almost could not comprehend what she was saying.

"Why are you picking on Susan?" Beth said.

"Because she was holding the car."

"Susan wasn't the one holding the car," Beth said.

Ella was standing off to the side, looking at nothing. She was a blond, hoarse-voiced, tan, toned cross-country runner. She was like a journalist in her thirties posing as a high school student. I had always admired her independence and had also been interested in her obsession with her body. But now she seemed younger than all of us, protecting herself, not telling what she did.

I had to give my name and phone number.

"Have you been drinking?" the policewoman said.

"No," I lied.

"Yes, you have," she said. "I can smell it on your breath. Come with me."

Fear rose up. "Why are you arresting me?"

"I'm not arresting you," she said. "I'm going to call your parents."

"My mother," I told her. Then I was in control: defiant, latchkey-tough. "My parents are divorced. I only live with my mother."

Once I knew I wasn't getting arrested, things were different. There would be nothing on my record, nothing permanent. I left the Dairy Queen with the cop, knowing that in only a moment, this would become the story of the night.

The cop shut me in the back seat of the police car, then stood with her arms crossed outside. People were on their way to Pogo's now. A girl from school noticed me. I saw her mouth go, "Oh, my God." A skater boy put his face close to the window and said, "What the fuck." I smiled and shrugged. It was like being in the back of a limousine, the special one, observed.

Then my mother came, and the high life feeling fell away. It turned out that she knew the cop, a parent at her school.

My relationship with my mother had been deteriorating all fall. I missed curfews. I lied and said I was going out "with Mormons." I rarely joined her and Betsy for dinner. The angriest she had been was on my sixteenth birthday. I'd asked for a cake from a favorite bakery, Treats. But I'd become a different girl in the two weeks between my mother ordering the cake and her picking it up. "What time would you like to eat?" she asked on the evening of my birthday.

"Oh, I'm not eating. I'm going out," I said.

"You're not eating dinner with us?" My mother had been sorting through the mail—she'd just returned home from school—but now she looked up, seeming both angry and wounded.

"No, okay?" I said. "I'm sorry." And I was sort of sorry, especially when my friend Meredith pulled up and, on my way to the front door, I glimpsed my mother and Betsy alone at the table. Outside, I climbed into Meredith's Wagoneer. We screeched toward the foothills, and I felt bad but only a little. Why couldn't my mother understand? I had to go out. My friends mattered. Not her. Why couldn't she see this?

But I felt bad again when I got home and saw the cake box in the refrigerator.

Hostility toward my mother was my new stance. Over the summer I had wanted to be close to her. This time last year, we'd phonebanked together at Colorado Freeze Voter and cheered at a Michael Dukakis rally. Even in ninth grade, when I'd been insolent and combative, I'd softened when we went shopping and to lunch. But now I was shutting her out.

"Mom, it was the first time I ever drank," I said on the way home in the car.

"How am I supposed to believe that?" she said.

"It's true," I lied.

Actually, it was pretty close to the truth, since I'd only been drinking for a few weeks. But I wanted my mother to assume that I'd been drinking for much longer than I really had. I wanted her to know that I was not the girl she'd been in high school, home on Saturday nights, reading Dickens and listening to Bach. I was smart *and* cool, which was harder. It gave me power to believe that I was something she was not. I wanted to flaunt this distinction, and so while I pretended my mother didn't matter, in fact she mattered so much that I was pleased that she had received a call about me from a cop.

We were driving on Arapahoe, on the narrow part where there were trees and it was only two lanes.

"What did she even say to you?" I said.

"She said you were drunk and disorderly and that you talked back," my mother said.

"That is not true," I said. "I was not the one holding the car." Then I genuinely wanted my mother on my side. But I was stuck in my role. "So you're going to believe her over me—fine, great," I said, as Arapahoe opened out into four lanes. It was our familiar way-home landscape of shopping plazas and the prairie-dog field and Ball Aerospace. "Believe this random policewoman over your own daughter, don't think twice, it's all right." I was saying the words as if I were already repeating the conversation to a friend.

Only a year later I would wonder if my mother had felt scared or ashamed that night. She would have fallen like a stone into bed at nine or ten. She would have still had wine in her when she got the call at midnight. When I went over the story after I was aware of her drinking, I wondered what calculation she had made. Which would be more revealing—not coming or getting behind the wheel? She kept her problem secret, and it would still be a while before I would notice it. By the time I did, I had a secret of my own.

11

WINTER

BY WINTERTIME, EATING HAD changed me. I had no control, and I hated myself for it. Once I would have come home from school and carefully prepared hot chocolate. Now I dug into bags. I stuffed things in my mouth and chewed them fast. Wheat Thins; blue-corn chips; a candy called Rainforest Crunch. Sunflower whole wheat bread that balled in my chest. Gruyère, which I sliced down to the rind, tasting the hard, gluey edge. Sometimes I would think of how my grandfather had once remarked on the quality of my chewing. I was a good chewer. I chewed slowly. No longer. I chewed as little as I could to get to the swallow. I hated imagining my grandfather. I hated imagining him ever seeing me like this.

I resolved to fix myself, always swearing, *Tomorrow I'll be better,* and sometimes I was. I didn't "eat bad," as I called it, every day, and while I was gaining weight, this actually made me look good. It saddens me that I could not see this. I was no longer anorexic, and I looked healthy. I went to Winter Ball with Cord in a crushed-velvet dress that hugged my curves. At the end of the night, the two of us buckled into the same seatbelt, he pulled me close and whispered,

"You look so hot tonight," and I knew it was true, because I felt it. But by the next day, I'd turned back into a pumpkin. My jeans, as predicted, now had holes in them, my knees having burst through the denim. I felt thick and sad and puffy. Everything was stuck inside me. I couldn't explain, couldn't get anything out. One afternoon at rehearsal for the winter musical, we were doing a warm-up exercise and people got the directions confused and Rita said, "No, no, you can show the connection another way, you don't *have* to touch," but Cord came over and held me anyway.

"I want to touch you because you're bumming," he whispered. "What's wrong?"

Everything was wrong. I ate in this weird way. I was always down. I was worried that my friends didn't want me around. I wanted to go back to the fall, when life had been magical. None of these were things I could say.

"I'm just depressed," I said.

At the end of the exercise, Cord moved away.

When, a few moments later, he flung out his arm and sang, "Try to remember the kind of September," I yearned for my own September, for September beside Cord in his black pickup truck, for September at parties under the moon, for September when I had been sparkling. The lightness and charge of the fall were gone, and a demon-drop of mood had descended. I loathed myself and was stirred by nothing. I tried to find a way out. Exercise helped. So did writing in my journal.

"Writers keep journals," my English teacher, Mr. Rothberg, said one afternoon in January. This semester, we'd all keep our own. The journal I chose was a green half-size spiral notebook, college ruled. Immediately I was carrying it everywhere. I could feel it in my bag as I walked into school from the parking lot. It was an object that pulsed with its own power. It was like having a large amount of money, or drugs. There was comfort in knowing I could shove up against my locker and scrawl or hide in the library when someone had left for lunch without me. At home I would lie on my bedroom floor, listening to the Smiths and composing prose poems about

Cord. (My attachment to him—still platonic—had escalated into obsession; not long after that day at rehearsal, he'd told me, seemingly exhausted by my neediness, "I think our friendship is becoming really intense and overwhelming," and we weren't speaking.)

I used the journal to sort through everything in my head. I would write, *I just have to figure out my life,* and I believed that in that green notebook I could.

Mr. Rothberg was my favorite teacher at Fairview. I'd taken every class I could with him, even a noncredit after-school class called the Creative Mind. There was a stillness to Mr. Rothberg but something appealingly agitated underneath, and though he was close to my mother's age, he seemed younger than a parent. He had an interest in kids who'd gotten into trouble, and sometimes I worried he found me less interesting because it seemed like I had it all together. I wanted both to maintain that impression and to complicate it.

From the first day of sophomore year, it had been clear that Mr. Rothberg would be the formative teacher of my adolescence. I thought of him as *the one who taught me how to write* even as he was still teaching me to do it. One of the earliest assignments he'd given was a paper defining a word. I'd picked "reality," hoping to distinguish myself by choosing what I thought was an especially difficult word to define.

Sometimes I fantasized about him giving me a ride home from school, like in the teacher–student song by the Police. I would be standing alone in the rain at the bus stop. Through a mist I'd see headlights, and then Mr. Rothberg would pull up. He would lean across and roll down the window, and I would climb into the front seat of his hatchback. And then the fantasy thinned, became innocent but also more exposing, because what I wanted from him was what I wanted from anyone I cared about. In the car we wouldn't kiss or touch. Maybe there was a weak subtext that this could happen. But the furthest the fantasy went was my driveway. He would drop me off and I would go in through the front door. Alone in the car, he would idle, staring at the steep angle of our tract-house roof and imagining the life that went on inside.

That was what I wanted most of all. I wanted to be known by him. I wanted to be in his head. I wanted to show him my own reality, but I wasn't sure how to do it.

One day at the end of class, Mr. Rothberg said, "Susan, can I see you for a minute?"

Shit. The way he said it, I just knew. It was about the ditching. A few days earlier Meredith and I had cut his class. We'd walked to the parking lot on the path right outside his window—a sunny day, the Flatirons glorious before us, Meredith tossing keys. Part of me had hoped that Mr. Rothberg might see us leaving. I wanted him to think of me as brilliant but also a little bad. I'd leaned close to Mere, acted urgent, conspiratorial.

In the classroom, Meredith was picking up her notebook. I wondered if he had already talked to her separately. Why hadn't she warned me? Inside me, things were collecting. Oh, God, this was real feeling. It came to me in a flood. I felt too nervous, too sick to eat; and so, even though I was certain I was about to get in trouble, relief coursed. I'd be perfect now; I'd never eat again. Real feelings, even horrible ones, raised me up above my dull mess. I ate not when I felt things intensely but when I didn't. I ate when I felt nothing. I ate when I felt low, and then I hated myself and I ate more in that hate. If I could just sustain heightened feeling, of any kind, would I not have to do this? Not have to eat?

I gathered my things and walked over to Mr. Rothberg. He was holding a printout of excerpts from my journal. At regular intervals we had to type up five pages' worth of entries and hand them in.

In the instant before he spoke, I scrambled to assess. He'd said you could change names, but I hadn't changed any of them. I wanted him to know who I was friends with. So I would just say I hadn't realized. Somehow I had missed the guideline. Obviously, I would prefer to change names. I wouldn't do it this way again.

"Susan, there's a lot in here about drinking, and it's not the first time you've written about this. Is there a problem?" Mr. Rothberg said.

I almost wanted to laugh. My only problem with drinking had been last year, when I didn't do it yet. My real problems—the sad, gray-blanketed way I felt; the way I ate; the way I was obsessed with Cord—I would never have revealed to him. I knew about cries for help. This wasn't that. Drinking! That was nothing. The sections I'd given him were safe.

"No," I said. "It's not a problem."

"Okay," Mr. Rothberg said.

I had a glimpse then of how he would be with kids with serious troubles. He was very still. He presented the situation plainly. He didn't go overboard. He didn't reach out a hand.

For a second I wondered what you could turn in that wouldn't give you away—current events? But was anybody really writing about apartheid, or the ozone layer, or Dan Quayle? I wanted to ask him what other people did.

There was another reason I'd chosen those entries. I saw that notebook as a place where I would find my voice, which was related to, but separate from, finding myself. A week earlier I had sat at the computer in the middle of the night, my notebook open beside me. When I reread my journal, these were the entries that gave me a little flare of pleasure.

But that I had wanted to show Mr. Rothberg my best stuff was also an embarrassing admission, and I left the classroom without saying anything further. I had already revealed too much of myself to him, not so much in what I had written as in what I had picked to share.

I WAS STARTING TO do a lot of work in the middle of the night. Most of the time it wasn't shot through with pleasure. Often I would eat so much in the evening that I couldn't do anything but go to bed. I wouldn't even get into pajamas. I'd climb into bed at nine, fully clothed, and set the alarm for three.

One morning I woke to that three-A.M. alarm in the same sweats and bathing suit I'd worn home from a swim meet earlier. I couldn't even say "the day before" anymore. I'd ruined boundaries. Rarely did I have the new-dawn fix-everything sensation. There was just one hour, one hour, another hour, the next. I had a paper to write, so I got out of bed and went downstairs to the computer. As soon as I sat down at the keyboard, I got up because I needed energy. I had a spoonful of granola from the tall clear canister and then put the spoon in the sink so I wouldn't be tempted to take another. But then I just uncapped the jar and poured some into my palm and gobbled it up like a pet. Oats fell on the floor, and I hated myself for not caring. Then I decided, as long as I was doing this, I might as well have something worth it, so I switched to ice cream. In the freezer there was Heath Bar Crunch. After one spoonful I realized it would make sense to eat the whole pint and not have breakfast and then start my good eating habits for real later in the day. Then I sat down to work, buzzing with sugar, and had to type fast to escape myself, to outrun the thing I'd just done.

I never threw up. I knew once I did it one time there would be no reason not to do it every time, even if all I ate was one cracker. It was self-knowledge, not self-control, that kept me from purging.

By five, whatever lift and brilliance the sugar had given me flattened. I was solid and disgusting again. I needed to sleep or to eat something, but I couldn't do either, because it was time to go swim. I went upstairs to change. There was a sophomore who slept in her suit so she would be ready to go in the morning. It was because she was nerdy and careful and organized. Not because she was an awful, flopping, desperate wreck. The suit in which I had awoken was the wrong one, my racing suit from the afternoon meet. My training suits were still balled in a towel in my swim bag from the previous morning's practice. They were damp when I pulled them on. The sensation reminded me of childhood: of being inside a glossy yellow bathroom stall at the club, hopping off the toilet, hiking up my damp suit, and running back out into the sun. A wave of feeling for the old, small Susan came over me, and I hated myself for failing her.

In the bathroom, I tried not to look at myself in the mirror. A week earlier I'd gone into my mother's room and casually observed in her mirror another girl, sour and defeated. Then I'd realized, *That is me*. There had been a lag before I registered my own image. It was startling and terrible not to know yourself.

I came out of the bathroom in my clammy suits and my sweatpants. My mother was in the dark hallway.

"Hi, sweetie," she said.

"Jesus, Mom," I said.

"I'm sorry I startled you," she said.

My mother was wearing her thin flannel bathrobe. It was one she'd had since Michigan. The tie at the waist was fraying.

"Well, you totally did," I said.

I was sure my mother didn't know what was going on with my eating. Her boyfriend, Bruce, was at our house a lot. He was here right now, on the other side of her door. My mother said Bruce didn't live with us, but his shirts were in her closet, and his Scotch and steel-cut oats were in the cupboard. My mother did not require me to join them at dinner, and at first I'd assumed I was getting a pass because she felt guilty about him. Then I realized that maybe I was so sullen that they preferred to eat without me.

"Sweetie," my mother whispered, as I headed toward my room.

I turned around. "What," I whispered fiercely.

"I just wanted to say goodbye," she said.

"Well, don't, it's bad luck," I said.

"What?" My mother was confused.

"That's the whole reason why people say 'see you later' or 'take care.'"

My mother stiffened. "Well, have a good day, then."

"Okay, I have to go," I said.

"Susan, what's wrong?" There was a note of pleading.

"Nothing is fucking wrong except that I have to go to swim team!" I said. "Lexie is going to pull into our fucking driveway and I am going to be late."

I was desperate for her not to go any further, desperate for her not to say "You seem unhappy," or "Is there something going on?" or, the worst, confirming everything, "You don't seem like yourself."

"Why are you so angry?" she said.

My anger had been talked about before. And, yes, I had plenty of it, but it was all at myself. I was angry at myself for all the wrong ways I was. I wouldn't be angry if I were better! If I could just fix myself, this would all end.

"I'm angry because you are making me late," I said.

"Susan, you act like you are the only person in this house." This, too, was familiar ground. It was true. My selfishness wasn't the demanding kind. I didn't draw my mother and sister into my dramas; I shunned them, which was worse. "We are a family," my mother said.

"Oh, really, we're a *family*," I said, mocking the word, because of course we weren't a family anymore, not the way we had once been, and my mother knew this as well as I did.

"Fuck you, Susan."

My mother stood across from me, steady, unapologetic, in her worn flannel bathrobe. I was startled—both because she had never said anything like this to me before and because the words had the potency of having long been bottled. She had at other times restrained herself.

"Fuck you, too," I said. A stagy whisper, the unreality of this. "And if you're going to fucking treat me like this, I can just go live with my father."

She knew I would never do it. But it was my thing to wield against her.

In the window downstairs was the swoop and spread of high beams.

"And now I am fucking late," I said. "Lexie is here."

I went into my room and stuffed my books into my bag. When I came back out to the hallway, my mother was still standing there. I thought of Bruce in the room behind her and knew that he'd heard everything and would take her side.

"Hi!" Lexie said when I got in the car. She was a sophomore who lived nearby.

"Hi!" I said. My heart was still beating, but this was the transition. Nobody at school ever saw me act the way I did at home.

In the water, I felt sick from the ice cream. I felt both stuffed and limp. But every stroke was redemptive. I was doing nothing wrong by being here. It was making me better every second. I never missed practice unless I was extremely sick. Now, holding a kickboard and watching the sky go pink outside the glass wall of the rec center, I thought, *This is the only thing keeping me afloat.*

IT WAS MELODRAMATIC BUT true. Exercise was a daily, reliable relief. I'd slip into the water and the arm-over-arm motion would restore me to myself. Running hard over an unpaved trail, I'd discover that *everything will be all right.* I liked the exertion as well as the euphoria that followed. In health class we learned about endorphins. In this aerobics-junkie town, it made sense to think of exercise as a drug.

I laid down so many bad habits during my adolescence, but exercise was a good one. It got me out of the house; it showed me that my body could be a source of pleasure, even on days when I hated myself for what I ate. It had its downsides: For years I exercised compulsively. The runner's high made me feel omnipotent: Why talk to anyone about my problems? I had my own way of solving them. And swimming, the sport that kept me sanest as a teenager, put my body on display. A friend once told me a story about a coach who said, "Did you have pasta last night?" The swimmer, a girl our age, nodded. "You ate too much of it. I can tell by looking at your abdomen." It was my nightmare, the idea that someone might see not only my stomach but all the things I'd shoved in.

Even before these new problems with eating, I had often been uneasy in my body. "You're very stiff," Rita had recently observed. "You have trouble physicalizing. You don't use your whole instrument." It was true. While I could convert myself into another with my mind, my body would not follow. But when I exercised, I did use my whole instrument. This sensation was radical: Usually my body was a single part, that abdomen filled with starch.

I'm just depressed, I'd said to Cord. I felt bleak that winter, and I found ways to cope with that: eating, writing, exercise. Later, eating would change to not eating, but that was the same thing, just another way of using food to manage feeling. I believed that if I ate in a ritualistic way, I could reach an exalted state. I believed this for most of my adult life, stayed in the church despite clear evidence of its hypocrisies. Writing and exercise I also maintained. But these were adoration, thanksgiving, penitence: purer kinds of prayer. That low winter of junior year proved to be foundational. Those were the months in which I laid down the faithful habits that, for better or worse, I kept.

12

ACTING

RITA'S COMMENT ABOUT THE way I moved stayed with me, and at my summer acting program, the first class I signed up for was Being Aware of Your Body. The program was at Northwestern, and it was only for rising high school seniors. I'd planned to apply for years and was thrilled to have been admitted. I was going to fix everything there, including my eating. I was determined not only to stop "eating bad" but to start eating well. On the first morning in the dining hall, I ate an apple. At sixteen, this was the first piece of fruit I'd ever had. A standard dry, mealy, tough-skinned Red Delicious. I wrapped the core in a paper napkin and shoved it under the plate on my tray. I felt weirdly proud and forward-looking.

The program divided us into groups, and every group was going to put on a show. My group was doing *Less Than Zero,* and I was cast as Blair, the main part for a girl. I threw myself into the role, into all of it. *Commit to the gesture* was one of the summer's mantras—and I did. They scheduled us late into the night and had us up first thing in the morning. It was like med school, or a cult. (Being Aware of

Your Body, the class that was supposed to stretch me, turned out to be the least challenging of all: The main thing we did was practice massage. "Open out from the spine," our extremely mellow teacher advised. "Don't pinch.")

One morning in an acting class, we did an exercise. We were in a hot room with filmy curtains and a black stage a couple of feet high. When it was your turn, you stood on the stage and the teachers battered you with questions. In theory it was about allowing yourself to be vulnerable. In practice it was about breaking people down and making them cry.

A girl named Amanda went. She had on mascara and it ran. Then Tim, who'd been cast opposite me in *Less Than Zero* as Clay. Tim was a tan, thin, long-distance runner, aloof and self-contained, but after a while up onstage, even his voice cracked.

I wasn't sure how I would behave when I got up there. Part of me wanted to reveal myself to others, but part of me was reluctant to. I was committed to losing myself as Blair. But losing myself as Susan seemed ill-advised. I didn't believe, as these people seemed to, that one was predicated on the other.

I was often suspicious of the exercises in drama. This one seemed like the psychological equivalent of the trust fall, the acting-class staple where you stood on a table and fell back into a net of arms. I didn't understand how teachers could claim that complete surrender was not without hazard.

When it was my turn, I climbed up onto the stage. I stared into the dusty light. It was how everyone did it. You looked into the middle distance, not at the people on the floor.

"Susan, how are you today?" said the teacher, a woman named Sam. Sam was tall and curvy and younger than much of the staff, still a student at Oberlin.

"Fine," I said.

"What's on your mind?"

"I'm thinking about when I'm going to go running." It was my honest, witness-stand response.

"Why do you go running?"

"To stay in shape."

But this was a question that made me protective. I went running so that I wouldn't get fat; I went running to lose the fat I already had; I was fat because I ate things in secret.

"Why else?"

She knew! She was trying to get me to say, *To lose weight.* Or, *Because I feel fat.* I wouldn't do it.

"Because of stress," I said.

"Stress," a health-class word. An insipid response. I felt a little fresh, combative. This is how it would go: I would ping back, deflect Sam. It was like Little Brick Out. I would move my bar up the side of the monitor every time she came at me. I would win.

"What are you stressed about?" Sam said.

"It depends," I said.

"What are you stressed about this summer?"

"Getting enough sleep."

"What are you stressed about right now?"

"Wondering when I'm going to be able to go running." I was getting hot up there. I was wearing a lavender T-shirt and floral leggings. We all dressed like dancers for every class.

"Susan, what's something that makes you sad?" Craig said. He was another one of the teachers. They were trying a different tack.

"My parents' divorce," I said. But thinking about my father made me stronger. *That which does not kill makes us stronger:* another of the summer's mantras. Up on this stage, I would be my father's daughter, Susan Mason Burton. *Quite simply, Susan is smart!* I would give clear, strong, direct answers in a powerful, disarming voice.

"What's the hardest thing about your parents being divorced?" Craig said.

"It's not hard," I said. "It's better than if they were married."

Then they made me wait for many seconds. I stood as straight as I could. I was the disciplined daughter of my squared-away father.

"Relax, Susan, let go," Craig said.

Nothing made me more rigid than being told to relax.

But then it was strange, because I felt a little sad. Up until now there'd still been a chance that I'd yield. Now I was so stiff that I could no longer give myself over to the exercise even if I'd wanted to.

Finally they gave up and I got off the stage. Back on the floor, I was conscious of myself as the noisy reentrant settling into position. I shifted, bumped my foot against Amanda, who turned. "Sorry," I mouthed.

I thought the teachers would see that other people were reluctant to do this, too, but by the end of the morning I was the only one who hadn't submitted.

We went out of the room into the bright day. On the path I hung behind and pretended to be having deep thoughts. But really I was mounting my defense. *Relax, Susan.* So fucking annoying! It wasn't that I couldn't open up; it was just that I needed to control the information. I needed to think about it in advance. I needed to look at the pages of my journal in the middle of the night and consider which ones to type.

But I was disappointed. I wished I could do it over again and feel what it would have been like not to hold back. I had been given a chance to be known, and I had not taken it. It was contrived, but it still counted. Everyone else had taken a risk—*take a risk,* another mantra—and come out closer.

Looking back, I can see that I showed strength. I was wary—rightly, I think—of manipulation. Yet that morning remains one of the most vivid of that summer because for years I'd still be standing on that stage, not knowing what I wanted, to withhold or to reveal, to yield or to protect. Refusal was safer: less risk. You can think of it as the anorexic choice, and in that way it was predictive of the one I ultimately made: The gestures I committed to were self-denial and containment. But was that really what I wanted? Because for years I'd still wonder what it would be like not to hold tight; what it would be like to join the group instead of maintain distance from it; what it would be like to *say.*

———

THERE WAS A SCENE in *Less Than Zero* where Clay and Blair kissed. It was the one moment I had trouble staying in character. I always let Tim take the lead, and the whole time his mouth was on mine, I was assessing whether he was into it. Whenever we parted I was always mad at myself for being lowly and submissive, which at least snapped me back into the correct frame of mind for Blair. By now I'd kissed enough boys to know that when I kissed Tim I was doing it "right." But I wasn't sure whether he was turned on by the kiss, and it felt like a failure that he didn't want me.

During the final week, my father and my sister drove down from Michigan for the performance. Now I had an additional reason to be nervous. My father was going to see me kiss a boy. My father had never picked up the phone when a boy called. He had not been there when I went off to Winter Ball with Cord in the skintight crushed-velvet dress. On the night of the performance, I felt like I was about to make my debut not only as Blair but as my father's teenage daughter.

The show opened with Blair and Clay in a BMW, which was represented by folding chairs. I spoke the first words: "People are afraid to merge on freeways in Los Angeles." Throughout the play, this and other repeated phrases—*Disappear here; I feel nothing*—echoed over a sound system.

After the show I met my father and sister in front of the theater. I hugged them both. My father was wearing a navy sport coat and pressed khakis. Betsy had on a floral Laura Ashley dress. She was twelve now and taller than I was.

"I couldn't believe it," my father began. I braced inside. He was going right to the kiss. "I couldn't believe when you picked up that cigarette. I said, 'Betsy, I think Susan actually inhaled!'"

"Yeah," Betsy said, "he did."

"Yeah," I said, "I did!"

And then we just all smiled at one another. Would this be it?

My father got out his camera and took photographs of me, the same way he had at my performances since I had played a rat and a village child in *The Magical Pied Piper* at Circle Theater at the age of eight. I wasn't sure if I believed that it was really inhaling, not kissing, that had startled him, but I was relieved that he had addressed the shock of my development so tactfully.

A FEW DAYS LATER the program ended and my father returned to pick me up. I would spend a week with him in Michigan. We headed south down Lake Shore Drive. On a path alongside there were runners and cyclists, and on the water the white triangles of sailboats. My father was listening to WBBM. On a bureau in my parents' bedroom, a boxy shortwave radio had played WBBM throughout my childhood. The sound of shortwave radio was echoey, as if WBBM were broadcast from outer space.

Now they were talking about Iraq. My father raised the volume. I knew nothing about Iraq. A day earlier, it had invaded a country named Kuwait. When the news brief finished, my father turned the radio down and said, "This is going to be big." His words made me solemn. Partly it was his broadcaster's voice. The simplest sentence from him carried the authority of the anchor's desk. But it was also that he was a baby boomer. Because he had lived through history, he could identify when it was being made.

At my father's house—the new one he and Donna had built together, large and skylit—I read *Native Son* for AP English and made late-night long-distance calls to my best friend from Northwestern. One afternoon my father took pictures of me on the lawn. A year earlier he'd taken photos of me on the boat. When the prints came back from the shop, I'd been pleased: my tan face bony like a fashion model's, my smile open, my white-blond hair windblown. I knew what I'd see when this film was developed: my pale, wide, pimply face; my heavy eyelid, damaged by my contact lens; my removed, guarded affect.

On the last morning of my stay, my father came into my room as I was packing. Standing near the bureau, he watched me roll my clothing. It was supposed to work better than folding.

"How much was your speeding ticket?" my father said. I'd been pulled over for going 56 in a 45 on Foothills Parkway in Boulder, and I'd mentioned it to him. It seemed like something my father would appreciate, a teenager whipping past mountains with windows down.

"Forty dollars," I said, and my father reached into his pocket, opened his wallet, and gave me two twenties.

"Thank you," I said.

It was the way my father usually gave me money, surreptitiously, so that Donna wouldn't know.

My father sat down on the bed. "I probably drove too fast when I was a teenager and as a young man," he said. "In the Healey." This was the Austin-Healey, a slate-blue convertible my father had kept in every garage of his life. "You can ask your mother." I nodded. I liked any mention of my mother in this house. It made my father and me complicit. "I probably drank too much, too, but I never did drugs. Don't do drugs, Susan," he said. "The culture is bizarre and unappealing. People get into that and they're never the same again. They just stop functioning. It's abnormal."

"I know, Dad," I said. "I don't do drugs."

With my mother, I wanted to be defiant. I wanted her to know that everything she thought was wrong, even if I actually agreed with her. With my father it was different. I wanted to be who I thought he wanted me to be. I wanted to misbehave only in ways he approved of. I wanted to be good for him.

The truth was that I had smoked pot. But it was too hard to explain that this didn't really count. My father wouldn't understand that in Boulder, marijuana was like beer.

"That's good," my father said. "Now, what about cigarettes?"

That cigarette! Had it really alarmed him?

"I mean, I've had cigarettes," I started.

"You knew how to inhale," my father said.

"Yeah, but I'm not a smoker," I said.

"Your mother can tell you I smoked cigarettes," my father said. "But I quit, and it was the healthiest thing I ever did."

"What about *Fit or Fat?*" I said. This line had long been a staple of our comedy act.

"Now, don't get technical," my father said, which was another part of the shtick.

Later, at the gate at the airport, I gave him a hug. His bulk, his scent, his skin that was extra–clean-shaven, like a U.S. president's: all so primordially familiar but so infrequently encountered.

I always wanted to cry when I was about to leave my father. He was my father. He should be near. But while in those moments our separation felt so wrong, in a daily way I did not think I was distressed by it. In fact, I was grateful for all he missed. I felt like I was getting away with something in Boulder. Felt like my father didn't know the worst parts of me, which in a way was true. A thousand miles away, I did everything without him knowing. He took those photographs wanting to see me, but my primary goal was to hide.

My apprehension about my father seeing me kiss a boy in a play seems so misdirected as to have almost been false. Him seeing me act was safe. Him seeing the real me was the risk. My father saw none of my troubles. He saw me as the golden girl I'd started as, and there was safety in being able to return to his gaze.

It doesn't give my father enough credit, of course, to assume his view of me remained rosy. A parent sees changes and makes different notes than a child expects: a check mark beside the cigarette, not the kiss. And parents have been teenagers themselves, which is part of what my father was trying to tell me that morning. But he wasn't witness to me on a daily basis, and all in all it was a relief that he wasn't there to watch me fall apart.

13

INDEPENDENCE

RIGHT BEFORE SENIOR YEAR started, I got a job at Alfalfa's. Alfalfa's was an organic food store but not the kind that smelled like wheatgrass and vitamins. There was less hummus and more pâté. There was steak, shrimp salad; fresh flowers, cappuccino; premium ice cream, free-range chickens turning on spits. Overhead were banners—a picture of the rancher who raised natural beef, a photo of the farm where the lettuce was pesticide-free. While this type of store is familiar now, back then it was not yet the American standard. I was a courtesy clerk—aka a bagger. At any other grocery store, the bagger job would have been lame, but Alfalfa's was a local institution. Its virtues would one day be extolled in a song by a jam band called Leftover Salmon:

> *When I grow up, I want to work at Alfalfa's*
> *Where the cheese is dairy-free*
> *A Birkenstock, spandex, necktie, patchouli grocery store . . .*
> *I'd be a working moderate-income socially conscious Boulder*
>   *hippie*

While I'd been able to control my eating at Northwestern, I'd messed up the moment I walked into the house, my luggage still in the kitchen. Now eating was bad again and social life was no better. Around my friends I was clenched and sullen. The night before the first day of school, I wrote down resolutions, as I'd done a year earlier, but I was no longer the quietly confident girl who could decide to transform and just do it.

The first day of senior year was everything I'd feared, dull and alienating. But after school I had a shift at Alfalfa's, and as I walked up and down the front end in my turquoise apron, my mood improved. It was as if the mission statement in our employee handbook, "Making People Feel Better," applied to the experience of working here, too. I became benevolent. I loved everyone. "Have you checked your eggs?" I said to one woman, and made a show of looking into the carton for cracks. To another customer, "This eggplant has some mold on the top. May I run and get you another?" Into paper bags I built groceries like a house. On the bottom, a quart of Mountain High yogurt, fresh-squeezed grapefruit juice, the season's first Western Slope apples; basil and lettuce up top. Driving home in the car I felt better, spent.

But as soon as I was in my room the unease came back. It was eight-thirty, and I'd been expecting phone messages because clearly on the first day of senior year there would be a party, but not a single person had called. I tried to gird for a year of being alone, but I wasn't as strong as I had been as a sophomore. I didn't think I could do this again.

I sat at my dressing table and began a letter to my best friend from Northwestern. *The first day of school started out absolutely from hell. My first class was psychology & just basically all the superficial girls from the senior class were there, my friends among them, and I just felt like such shit and I totally wanted to cry.*

Then my phone rang.

I stayed still. I usually didn't pick up until after the second ring. This was to show that I was busy. People who got calls all the time would just pounce. They didn't have to pretend anything.

"Susan? It's Julie Gray."

The two names, the formality: a way she wouldn't identify herself again until twenty years later, when we first spoke after a separation nearly that long.

"I was wondering if you wanted to come to Neva Road."

I thought of Neva Road, so far away that our rocky foothills turned grassy. We would hurtle down a slope to the meadow. We would park and see guys in the pavilion crouching over a keg. I would slam the car door shut and our feet would crunch together over the gravel.

"I would love to," I said.

And that was when I became friends with Julie Gray.

JULIE GRAY WAS THE friend, the one whose friendship still rose in me like a romance even decades on.

There's a photograph I love called "Girls in the Woods." It's by an artist named Jerald Frampton. In the photo, two girls are sitting on brown leaves on the ground. One of the girls is drinking a beer. It looks like she's chugging it, like she's used to drinking fast. The other girl is holding a cigarette, but what she's mostly doing is watching her friend. I first saw this image in my early twenties. I was in an art meeting at the magazine where I worked. I bent to the lightbox, put my eye to the loupe, and as soon as I raised my head asked, "Who is Jerald Frampton?"

I went to the gallery in Chelsea where his show was up. The photograph cost $375, an impossible price. But "Girls in the Woods" was the postcard for the show. That was lucky. I had that to frame.

Sometimes when people were at my apartment, they'd see the image and ask, "Is that you?" No, but yes.

It wasn't just that Julie did bad things or that she was daring, or ahead. These things were true of all of my friends. With Julie it was different. The force of what I felt for her: I wanted to be with her and also, in a way, to *be* her. I wanted her womanly way of blazing through the world. So many nights we would drive in her little car deep into Denver, always for no reason, always just us. "Lips Like Sugar" would come on, a song that made Julie nostalgic for sophomore spring, when she had dated Liam. Soon "Lips Like Sugar" made me think of Julie's spring with Liam, too. And still later I would be nostalgic for having had the kind of friendship so close that a song could trigger for me something out of another girl's head.

The closeness I yearned for: I believed I finally had it with her.

FROM THE START, OUR bodies mattered in our friendship; at least they did to me. Julie was a lot taller than I was, seven or eight inches. For years she'd been willowy and flat-chested, but now her breasts were enormous. She was so transformed that I marveled how at home she seemed to be in her new shape. I'd sit in her room on a Friday evening as we prepared to go out and she would change tops right in front of me. Wearing only a bra, she'd bend to reach a towel on the floor and her stomach would collapse in rolls. I'd avert my eyes, instinctively. But rolls didn't seem to bother Julie. It didn't seem to occur to her to want what I did: a stomach that folded in two, like a piece of paper. Watching her, something would flicker—*what I want is freakish . . . I don't have to hate myself*—and then short out. Julie's confidence in her body captivated me but also made me feel inferior. She was the grown girl, and I was her small sidekick. She embraced her body, and I was defeated by mine.

Julie had been a violin prodigy. She'd quit, abruptly, when she turned sixteen, but for years she'd practiced every afternoon for hours. I wondered if violin was what made her slightly distant from our group of friends. Sometimes another girl would yell out an inside joke and Julie would look confused. She would make it clear that this was something she had missed. When she did participate, there was almost always a moment when she withdrew: all of us still sitting in the car but Julie now somewhere outside it. I wanted to know where she was in these moments. It might have been one of the things I was most drawn to, that she went somewhere I couldn't reach.

"If you push on the wall, it does not push back," I said to her one night in my room. We were on the carpet with our notebooks, doing AP Physics homework. "It just does not."

"But it does, honey," she said. She was always doing that, saying "honey," "sweetheart," touching your wrist. Sometimes I tried it out. But I was awkward with endearments. It was like when a Mormon swore. They didn't say it right, and you felt embarrassed for them.

Something about physics class made me stubborn. I pushed back against the laws of the universe. Except the one about how molecules tended toward entropy. That made sense. The inclination toward chaos, the daily combat against it.

I looked in my bag for a sharper pencil. A lamp blazed high up on my dresser. Julie's school bag was on my floor. It was the first time I'd had a close friend like this, one serious enough to do physics homework with at eleven at night but also wild enough to drink and mess up with and not be careful.

Julie yawned and stretched her arms over her head. She stretched like a dancer, like someone who knew her own musculature. "I am going to fall asleep unless we have caffeine. But I'm guessing you don't have any Diet Coke."

"We don't have any Diet Coke," I said. It was no surprise that I'd gotten a job at Alfalfa's. Mine had always been the house without regular junk food.

"Coffee?" Julie said.

"Coffee," I affirmed, and we went downstairs.

But neither of us had ever used a coffee maker.

"And the water goes . . . where?" Julie said. We unplugged the machine, a white plastic Krups. We turned it upside down and put our faces in it. We felt daft. Julie gave her high, tweety laugh.

"We could ask my mother," I said, but immediately regretted

this. My mother would be sleeping heavily. If we woke her, she might smell like wine. It was possible Bruce was in her bed.

"No, let's not disturb her," Julie said.

But I wondered if at Julie's house we would have gotten her mother.

I found the coffee-maker instructions in the wet bar, with bills, my SAT scores, and my parents' divorce agreement.

Into her coffee Julie poured milk and sugar from our five-pound bag. I hadn't ever had coffee, but I knew I took it black because of my parents. We dimmed the lights in the kitchen and carried our mugs up the stairs.

The coffee was insane. I couldn't believe it worked the first time. I thought it would be like pot, where I might not feel anything. But I was awake and conquering. Even with a friend in the room, I was focused. I was blazing down the page. It seemed to me we had done things in the wrong order. We had all started with alcohol. But coffee, which was actually helpful, should have been the first thing we learned.

THE FIRST FEW WEEKS of drinking coffee, I was as altered by it as by alcohol. I liked coffee better. Coffee sharpened as well as disinhibited. Alcohol was slurry love, girls being sentimental, talking about friendship. Coffee was the city. It was getting information out faster, so the person you were with would know everything. Also, I found out that coffee had no calories. Literally to coffee there were no negatives.

Alone in the afternoons I'd park at a meter, then come out of a café brandishing my thermal mug. Sometimes I felt thin in my jeans, composed; other days were mess-up days, and the coffee was going to propel me forward into betterment. I'd get in the car, pull the seatbelt across my chest, and peel out into the sunny afternoon.

Freedom, independence: those keywords of adolescence. I didn't feel loose enough to embody freedom, but for the first time I had a firm hold on its partner, independence. That was the temperature of that fall: yellow aspens and cool days and driving over dry streets. There was something mature and strengthening about being alone in the car. One hand on the wheel and the other on the radio. Scanning through station presets and cresting the hill on Broadway. The feeling of the road rising up to meet you when you found the perfect song. Racing toward the stoplight on Table Mesa with the sun bright behind the foothills and *In a big country, dreams stay with you* blasting. These were radio stations from when radio stations were still good. They weren't owned by conglomerates. Smart DJs chose perfect songs. Later, when I wanted to hear the songs of my adolescence again, what I wanted did not exist on Napster or iTunes or Spotify. I didn't want the songs back by themselves. I didn't want singles for 99 cents or Sirius 1st Wave or even my own perfectly curated mix. I wanted radio back. I wanted air checks. I wanted them so bad I thought about taking the train to the Library of Congress, where, somebody had told me, this was the kind of thing I might be able to get. I wanted the texture of those afternoons, wanted them narrated by the DJ who herself had the rough sexy sound of a singer in a band. I wanted the weather. I wanted traffic on the turnpike. I wanted the ad for F.A. Ski and dollar Molsons. I wanted the ad for *Re-cycled Cycles . . . roll on!* I wanted Tom Petty's "Free Fallin'" again and again and again.

As a new mother in my early thirties, I toyed with moving back to Boulder. On a visit to town, I called a real estate agent. "We'd want to live downtown, because in Brooklyn we're used to walking everywhere," I said. But when I drove away from the showings, in a car by myself with the radio on, I realized both that *Holy shit, I like cars* and also what I really wanted: not a house, not a yard, not locally grown everything, not skiing every weekend, but this, this motion. What I wanted again were these streets, this map that was a part of my heart. The enduring topography, and the bendable rules—where Arapahoe changes from 35 to 45, meaning you can floor it to 50. I wanted the feeling of senior-year fall, the land rushing under me and the conviction that I would *get through this,* that I would transcend whatever trouble.

The happiness of that fall feels more authentic, more reachable, than that giddy, golden junior year. It was tempered with daily struggle.

Sometimes I would come home in between school and my shift at Alfalfa's. And as happy as I might have felt in the car, arriving home almost always brought me down, because it brought me closer to what I didn't want to do but would almost certainly do anyway.

In the kitchen I would put down my school bag. I would open the cupboard for just one thing. But inevitably one handful of granola would lead to another, and then all I would do was eat. I would walk around the kitchen shoving food in my mouth, even if I only had ten minutes. Ten minutes was enough to ruin everything. How was it that in such a small unit of time you could make an entire day into a total wreck?

It maddened and crushed me that I was doing this. There was nothing I needed the food for. Not as ballast or comfort. By now it was clear to me that I often ate in uncertainty or disappointment. But the ten minutes between Alfalfa's and school was not a time of torment.

I could have gone straight to Alfalfa's and avoided my kitchen, yet I came home precisely because of it. There I would be able to eat the right thing, the thing that would fix the day at once, and me forever. The right thing was one Norwegian cracker with many layers, like cardboard. Or one slice of sunflower whole wheat spread with chèvre. Or one apple. Or one cookie, as long as it was *just one,* and as long as I didn't devour it straight from the freezer, tongue to the molar I feared I'd just chipped. *Fuck it, fuck teeth, keep going.*

Sometimes I ate during those ten minutes because I hadn't eaten since dawn. But one bite would ruin perfect emptiness, and then I would hate myself, and then I would continue. The predictable hunger I'd once felt between meals was not driving this, and in the moment I was eating, I was never thinking about what was. (In general I wasn't yet thinking too hard about the reasons behind it, just resolving to stop it.) So I'd tear around the kitchen, my urgency heightened by the possibility that Betsy might come downstairs. Then I'd look at the clock on the stove and, fuck—now I was going to punch in late. I'd become that girl, the one a couple of minutes behind. I'd feel stuffed and poky on my way to the car and slow and unpretty at the store in my apron.

But during my shift, I couldn't eat. While I was working, I couldn't stuff anything in. An hour would go by, another. Something would lift.

During my break I'd go up to the employee lounge, and even though I was shy, people would talk to me because they were curious about someone they thought of as a native. To my co-workers I was special, in the way kids who grow up in Manhattan are special to anyone who arrives later. The type of people who worked at Alfalfa's had come to Boulder as a destination. They would be professional mountain bikers, or students at the Jack Kerouac School of Disembodied Poetics, or majors in kinesiology at CU. A stylish girl named Jane from Seattle seemed to be employed at the store simply as an ambassador of cool; she was the one who, every Friday, handed me a clear-windowed envelope with my paycheck. After work I would go to the drive-through at the credit union, then continue home. But once I rounded the corner off 55th, approaching our house from the back, and saw the pendant in the kitchen lit—those were the last moments of feeling good. I'd downshift and make the last turn, then pull into the driveway of the earth-toned three-bedroom in which I'd planned to flourish but was instead self-destructing.

MY FAMILY HAD ALWAYS loved Alfalfa's. The hype, the pride around me getting this job—almost thirty years later it is nearly unrivaled. My mother and I both still wear the turquoise employee aprons I pilfered. Back then she was also happy about the employee discount: 20 percent.

"I could not believe it," she said. "I actually spent less than a hundred dollars at Alfalfa's." It was a Sunday morning, and she was carrying the groceries into the kitchen from the garage. As she went back and forth to the trunk, I sat at the kitchen table, eating toast and reading the paper, and did not offer to help.

Betsy came into the kitchen, wearing plaid pajamas. She was a seventh-grader in an awkward stage: curling-iron bangs that covered acne. But her awkward stage was nothing like mine. She had never been an outsider, and her problems at school were popular-girl problems—friend betrayals and slumber parties where everyone cried. Where you saw Betsy's instability was at home. She cared too much about things we no longer had (e.g., money, a live-in father) and things my mother no longer did (e.g., bake). I knew the perfect-looking family in the perfect-looking house didn't guarantee happiness, because I'd lived it. Betsy had lived it, too, but only briefly, and the consequences of her having not known our family reality were starting to manifest. A year from now she'd use a small inheritance from a great aunt on a new kitchen table and chairs, one that matched her idea of the kind of furniture found in a traditional home. I am not sure why my mother let Betsy buy that dining set, except that her guilt, ever-present, was increasing. First her guilt had been about the divorce and the move; by that stage it might have been about drinking. Or maybe my mother's feelings were as conflicted as mine, rejecting the idea of the perfect home but longing for it, too.

Betsy stared into the refrigerator. "There's no more milk."

"Mom just went to Alfalfa's." I pointed at the bags on the counter.

"Oh," Betsy said, and sat down.

I observed that the refrigerator door was still open a crack and returned to the newspaper as if I hadn't.

In the garage, the trunk thudded shut, and then there was the rumble of the automatic door going down. My mother came inside with the two last bags. "Oh, God, did I leave this open the whole time?" she said, seeing the refrigerator.

"No," I said. "That just happened, with Betsy."

"Then why didn't you close it?" my mother said. She felt the temperature of a plastic bottle of fresh-squeezed grapefruit juice before pushing the door shut.

"I knew you were coming right back," I said.

"Lazy, Susan," said my mother.

"Is there fresh granola?" Betsy said.

"The granola in the jar is perfectly good," my mother said. "I ate it this morning."

Betsy said, "I'll wait for the fresh."

I went to the refrigerator and poured myself a glass of water from the pitcher that filtered out impurities. Ordinarily I would have put the pitcher back without refilling it for the next person, but because my mother was watching, I took it to the sink.

Would it be any surprise if Betsy wished for a family unlike the one the three of us made? There had been a brief but solid era when we'd cohered. Our first fall in Boulder we'd made waffles every Sunday with a heart-shaped press. High-altitude sun had streamed into the kitchen. On those mornings I'd felt the freedom of living in a house without my father, of no longer bracing for his explosions. Now, three years later, we had become grouchy and separate. We were like roommates, each with our own lives. Even out in the world, we were Nancy, or Betsy, or Susan; nobody knew us as a family. "It's so weird," a teammate of mine had said to Betsy at a summer swim meet. "There's this girl who looks just like you, except she has blond hair."

"That's my sister," Betsy had said.

This was another, uneasier kind of independence.

I often wondered if I had caused the separation. I knew it could not be entirely my fault, but I believed I was probably the worst offender. I was the only one who spurned the others. I was the only one who was mean.

My mother moved around the kitchen, unpacking. When she came to the granola, she handed the plastic bag to Betsy before pouring the rest into the tall clear canister.

"There," said my mother, sliding the last paper bag into a cupboard.

A few minutes later, she left for a walk with a friend.

I waited until she was gone. I even rose from the table so that I could see her disappear around the corner toward the Centennial Trail. Betsy was in the bathroom. I opened the jar of granola, stuffed a handful of it into my mouth, then, like a quivering, cheek-filling rodent, another. The toilet flushed. I chewed, wiped my hands on my shorts, and scurried away, leaving Betsy alone in the kitchen.

14

COLLEGE TOUR

MY MOTHER'S DRINKING PROBLEM had been building. Maybe slowly, or maybe it had spiked. An evening softness had shifted into something frightening and inept. I had not charted this progression: I'd been self-absorbed, or naïve, or both. Or just habituated to adults having too much to drink. I worried about my father only when I thought of him drinking in the car, but with my mother it was different. The feeling I got when she was drunk was the same scared feeling I'd had as a child when she got sick. I hadn't liked seeing her muffled or altered back then, and I didn't like it now.

One morning in October I pulled into our driveway, and my mother, gardening by our front step, watched as I opened the trunk and removed an enormous clear garbage bag of beer cans.

"They weren't going to get recycled," I told her.

We stood there, she with her trowel, and me with my bag of cans.

"I'm going to take them to Alfalfa's," I said.

Inside, I went straight to the shower. There'd been a party the night before and I'd slept on the floor with my head on a couch cushion. I felt grimy and stiff. Afterward, I stood on the bathmat, rubbing a towel over my wet hair, and in the silence when I finished, I heard my mother on the phone in her bedroom: "An amount of beer cans I've never seen. . . . No, not by herself! There was a party. . . . But the thing is—she was going to recycle them!" There was a little pride in her voice.

Our own recycling bins weren't big enough for all the cans. They were small and blue and labeled ECO-CYCLE. They were in the garage, and I tried to ignore them whenever I went out to the car. I didn't want to see my mother's wine bottles. Sometimes I forced myself to look, because maybe there weren't as many as I assumed; but it was always even worse than I imagined.

Occasionally in our bins would be the little bottles like they gave on airplanes, and these produced in me the greatest sadness. It was what a girl like me, an eater, would do, buy something in individual serving sizes to prevent yourself from going further. It was what you did when you couldn't control yourself or keep yourself in check. It was what you did when you were trying, futilely, to quit.

The first time I'd seen my mother drunk was in Florida when I was in ninth grade. At dinner one evening she'd begun crying and then, with my grandmother holding her elbow, had gone to the bedroom and not come back. My grandfather told me, "Your mother got too much sun."

That this night was not singular had dawned on me only gradually. At the tail end of junior year I'd started to notice a difference. I'd felt tough about it then and even, despite the evidence of a problem, thought I might be exaggerating it. "Mom, I'm on the phone," I would yell when she picked up in the middle of one of my conversations. "Sorry," she would say, drowsily, and it would take a second for her to return the receiver to its cradle. Sometimes she wouldn't do it all the way and I'd have to go into the kitchen, glare at her, and slam it down myself. Then I'd run back upstairs, get back on with Johanna, and say, "God, my mom is totally drunk."

But now I understood that her problem was a real problem. Now it just made me sad and scared when she picked up the phone in the middle of my conversations. Yet I had stopped agitating for another line, because as long as Betsy and I were on the phone, she was not. I felt like I was protecting her. Parents of the children she taught sometimes called at night. I couldn't imagine that they didn't notice she was drunk, unless they were drunk, too. Betsy would take the bottles of wine my mother hid in her closet and pour them down the sink. I stopped going into her closet to borrow things. I would only huff when I opened a kitchen cupboard and saw the juice glass full of chardonnay she'd hidden the moment I came in, "Jeez, that's funny, there's a fucking glass of wine in the cupboard," etc.

I wanted to look away, but I couldn't. I would glance at those recycling bins and then flop into the car and back out fast.

I could no longer pretend I was not like my mother, because I knew I was. I was like her in this way that seemed deepest of all.

My identification with her both drew me to her and repelled me. She was a model for me in so many ways: of strength, generosity, sensitivity, independence. And of the hidden life. Of how to maintain it. Of how to be one highly functioning self in the world and shrink into another at home. I sometimes wondered if it was because my mother tended her own hidden life that she accepted mine; or maybe she just didn't know about it, or didn't want to. Maybe we normalized secrecy for each other: I wouldn't bother her when she retreated into her thing, and she wouldn't shame me by barging in on mine.

My mother has been sober for a long time now. While I remained in hiding, still furtive and resistant, she stepped out and conquered her problems. After she got sober, she told me that she'd started drinking heavily in Michigan during my father's affair. At night, after everyone was in bed, she would sit on the kitchen floor, her back against the cabinet, a bottle beside her. By the time she told me this, I was familiar with the particular desperation of being a woman alone at night in a kitchen. I felt as if I had been her; as if I'd sat on that floor, not wanting to get up, because once I did I would have to return to my life and all that I was incapable of solving in it. And I also felt as if I had seen her; as if I'd come downstairs in my plaid-flannel middle school nightgown and stumbled upon my mother, wrecked and altered. Picturing the scene she described, I was at once a defeated woman and a frightened child.

THE WEEK AFTER I brought the beer cans home, my mother and I went on a college tour. We flew into Bradley and picked up a rental car. Though this region was my parents' orientation, the New England landscape was largely unfamiliar to me. The roads were narrow, the states close, and whenever NPR faded out, I could always find another NPR elsewhere on the dial. There was so much more of everything here.

We worked our way through the Massachusetts schools and crossed into Connecticut. On a blue, sparkling afternoon, we stopped at an orchard's roadside stand. There were doughnuts, cider, and apples in dark-green buckets. We bought two apples.

"Yum," my mother said in the car.

I said, "This is even better than Gala," which was the most popular apple variety at Alfalfa's. When it was four o'clock, time for *All Things Considered,* the familiar trumpets announced the show, and there was the teletype fade into the stories. I felt cozy in the car then, as I did in our kitchen at this moment of the fading day. If my mother was drinking in secret at night on the college tour, I didn't know it. On this trip we were our old selves.

My mother and I had traveled together like this once before. The summer I was twelve, we visited Andover. We drove down from the Adirondacks and stayed overnight at an inn. In the morning I went to my interview. The admissions office was in an old house, and the interview room had an Oriental rug, a fireplace, and lamps with fluted shades. A window-unit air conditioner was going. The two interviewers pulled their chairs close. At my father's insistence, I had brought the Sunday-magazine insert in which my story "Bellamys" had been published. One of the interviewers said, "I love it when people bring stuff." He picked up the insert. "Do you know who this is on the cover?" He pointed to an illustration of a long-haired scribe dipping a fountain pen in a barrel of ink. "I don't think it's anyone," I said. "I think it's just a guy they put on there to, you know, show writing." The man nodded. "Actually, it's Shakespeare," he said. "It is?" I said. "Oh, wow."

"Oh, no!" said my mother when I told her. We were walking into town to buy my father a T-shirt. "You didn't know that was Shakespeare?"

"How was I supposed to know?" I said.

But, still, I got in.

Recently I'd asked my mother if I could say on my college applications that I'd gotten into Andover. "Why would you put that down?" she said.

"I don't know," I said. "Just to show, you know."

"No," said my mother. "You can't put it down. It would only matter if you'd gone."

It should have been obvious: The only version of your life that counted was the one that had happened. Or it was the version that counted to other people, at least, even if something you hadn't lived counted just as much to you. Andover was an alternate life I'd inhabited since we'd left Michigan. Sometimes I'd sit in that other reality, in which my parents were still married and I went home on school breaks to my old house. More recently I had added a new setting to the fantasy, a dining hall. At Andover I ate like I did before any of this happened. I never ate bad anywhere but in my kitchen. I was banking on solving my problem next year, when I was away from home.

YALE WAS OUR LAST stop. When we got off the exit in New Haven, it was dark, and everything was a one-way street. "I don't remember this neighborhood," said my mother, who had grown up nearby. Soon we passed a long, brick colonial-style building with black shutters, and my mother said, "That's one of the colleges," and then at a red light she said, "Okay, there's Woolsey Hall," and turned on the left arrow. A lawn ran deep, helmed by a spired, cathedral-like building. We went through an intersection, and the same type of architecture unfurled in an unbroken span. The streetlight was ghoulish, the effect haunting. I had not considered what it would be like to see Yale, and I was startled by the sensation. It was like entering something out of my memory. Yet I was actually entering something out of my parents' memory, something out of my family's collective unconscious. Here my parents had started—met—and so, in a way, had Betsy and I. I was catching up to my parents, to the years in which they were people I could imagine. Their childhoods were formal and distant. But I'd never separated out my college-age parents from the grown-ups they'd become. They were still those students; it had all happened in a continuous line.

All separations healed then. For a moment, atoms came together, reunified.

15

SECRETS

ACK IN BOULDER, SWIM season started. Every morning at dawn we slumped on the pool deck in sweatpants. When our coach clapped his hands, we stripped to our suits. Then we moved through the water, still half in a dream. Once, I swam the first lap with my car keys clasped in my fist.

Midway through, the sleepy mood would change, and we'd yell things across lane lines. The sun would rise orange-pink through the glass wall. Something always turned over in me then. It was a tiny, daily experience of awe. We were already swimming, already doing. We moved into the day weightless, graceful, in water.

Julie Gray was also a swimmer; the most graceful one of us all. Sometimes, waiting at the wall in my lane, I'd watch her: the roll of her shoulders, the reach of her glide. There was a sensuality in her movement, a rhythm that made me self-conscious when I looked too long.

One morning in December, I got out of the water in a bad mood. Other girls just had their bodies and put food into them and didn't think. Or they did think but in a normal way. I could tell by the way they said it: "I am getting so fat." They weren't wrecked by food in the way I was; it didn't define them.

I was irritable all through physics. But I felt a little better afterward, driving with Julie to the Brillig, our favorite coffeehouse. The Brillig was housed in a narrow three-story building on the Hill, the college neighborhood. There were sloping wood floors, shafts of dusty gold light, and stairwell advertisements for practitioners of Reiki. I thought Julie and I had discovered the Brillig, but then one time I mentioned it to Mr. Rothberg and he said, "Does that place still exist?"

We'd been awake for hours, but CU students were just getting started. We stood behind them in the line and looked at the muffins in the case.

"What are you going to get, hon?" Julie said.

"I think the triathlete," I said. "Because of the no-dairy." The triathlete was a vegan muffin with cornmeal and tiny blueberries.

"Right," she said. Then, dubiously, "How's that going?"

I'd been vegetarian since the spring of junior year (PETA presentation on Earth Day), but since starting at Alfalfa's I'd been drawn to the vegans. They were more moral, more extreme. Their carts were filled with soy-cheese pizza and a frozen treat called Rice Dream. Yet they were not superior but kind. "I'm vegetarian, but lacto-ovo," I would say. "I want to be vegan, but I'm worried I would miss dairy and eggs."

"You could do it," I had been encouraged. It was like running a marathon: You just had to train.

Like all eating practices I adopted, veganism was intended to fix me. It offered limits as well as the promise of a higher plane. And it made me calm to cut things out. A diet that contracted rather than expanded felt like a way back to who I used to be. *Susan doesn't like pizza.*

Maybe working at Alfalfa's was inevitable: I was obsessed with food, and my job fed my obsession. At Alfalfa's we sold not only groceries but a fantasy that seduced me. Here, eating was a vehicle for personal transformation.

One of the things I liked best about Alfalfa's was that I didn't eat there but I got to see the way other people ate. Because food was deeply personal to me, I saw it as an intimate window into others. Groceries were revealing. Almost without exception, I imagined that the shoppers took care with and pleasure in the food they purchased. This could not have been universally true, but it was my assumption. Only once did I see a girl like me. She had the matted hair of a jam-band follower. I was working as a cashier when she came through my line. At nine in the morning, she put a pint of Ben & Jerry's on the counter. I punched in the price without even looking: $2.39. Then she asked for a spoon. Someone else might have thought she had the munchies, but I was pretty sure she didn't. Her aspect wasn't airy but sad, and she had asked for the spoon in a kind of aggressive mumble, as if she was embarrassed but also did not want to be challenged. I might not have thought about her again, but in ten minutes she was back in my line with another pint. My heart raced. Now I knew for sure. Where had she eaten the first pint—at the edge of the Creek Path, or across the street in the municipal parking lot? She looked like she hated herself to death. I tried not to make eye contact. I knew what it was to not want to be seen. As I scooped her change from the little pockets in my drawer, my face got hot. There was a charge in being so close to her, in seeing my own shame reflected in another. I handed her the coins and she stuffed them into her pocket. Her eyes were watery and red. *She threw up the first pint.* But by meeting her eyes I'd gone too far; she was angry then, it seemed like she could tell that I knew. My heart was still beating fast as she left the store.

"The vegan thing is going fine," I said to Julie now.

She put her hand on my wrist. "Really?"

"Really," I told her. The way she asked, it was almost as if she knew about my eating; but she couldn't, no one could know how dominated I was by this. They couldn't know, because I wouldn't tell them.

"I worry about you," she said, removing her hand. Relief flowed; we would not continue talking about this.

Julie took her mug to a small ledge. I liked watching her fix her coffee. The cream billowed. She shook in a packet of sweetener, stirred with a flat wooden stick. I sipped from my mug; they filled to the top if you said black. It sloshed when you climbed the stairs if you didn't drink a little first.

Up on the sunny third floor, Julie and I sat at a table with uneven legs. I had her to myself, in our place. We would drink coffee, grow closer. No one else from Fairview came here. At the Brillig, Julie and I were adults. High school was just an institution around which our current social interactions were arranged.

"So do you like him?" Julie said. She was talking about Will Carey, the boy I'd taken as my date to our friend Amy's Christmas party a few nights earlier.

"I mean, vaguely," I said.

"I like that," Julie said. "Vaguely."

"Honestly, I'm still not over Cord."

"You need to get over him," Julie said.

"I just need a new obsession," I told her. "Someone to get him out of my head."

"How about . . ." Julie said, trying to think.

"But not right now," I said. "I'm just going to indulge it a little longer. Because he's coming back."

"He's coming back?" Julie said.

"For Christmas break," I said. "They're all coming back."

"How do you know?" Julie said.

"I mean, I'm just assuming," I said.

"Sometimes I think about Cam Fisk," she said, naming a boy in Cord's group of friends.

"Oh, really," I said, leaning in.

"Yeah," she said. "We got together once." Then she widened her eyes. Was it possible that every episode in her life was imbued with this much drama? "Did I ever tell you about that?"

But I loved these openings. I loved learning about her years before now. As a sophomore, Julie had been wild. There were stories about her and Amy and Eden. Before going out, they would do shots and Julie would say, "Ready, set, you bet. Can I still feel my face?" and press her fingers to her cheeks.

Eden was Julie Gray's real best friend. This year I had paired off with Julie, but it was like having an affair: She would go back to Eden in the end. It wasn't like she was cheating on Eden; it was more like an open marriage, they were so evolved and securely attached.

I acted like I was cool with this, but being second-best bothered me more than I acknowledged. And I can see now that I used eating to cope with that feeling of mattering less to Julie than she did to me, not just in terms of Eden but in general. I remember Julie pulling me close at a party on a humid fall night and the delight of being drawn near—but it was only to tell me about a drama with a boy. I got together with my own boy in another bedroom and then left the party in a funk. I knew that my boy was a reaction to hers: I was rivalrous, smarting. What I didn't understand was that the food I ate when I got home was a reaction just as direct. Eating was an attempt to fill a need not met—one that would never be met, because the exclusivity I longed for was impossible. "One of" wasn't enough for me. I wanted "only."

We stayed at the Brillig until the end of third period, then got in Julie's car to go back to school. She fished by my feet for a CD, one arm low, her shoulder sloping, her head poking up to see the street. She found what she wanted, slid it in the deck, and then, with an elegant flick of her wrist, palmed the knob and shifted into third.

There were people who drove all the time and people who didn't. If they did, their cars—way more than their bedrooms—felt like their world. Seeing the town through Julie's windshield was like being inside her eyes. Behind the wheel, Julie relaxed, gave herself over to the pleasure of zooming off into our mountained universe. None of us had been drivers for long. The person at the wheel was still more like the grown-up, more like the mother. It made the driver powerful, and the passenger dependent, which was a freedom of its own sort. You succumbed to the ride.

Back at school I saw a girl I knew from theater, named Iris. She had perfect snowy skin, which I attributed to her Buddhist practice. She came up to me on the ramp and announced, "Cord's back."

"Are you serious?" I said.

"I saw him," she said. "And also Cam Fisk."

"This is a total omen," I said.

I had the levitating feeling of junior year again. It was that easy, that quick. Cord on these streets, the chance of an encounter. Something racing inside me, an orientation to my day.

I went straight to the senior balcony and tapped Julie's soft shoulder. "Cord's back," I told her. "And Cam Fisk."

"Cord's back?" Julie said. And then everyone was squealing and teasing me, and I felt loved and known.

The day shifted to hold this information. The lightness stayed.

At the afternoon swim meet, I was bouncy, stagy. I was one of the three captains, and on the blocks we did a cheer in which we each made our body a letter, F H S. I was F. I was the girl the other girls watched: the girl who ran things, the girl whose life was all fixed. And in those moments my life did seem fine.

In the hundred free, I got my best time ever. When I got out of the water, Julie was waiting. She hugged me, she in an oversize gray sweatshirt, me still wet in my suit.

After the meet, the team gathered at Round the Corner, a hamburger chain where you placed your order from a phone in your booth. When I hung up, Julie said, "We have been together all day. We have essentially been together since five-thirty A.M."

"Wow. Yeah, you're right," I said.

I worried, as I always did, that she preferred the world to expand to include more people, while I preferred it to narrow just to her, to contract. But I also wondered if she had made the comment in the same way I would have: to deflect real feeling.

A girl named Shannon slid in. "What's up, ladies?" she said, and I had the sense of receiving her, of being a couple with Jules, together in our booth.

———

"HE JUST TOTALLY DIDN'T get me, you know? It was like he wanted Amherst to still be all men."

A week later, in the employee lounge at Alfalfa's, I was on the phone with Jules. She'd just had her alumni interview for Amherst.

"That's possible," I said. "But don't worry, honey, you'll still get in." On the phone I was better with endearments. I could slip them in.

"I really don't know," she said. "None of yours were like this, right?"

"My interviews were with, like, known dads." Princeton had been with Margot's dad, who was a psychiatrist with African masks in his office. Yale had been with Jenna's dad, who was a lawyer from my father's own class. "Except for Brown," I added.

"The hottie," said Julie. "The hottie who is going to write, 'Susan is something really special,' on your form."

"Stop it. I'm at work. You're embarrassing me," I said.

But the alumni guy from Brown had been hot.

"He is going to come find you at Alfalfa's and take you to—to the basement, and—"

"Stop it! There is no basement."

"All right." She sighed. "This is going to be okay, right?"

"Totally okay."

"Okay," she said. "What time do you get off?"

"I get off at three," I told her, "but then I'm going to get my hair cut."

"Call me afterward," she said.

"I will," I said, and reached up to the wall to replace the handset in its cradle. Then I resettled on the torn leather couch with a magazine. But suddenly I was self-conscious. When you were on the phone you could trick yourself into thinking the conversation was happening in an isolation booth, but really it was like a broadcast. A cashier named Zoe sitting at the table in the center of the room had been listening the whole time. She flipped a page in the alternative weekly and said, "Was that your boyfriend?"

"No," I told her. "It was my best friend." I felt gratified that the

depth of my connection with Jules had been verified by an independent observer.

But later, bagging groceries, the question made me nervous. Zoe
was a lesbian. Had she recognized something in the way I talked to
Jules? *Was* there something in the way I talked to Jules? I looked
over at Zoe. She was tiny, with pixie hair that showed the many
piercings in her ears. She wore thin black clothes and huge black
oxfords and a Guatemalan knit hat with strings. This December it
was as cold as it had ever been. The daily temperatures were outrageous, such as a high of minus 8.

But the startling weather made the world feel new and spare. I
would start over now, do better going forward. The town was a
frost-dusted grid on which I was about to begin.

After work I got my hair cut and then drove up to the bookstore
and bought a box of Sierra Club cards, and when I got home I sat
down at the dining room table with a pen.

I still have the cards—long, detailed, heartfelt notes I never gave
to my friends. There I am, wanting so desperately to connect but
deciding in the end to hold back for fear of how my gesture would
be perceived. And in the initial impulse there had been such joy! It
wasn't duty or trying to be like anyone else. It was the thump-
thump-thump of "It's Christmas time in Hollis, Queens" and driving around Boulder on a clear winter day all by myself.

The box of Christmas cards I never sent in 1990 also contains the
cards that I received. Even twenty years later my heart sped a little
when I picked up Julie Gray's. I wondered what she'd said. But
she'd written only a few sentences. *I am so glad we talk more this year,
I hope it continues.* As soon as I read the card, I remembered getting
it. I remembered feeling deflated and glad I'd held on to my own
effusions.

I DIDN'T KNOW HOW it had started, but it had. Before I went to sleep, I
thought about Julie the same as I did a crush. I imagined kissing her.
I imagined it happening in her bed. Her soft bed—I knew its con-

tours; once, after drinking beer in the middle of the day, we had napped there. "Why is your bed so soft?" I'd said, and she'd said, "I have an eggcrate." She pulled up the fitted sheet so I could see. It was a queen-size piece of khaki foam. At Target, I hesitated before the thing in its plastic pack. Hard beds were better for you, like standing instead of sitting, or keeping your house colder than 68. But I bought it anyway, and for the first time my bed in Boulder felt snug and soft.

At night in my bed I'd imagine us in hers. I didn't want to admit I was doing this. Even in my own head there was avoidance, dissembling. I proceeded carefully with the fantasy, as if I might be discovered. I would say calmly, as if to a therapist I'd seen in ninth grade, that I had to admit that I sometimes imagined kissing Julie. I imagined it happening in sleep. It would have to occur in such a way that each girl could think to herself of the other, *She was the one who started it.*

Beyond the kiss I didn't have much. I would start the sequence over again or move on to the aftermath.

"So, last night," Julie would begin. "I—it was—are you okay with what happened?"

"Yeah," I would say, "I'm okay with it."

"Okay," she would say. It would be sunny. She would be driving. My heart would be galloping. I'd feel myself to be going faster than the car. It would be like a story problem: *If my speed = x and the car's speed = y, I will arrive at our destination z minutes before my body.*

There would be a pause.

"It was nice," she would say, and touch my wrist.

I would look down at my braided silver bracelet. Then I would look back up and meet her eyes.

"It was nice," I would say, in an echo of her way, emphasizing simple words to signify you were really saying something deeper underneath.

I wanted the kiss fantasy to remain a fantasy but for the aftermath to exist. That way I would have done nothing that would implicate me. That way our closeness could be acknowledged without shame or confusion or risk.

I imagined that the kissing would happen maybe a couple of times again. We'd go through the course of a regular night—driving, Taco Bell parking lot, trailhead keg—both excited for it but not saying. We'd find our way to each other at the end.

At maybe the third or fourth time, she'd say, "We have to stop doing this," and I'd say, "I know," but still lean in.

If I imagined this in the day, my heart would race and I would turn to my homework, something responsible and calming. Or I would pull on my tights and go for a run and on the trail feel returned to myself and able to look upon the situation rationally. She was the main person in my life right now, and I was projecting. These feelings were just a novel expression of the intimacy I craved. What I wanted from her was the same thing I had wanted from Cord: acknowledgment that there was something between us. It was a fantasy about reciprocation, about having your feelings confirmed. Yes, this was all I wanted, an affirmation of our closeness.

I remember seeing an advice column around this time, maybe in Betsy's *Seventeen,* that addressed a question like, "I think I'm attracted to my best friend. Does this mean I'm a lesbian?" The answer was essentially: "Don't worry. You are not a lesbian. You think you want to kiss your best friend, but that's just because your hormones are going crazy. Really you just want to be close to her. Like, emotionally close."

I found this answer unsatisfying. First of all, I was sick of hearing about hormones. They were the excuse for everything in adolescence. They seemed to me less like chemical messengers and more like marketing tools. Second, there was the response's general tone. Same-sex attraction wasn't something you were meant to celebrate. It was not bad, but it was also not great. This was troubleshooting. This was in the event of. And finally, how to make sense of the implication that your feelings weren't real feelings? *"You want to kiss her, but you don't."* Such a statement was, literally, nonsense.

Theoretically the answer should have comforted me. "You just want to be emotionally close" was what I wanted to hear. But beneath my fear of my feelings was curiosity about them, and I would have benefitted from an answer that acknowledged their complexity: an examination of how strong feelings of all sorts—identification, admiration—can manifest as arousal; of how you really might want to kiss your friend and how it really might mean that you are attracted to women, in addition to or instead of men; of how sexual response is variable and complex—over time, across circumstance.

Still, I did feel a little better. By choosing to publish the question, the editors had identified it as one of broad interest. Either a lot of girls were asking it or it was something they themselves could remember feeling and were still thinking about, too.

Years later, I read that G. Stanley Hall, the psychologist who, early in the twentieth century, established the modern conception of adolescent development, had characterized adolescent girls as "prone" to "idealize unfit persons." Teenage-me would have bridled at this assertion. The people I'd longed for weren't unfit! They were the most fitting people imaginable. It was amazing, that I had found them; that the universe had worked this way, to allow me to. The longings themselves were unfit, not the people they were directed to. It was their force; their provocations; their demands on my attention. The depth of the longing itself was what was taboo.

Of course, there was another longing whose power I feared. When I submitted to it, I tore around the kitchen; but then no matter how much I ate, the longing was never satisfied. Maybe I ate because I didn't act on those other, human longings; maybe I didn't act on those human longings because I feared how I'd handle myself if I did. What I do with food has always reflected in some way what I do with people, and my secrets have never been just about facts but about intensity of feeling. I have never been hiding only what I want but how much.

I WANTED JULIE. BUT as real as that was, and as scared as I was about it, it was nothing compared to eating. By now, winter of senior year, nothing could compete with that. Everything else was a distant flare. Sometimes a flare would attract my attention: When Operation Desert Storm started, I marched and protested and spoke at a rally at school. There was a quote from me in the *Daily Camera*: "It doesn't matter what you get on your finals. It doesn't matter what you get on your Algebra II test. We are going to go to war. What's more important, grades or war—people dying? I don't know, you make the choice." My mother hung the article on the refrigerator. The same refrigerator to which I'd inevitably return. Afterward— bloated, sated, hating myself—the flare mattered less. It could continue burning or it could extinguish itself; who the fuck cared.

So much in this stage went unexamined or undone, from feelings to schoolwork. I did approach writing with purpose and consistency. But even writing was compromised by eating, both because it was secondary to eating and because eating was its primary subject. Eating always needed to be figured out first, always had to be fixed before anything else could begin. It was always the thing that got in the way.

Mine was the compulsive focus of someone with a disease. Yet for a teenage girl of my era, my subject was not atypical. In my thirties I read a history of the adolescent female body. The book's author had read hundreds of diaries kept by adolescent girls over almost two hundred years, and a pattern emerged: While nineteenth-century girls used their diaries to write about their goals for character improvement, girls at the end of the twentieth century wrote almost solely about the ways they wanted to improve their bodies. The shift in focus from "good works" to "good looks" was remarkable, and the new focus on the body "all-consuming." I, too, had moved from one mode to another. My problem had seized my daily life and my inner one, too. A year and a half earlier I'd wanted to be "confident, happier . . . friendlier, outgoing, mature." Now I was examining little other than what I ate, how much I hated myself for the way I ate it, and how desperate I was to stop.

16

THE OBSESSION

LIKE ALWAYS, I WAITED until my mother was in her room for the night. Sometimes it made me hate her, how long I had to wait. Then finally: her feet on the stairs, the click of her door, the fuzz of her sink.

Even as I was going downstairs, I pretended there was a chance I wouldn't do it.

Once in the kitchen, I turned the dial for the overhead light. Our sunny kitchen looked different at night. You saw the dead flies on the fixture, the refrigerator's coiled back. I went to the freezer calmly, as if I were a normal girl considering the possibility of a midnight snack. Then I opened the door and took out a pint of ice cream. A bite fell on the floor, which I rued, because now I would have trouble judging how much I had eaten, and also I would have to pause at some point to clean it up. I finished the pint, returned to the freezer, pulled out a ziplock bag full of muffins, ate one that was still frozen—an oat-bran muffin from Alfalfa's with a hard, grainy edge. Then I opened the cupboard, ripped off the gold wrapper of a malt-nut PowerBar, which was like pressed taffy and made my jaw

THE OBSESSION | 149

sore. Then I turned the light off quickly, my heart racing with sugar. On the stairs I had a labored feeling, my body dealing with all that had gone in.

I didn't brush my teeth. I had to get in bed, to hide from what I had done. I would sleep it off, wait for the next day to begin.

In the morning, I was right back in the kitchen, feeling my over-age move through space. I ate breakfast immediately, even though I was still full from the night before, because today was the day I was going to fix everything by eating three normal meals. But as soon as I got up from the table I felt sluggish, and by the time I was out of the shower I was as exhausted as if I'd never slept. Food didn't give me energy anymore. It depleted me. I'd messed myself up, altered my own factory settings. In my room I opened my towel and ran a finger over the white threads on my hip: stretch marks, new from eating. *Disgusting gross hate myself kill myself want to cry.* The day was already ruined. *Want my mom,* even though she was here and I didn't want her, even though that didn't make any sense.

Back downstairs in the kitchen, my mother was pouring a cup of coffee. I walked past her without saying anything, took my car key from a hook on a wooden rack. She was probably doing the same thing I was, making resolutions, *Today is new, never again.*

My mother's drinking and my eating were both forms of what was then called "substance abuse," a term I disliked. "Abuse" implied you were choosing night after night to do damage. But that wasn't the whole story, because you were fighting it, too. You were wishing, more than anything, to go back to a time before this was something it had occurred to you to do.

ONE NIGHT, MY STOMACH against my waistband, feeling hectic and sick, scared that I'd cycled through so many nights like this, I called the Boulder Women's Clinic. Almost every day I saw the ad for their eating-disorders group in the *Daily Camera.* The phone beside my ear, I felt better already. My heart slowed, the airplane finally descending. It was the turning point, the action you take that makes it right. I was already placing it in my story. *And then one night my se-nior year I called this clinic, and I never ate bad again.*

"Hello?" It was a man, which surprised me.

"Hi, I'm calling about the eating-disorders group?" I said. I was calm. This was just a task on my list. I was reporting a newspaper that hadn't been delivered, making a reservation for a trip.

"Oh, you'll have to call back tomorrow. This is the janitor," he said.

"Oh, okay," I said brightly. It was a sign, obviously. I wasn't meant to do this. I never got the courage to call the clinic again. But I was increasingly anxious that I had a problem too big for me to fix, and I was wondering if I could tell Julie. Possibly I could hint at it the way she hinted at her problems.

"Something is just weird with my body," she said one afternoon.

We were driving through pale winter light. Our brown town was spread around us.

"You mean, like . . ." I said.

"I went to Kaiser, and they don't know. But the doctor I saw isn't really my doctor. It's the HMO model, so . . ." Julie knew all the working-girl terms already: insurance, pay stubs, HMO.

"Is it still your . . ."

"My stomach," Julie said. Lately in the mornings Julie had been pushing herself up out of the pool, smacking wetly across the deck, and going into the bathroom, where, she said, she threw up.

"I throw up every morning, Susan." Her gray-green eyes wid-ened. "And I don't think I'm pregnant." Which left open the possi-bility that she could be.

There was something between Julie and a guy I didn't know well. Exactly what, I didn't know, either. She'd been vague about it. She would say things like, "I have a problem, but I can't tell you what it is," which made me so mad that I wanted to get out of the car. I thought this was rude, and I wanted her to know it. I wasn't good enough for all the information, only a partial share. I was hurt because I saw information as the primary indicator of intimacy. I believed that knowing everything about another would draw you close. Sometimes when Julie wasn't letting me in, it protected me to know I was also holding something back. It never occurred to me that maybe sensing there was something I withheld made Julie withhold, too.

"I haven't had sex with him," she said.

"I know," I said.

"But it went farther than it should have."

I got a little still then, waiting for her to continue. When she didn't, I said, "It's okay, honey, it happens. You're not pregnant."

In those days there was a Swedish pop song that went, *My body says yes, but my mind says no!* One afternoon it came on the radio when I was in the car with Julie and Eden. They screamed these lyrics. At the wheel, Julie lassoed an arm in the air like in a strip-tease. In the passenger seat, Eden lifted her pelvis. In the back, I looked out the window. I wanted to feel what I assumed they felt, wanted to feel that aroused. I suspected there was a higher gear I hadn't gone into yet, or, worse, one I was missing entirely. At seventeen I worried about sex in the way I had worried at eight about a heart attack. There was something wrong with my body, but I would keep mum about it and act like I was normal and eventually I would be; or maybe I wouldn't, maybe this was a permanent defect.

Though I felt sexual desire, I worried that I did not feel enough of it or in the right way. I see now that eating muffled desire, but back then I did not make that connection. Eating and sex were linked in my mind, but only in that I believed I was having a different experience with my body than a teenage girl was supposed to. My friends all seemed to know about sex and like it. They were reveling in their bodies; I was sabotaging mine. The way I ate was physically punishing, and my body was overtaxed. I was gaining weight rapidly now. Sometimes I attempted to like my body this way. I tried to see my body the way I saw Julie's—womanly, sensual. I tried to think of my flesh as beguiling. In the shower I'd look down at myself, move my torso, imagine my breasts as pendulous. But I couldn't change my perception. I saw everything on me as extra.

At the end of a frontage road, Julie paused at a stop sign. An obese woman with enormous white arms entered the crosswalk.

"Please don't ever let me get that fat," Julie said. "Please tell me if I do."

It meant so much to me that she assumed in the future we would still be friends.

"I promise, I won't," I said. "I mean, I will. I mean, you know what I mean. But you have to tell me, too."

"There's no way you could ever get that fat, Susan," Julie said.

I was silent. She would only say something like this if she had no idea what I did.

BY NOW I WAS significantly heavier than I'd been at the beginning of junior year. It was impossible that my friends had not noticed. Maybe at first their discussion of me had been almost catty: "Susan's getting kind of big."

But I was sure they didn't know how I'd gained the weight. I absolutely did not think they could have guessed. What I was doing was so weird and awful. There was no precedent for it; I seemed to have invented it. There was a line in Mona Simpson's novel *The Lost Father*: "I was the first anorexic in America. I made it up myself." I thought I knew what the narrator, Mayan, meant. Everyone said that eating disorders were because of magazines. They were culturally constructed. Maybe this was part of it. But you found it in you.

I was churning, crazy, unable to stop. It didn't make sense. I had always been small and controlled. I was betraying all first principles. As bad as this had been junior year, there had been nights I didn't do it. But now I couldn't go a day without it.

"What's wrong, honey?" Julie said one night on the phone.

I was going to do it. I was going to now. I would approach it her way. "It's—whatever, I know what it is, but I can't tell you."

But either she was hurt—she recognized I was throwing her words back at her and was trying to hide the sting—or she actually respected this.

"Yeah," she said. "I know how that is. But I'm here for you, okay?"

"Thanks." Then my throat got tight, because she was so kind to me; because I'd closed off my chance at telling; because I wondered if we were still in the moment where I could tell.

I wanted to tell, because maybe telling could fix it. And while closeness wasn't my primary motivation for telling, I did imagine that would be a by-product of it: a deeper understanding, a new tenderness.

I could still tell. I swallowed. "That means a lot to me, Jules."

"I'm always here for you," Julie repeated, and I felt like I might cry again. "Okay?" she said.

"Okay," I told her.

"I worry about you," she said.

EATING DISORDERS WERE IN the media then, but it wasn't like today, with the Internet. You couldn't lie in bed holding your phone over your face and access all the world's information. It would have been different if I'd been able to tap into that stream. I don't know that it would have changed the behavior, but it would have altered my thinking about it. I would have felt less alone, but I would have been even more mired in it.

My senior year of high school, information was still found in the traditional places. I went to Boulder Book Store. "Women's Studies" was upstairs, beneath the skylight. With my money from the health-food store, I bought a book called *The Obsession: Reflections on the Tyranny of Slenderness*. On the cover there was a girl in a Santa suit who seemed to be eating the snack meant for Santa.

As soon as I got home, I sat on the couch in the corner of my bedroom with a highlighter. It was exactly the way they told you not to use highlighters: It wouldn't help you study if you scraped the yellow marker over an entire page. But I couldn't help it. I was so relieved. This book about the body actually took me out of my body and into my head. It turned out to be a work of feminist theory that seemed only partially relevant. But it allowed me to engage with my experience intellectually instead of practically, to analyze it instead of trying to fix it. And it demonstrated how another woman, in another time, had struggled with a version of my problem and tried to make sense of her story in her own language.

MAYBE BECAUSE I WAS failing at changing the behavior, it occurred to me that understanding its origins might help. And so in physics, when we had to write a paper, I used the assignment as an opportunity for my own research. The paper didn't have to be on physics, just something scientific, and mine was called "Dysfunctional Familial Patterns and Eating Disorders."

The day Mr. Briggs handed back the papers, he asked me to stay after class. I looked at Julie and she raised her eyebrows. Mr. Briggs was a famous rock climber, and preternaturally calm. I suspected that at times he found our behavior irritating: We sat at a high lab table in the rear, twirling on the chairs like barstools, posturing with our coffees, which we always had now. Coffee was something of the adult world you could bring into the classroom. Sipping it while a teacher talked was almost like being allowed to smoke a cigarette.

While the class left, I had two thoughts. One was that my paper was so good that Mr. Briggs was going to accuse me of plagiarizing. I would deny it. I would show him. But underneath my bluster was nervousness. Sometimes it was hard to make sentences all that different. Even if you put things in your own words, it still sounded a lot like what the original writer had said. I was like many high school students, changing (modifying) words (language) here and there (now and then).

The second possibility was worse. He would escort me to his office. He would ask if I had a problem with this, with eating. It would be like being committed. A guidance counselor would have been alerted in advance. Now in the doorway, she would appear.

But when I came to the front of the room, Mr. Briggs handed me my paper and said, "This is very good."

"Thank you," I said.

He stood there, calm and trim, this man who free-climbed canyon faces, notching himself into cracks. "Is this what you want to do?" he said.

"Study eating disorders?" I said.

"No," he said. "Write."

"Yes," I said.

"Well, you're very good at it."

"Thank you," I said again.

As soon as I was away from him, I raised the cover sheet and flipped through for his notes. He hadn't made a single comment except on the top of the first page. _Well written!_ Underlined, with an exclamation mark. Then it said _99-2,_ and _97_ was circled. 100 would have been analyzing the problem and solving it, too.

A FEW MORNINGS LATER Jules and I again sat on our high stools in physics. She was glowing. She spread her hand over the lab table. "My fingernails are finally grown out. My mother says it's because of my new healthy eating habits."

The night before, Julie and our swim coach and I had eaten salad at a restaurant actually named Healthy Habits. Then I'd come home and eaten frozen oat-bran muffins and vanilla ice cream at ten-thirty P.M.

The whole morning I felt thick. Physics, library, play production, walking Jules to class, returning to an empty senior balcony, everybody having left for lunch without me.

I stood at my locker, stewing. Why had I walked her to class? Why did I cling to her, instead of looking out for myself? Now I had no one to go to lunch with—but even if I hadn't walked her to class, probably no one would have asked me to go to lunch anyway, which would also have sucked. I hated this, why did I even care, fuck, fuck, fuck.

I drove home in noontime light that made me feel low and wrong. I played music loud in my car and whipped around turns the way Jules did. But I wasn't a good driver like she was. Behind the wheel, she was assured. I was messy, about to explode. When I came to my corner, I blasted toward my garage and almost hit the station wagon driven by the young, fluffy-haired mother at the end of our street. For a second she looked frightened, as if there still might be an accident, and then something in her face hardened.

There was a problem right away: The garage was open and my mother's car was inside. I wouldn't be able to eat if she was home. And I needed to now, needed to shove something in my mouth. I needed, really needed, the kitchen. I wasn't planning to eat total amounts; I rarely was, especially when I came home at midday like this. But I needed to eat something, and I needed to do it alone. I needed not to be seen. Why did I need this? I just needed it. I just did. It was like a swell in my head. Later in life I would learn that one was often advised to slow down and record the feeling one had on the verge of the binge. If you had told me to do this then, I would have told you to go fuck yourself. What I felt on the verge: My God, were you an idiot? I felt bad, okay. Obviously! Actually, I did it when I felt bad and I did it when I felt good. But I did not want to stop to tell you any of this. I would not say what I felt because of that swell. I was in the tunnel and I would *stay in lane*. A million different roads took me into this tunnel every day.

My mother was at the kitchen table, eating a salad. There were tomatoes, cucumbers, feta, dill fronds.

"Hi, sweetie!" she said. She was friendly. It was a nice surprise to see me.

"Why are you here?" I said.

"I went to the dentist," she said. "And I'm having lunch before I go back to school."

I was already opening cupboards, looking around. I went to the glass jar of granola and took a handful, like it was a snack. Like it was just something to munch on while I decided on the real, healthy lunch I was going to have.

Once, my mother had said to me, "Your problem is that you

never eat a regular meal, so you're never satisfied." She had dispensed this advice casually one morning like a diet tip.

But that had happened a long time ago, junior year. She had never seen me like this, keyed up, desperate. I was bent over my hand, mouthing the granola like a horse eating oats. She had stopped eating to watch me.

"What?" I said. "What, I'm hungry," and then bent my head back, tossed the rest of the granola into my mouth, opened the refrigerator—the seal making a cheap, rubbery smack—grabbed a string cheese, slammed the door—heavy with bottles that jangled—and went upstairs, wiping oats on my pants, and waited in my room until she was gone. Then I went down to the kitchen, and when I was finished I felt roly-poly, full to bursting.

As I'd been eating, I hadn't felt anything. Now that I was done, there was a flood of feeling, mostly fear, because I'd have to get through the day like this, upholstered. Then came shame about what my mother had seen and more fear that I'd not been able to control myself. Eating like that in front of her, licking granola off my palm, was a new low.

It occurred to me that her reason for being home could have been made up. Why couldn't she have gone straight from the dentist to school? I didn't think she drank in the classroom—she couldn't drink in the classroom, please God, she couldn't. (And she didn't, ever. My teenage paranoia was not true.) I also didn't think she drank in the car, but I didn't know for sure: There was a squeezable bike bottle I wouldn't use, the white one that said *Specialized*. The inside smelled like wine.

Fuck her.

I turned. I left the kitchen. I went to the stairs.

What I wanted was to stay in bed for weeks. I wanted to hide out somewhere, like a pregnant teenage girl in the 1960s sent away to a convent until she delivered. Yes, that's what I wanted, a convent, white sheets, until all of this was out of me. It didn't belong, it was something evil. I would deliver it in a pile and begin again. The secret would be out of me, and I would be elsewhere, relieved and spent.

I felt ruined, like a girl who'd been spoiled, a girl who'd given it away. A girl who watched pretty, fresh girls flower while she stood behind a heavy drape, bitter and sallow. A girl was always ruined by her body.

I had math, but fuck math, fuck if I was going to go back for it. I would get an unexcused absence, but it didn't matter. For every unexcused absence your parents received an automated call, but my mother just pressed DELETE as soon as she heard it on the answering machine. She thought the school was a joke, except for Mr. Rothberg. ("Colorado has one of the lowest property taxes in the country," she would say. "It's ranchers and Republicans. They don't care about schools.") After a certain number of unexcused absences your parent had to sign something, but my mother didn't care if I forged her name. Something welled up in me; she couldn't be drinking in the day, she couldn't, I would do better, I would not be mean to her, I wouldn't.

I emptied my swim bag. I shook the suits and towel out of their ball and hung them in the bathroom. A task was done; one thing was better. This was okay. Then I sat on the floor and wrote a little in my journal. In a way it was like getting the food out of me, because it got thoughts out of my head. It was redemptive, always, even just a few lines. It made me feel better about what had happened. It made me determined to never mess up again. I stood up. It would be all right. This was just one thing in my long life. I had missed math, but I could make it in time for seventh period. I had the strength to go back to school.

When I walked into AP English, I conferred quickly with Jo. We didn't have our papers done and we lied to Ms. Koch about having misunderstood that today was the deadline. "We both had that down, so you must have said it." I felt cheery, naughty, bonded.

But once the class started, the little lift was gone, and I fell into my head again.

I always felt self-conscious when I was back in the world after a binge. I wondered if people could tell, if they could see the food on me. Did the new fat spread like frosting right away under your skin? I didn't think so. Your body hadn't had a chance to process the food. It was like stealing something and not being caught yet. But I knew I looked different when I didn't do this. One morning after a rare trouble-free night I'd gone by Julie's to drop off a sweatshirt, and as I stepped away from the door, she'd put her hand on my wrist and said, "You look pretty." One night of not eating, that was all it took! They said you got the chipmunk cheeks from throwing up, but I got them just from chewing. I would study this, prove it with research. On another singular morning-after-nothing, the English teacher, Ms. Koch, had said, "You look nice today, Susan."

I wondered if Julie and Ms. Koch knew and they were issuing a coded message: "This is how you could look all the time if you would change."

About other issues, Ms. Koch had been more direct. "This year you've done some of the most brilliant work I've ever seen," she'd told me recently. She was so impressed with one of my papers, "The Symbolism of the Vermiform Appendix in *The Death of Ivan Ilych,*" that she read the first two paragraphs aloud to the class. "But," she continued, "you've also done some work that's very bad."

My chest got tight when she said this. She was right. I nodded. She waited for me to speak, but I couldn't. I think her assumption was that I was lazy, or careless, but it wasn't that. Eating, and recovering from eating, took a lot of time: That was part of it. But, also, I didn't seem to be in control of whether things came out well anymore. My output was unpredictable. Was this the person I had become? Uneven, inconsistent, others always a little disappointed in me? Believe me, I was disappointed, too.

Back then I was drawn to stories about talented adolescent girls who experience traumas. Mick, the musical prodigy in Carson McCullers's *The Heart Is a Lonely Hunter;* Sylvia Plath's suicidal Esther Greenwood. McCullers in particular was drawn to the theme that, as one literary critic I read years later put it, "adolescence brings a paralyzing knowledge of inadequacy to the exceptional girl and bars her passage into the world of art." Eating was the first thing that made me feel inadequate. As I moved into adulthood, there it stayed, like a hovercraft. Sometimes I'd wonder, if I didn't have this obsession to distract me, to constantly keep inches off the ground, what could I be writing? Now that I am older still, the work I have or have not done seems far less important than the life that has or has not accommodated that work. The life in which I have often been distant or short with the people who loved me; in which I have often been distracted; in which my quality of attention has been diminished because of something I have not fixed.

BY SEVEN-THIRTY THAT EVENING, my stomach was emptying. It was a normal time to put food in. I stood up from my homework and opened my bedroom door. There was the sizzle of onions and peppers. My mother was making chicken fajitas. In the oven there would be flour tortillas. I hesitated, then closed my door. I would not eat. I would not eat again.

I sat back down on the floor with my journal.

I wish, I wish, I could tell people more.

17

LATE TEEN

JULIE WAS ONE OF those people with an absent sibling who seemed more like an only child, and I'd long been curious about her older brother, Chris. He was twenty-three and he lived in Austin. I finally met him when Julie and I took a road trip to Texas for spring break. Chris had just been admitted to the university's graduate program in English, and his small apartment was filled with books.

"What are you reading?" he said, when we established that I liked books, too.

"*On the Road,*" I said. "I read it last year, but because we're on a road trip, I'm, like, reading it again." Immediately I wished I'd had a better answer for Chris, because as drawn as I was to Julie, I was even more powerfully drawn to him.

All spring I looked forward to June, when Chris would arrive in Boulder to work for the summer. To my surprise, the end of senior year went by in a rush. We stole FOR SALE signs and planted them in front of the school. I wore skull earrings with my prom dress. One afternoon, the fat envelope arrived: I'd gotten into Yale. I had a brief knife of pride. Then came relief, which made me feel pathetic.

I knew from Julie that Chris would be at our graduation. Many nights I closed my eyes and imagined him hearing my speech. In a way, I'd written it to make him fall in love with me. "I liked your speech," he told me after the ceremony, and I twitched with hope.

Once summer came, the three of us hung out a lot. We'd get together after work—me after Alfalfa's, Julie after lifeguarding, and Chris after the library, where he stayed pale in the archives. At the Nepali restaurant, we ate vegetable momos. At the condo Chris was subletting, we drank pony beers and watched *Texasville*. We saw Chris so much that Julie said, "Do you mind that we always do things with my brother?"

"No," I said. "I like your brother."

"Are you sure?" Julie said.

"Yeah," I said. "I really like your brother."

One day Julie and I went to a concert on our own. I picked her up at her pool and we drove to Red Rocks, an amphitheater in a canyon near Denver. This was an all-day show, hot and bright and long, and early on I had some beer, but as it grew dark I stopped because I was driving. Julie was drinking a lot. It interested me whenever this happened. Was it a desire to lose control, or was it palliative? Sometimes her abandon was rough, frantic.

In the car on the way home she said, "I think I'm going to throw up," and she opened the passenger door and vomited.

For once I was in the position of caretaker. "Oh, honey, are you okay?" I said.

"Oh, God," she said, and closed her eyes.

For the rest of the drive she was quiet. And even though I was the one in the driver's seat, I felt young and dutiful beside her. When I got that drunk, it was an accident, and I was shaken. But Julie knew limits and purposely surpassed them.

I dropped Julie off and drove back to my house. The whole way home I told myself I was going to *get inside, hang my key, and go straight upstairs.* But once inside, hooking the key onto the rack, I determined it would be all right to go into the kitchen. *I will just have a bite. I will just see if there is any leftover chicken.*

And then it was awful. The worst night that had ever been.

My eating had worsened in distinct stages. Beginning each new level, I'd felt horror that *this is the worst it's ever been.* Now the worst felt medical. There were times I ate so much food I worried something bad could happen to my body. A line had been crossed: The fear of the harm I was doing was now worse than the humiliation of continuing to expand.

That night: scooping granola from the jar, oats falling through my fingers. (Every day my mother must have swept.) Ice cream, scraping the bottom rim of the pint. Clif Bars, which were sweet at first but then were like dog food, just a sticky brown nugget you were shoving in.

I never pretended to be a regular girl anymore, the snacky, chatty teenage girl or the one seeking a midnight snack. Now I was a head case being studied. The kitchen windows were two-way glass. In our backyard was a psychiatrist with a clipboard and a stopwatch.

I would call it a fugue state, but I don't want to imply that it was dreamlike. This was tearing things, a frenzy. This was metal clanking in my ears.

I always read something while I was doing this. *The Daily Camera,* or the J. Crew catalog. Reading gave my mind somewhere to rest other than on whatever I didn't want to face next. I ate more so that I could stay there, in the mindless copy.

That night I went up the stairs feeling my heart wild and dangerous in my chest. It was the way the heart is after the injection of a drug, something it isn't designed to process.

I couldn't wash my face or brush my teeth. I couldn't do the things of a normal girl, when I wasn't a normal girl at all. I didn't even consider them. I would go straight to bed. I needed to escape from what I'd done psychologically but physiologically, too. There was a medical indication, my body was overstressed.

In my room I pulled off my shorts. I got in bed still wearing my shirt and my bra. It was too much to change: too many steps, but also too awful to imagine pulling a nightgown over that hated mess.

Under the sheets it was always scarier for an instant, your heart louder, your breath thick. I closed my eyes. I would sleep while my body was processing this, roiling. I would wait until morning. I would be better then.

Then the phone rang. I didn't want to pick it up, but I had to. Otherwise my mother in her drunk oblivion might reach for it.

I pulled myself up, flicked on the lamp. "Hello?"

"Hey, sweetie," Julie said.

"Hey," I said.

"Oh, you don't sound good. Did I wake you?"

"No, I'm still awake." I laid my head back down on my pillow.

"Okay, good. Honey, whatever I had in me is out of me, and I feel so much better now."

Whatever I had in me is out of me, as if it were food poisoning.

"I just wanted to thank you for taking such good care of me," she said.

At other times this sentence would have made me spark with feeling. But I was so stuffed that nothing she said could get through. Nor could I properly respond to her: tell her that I hoped she was feeling better, that it was so not a big deal.

"That's okay," I said.

"Was it fun?" she said. "I don't even know if it was fun, that's how out of it I was. Did you have a good time?"

"Yeah," I said. But in my mind now: *You don't sound good.* She was standing in her lifeguard chair, throwing me the ring buoy. All I had to do was grab on. It was the worst night ever, and it was a sign that she had called while I was still inside it.

"You sound so tired. I think you were sleeping. I'm going to let you go."

"Okay," I said. She wanted to let me go: another sign. I lived by signs, relied on them. I was indecisive, and signs were easier. How else were you going to choose?

I hung up having missed my chance again.

I heaved myself—this was how it was to put so much in you, like a whale swallowing another whale—back under the sheets and slept.

In the morning the light came through the floral blinds. I felt sore. It happened sometimes after I ate. I wondered if it had to do with the work of the body having to expand the skin.

The phone rang, and the machine downstairs in the kitchen switched on. A friend's voice came through the speaker: *Susan? I'm just waking you up.*

We had an early swim meet. But I couldn't do it. I couldn't pull on a suit. I had never skipped a swim meet before. In my bed, I turned toward the wall. So this was a marker of the new stage, too. Now the *worst it's ever been* included not doing the thing that made it better.

THREE DAYS LATER JULIE turned eighteen, and she and Chris and I drove up to some land their family owned in the mountains. We got out of the car and stood in the sun in an empty meadow. A little breeze shook the trees, and there was the smell of pine.

"Eighteen is a big deal," Chris said. "It's like thirteen, an age that puts you into a new category."

"Not as big a deal as twenty-one," Julie said.

"The summer I moved here, the drinking age was still eighteen," I said.

"I *was* eighteen when that was still the drinking age," said Chris.

"I mean now, eighteen, what?" Julie said. "You can vote. Actually, that does matter to me."

"You're an adult," Chris said, "in the eyes of the law."

"In a way, twenty-one seems younger than eighteen," I said. "At eighteen, you assume responsibility. When you get to twenty-one, you go back to being frivolous."

Chris and Julie were both looking at me. I felt like I'd said something insightful.

Then Julie said, "You know what Chris said? 'I wish Susan was eighteen so I could wine and dine her.'"

There was the hum of insects in the thin air. I wanted the world to stay where it was, all of us motionless in this meadow. Julie had been testing those words, seeing if they were true.

Chris looked blank. These words meant something to him. His discomfort made me confident enough to speak.

"The age I least want to be," I said, "is twenty. You're not twenty-one, but you're not a teenager. You're not young anymore, but you're not an adult, either. Twenty seems like the most depressing age there is."

Honestly, even eighteen seemed depressing, though I didn't want to say so in front of Julie, given that it was her birthday.

Eighteen and nineteen were teen in name only. These weren't the ages of girls with pom-poms and textbooks and lockers. They were the ages of girls with apartments and birth control and lingerie. If somebody that age was raped, a crime often committed in Boulder, she wouldn't be called a teenager in the newspaper. She would be "a woman, 19, jogging at noon in Boulder Canyon." Even though the rape victims were close to my age, they seemed much older, because of that word, "woman."

But if "woman" wasn't right, nor "teenager," then what were you to say? In my thirties, when I read Dana Spiotta's novel *Eat the Document,* I liked her term: "late teen." She used it as a noun: "Nash remembered being a late teen." Maybe she'd made it up, or maybe it was something from psychology. Wherever it had come from, now I had a name for the way I felt that summer when Chris and I were dating.

THE FIRST NIGHT WITH him, I felt the desire I'd feared I lacked. Something broke open in me, urgent right away. Driving home from his place, I reached for the radio, then decided not to turn it on. I wanted nothing else, no other inputs. I felt electric, connected, and content. At home I bypassed the kitchen. That hadn't happened for months.

(And it wouldn't last. The pull he had on me was strong, but the pull food had on me was stronger.) In my bed I replayed the night's events; and then I reached for myself. I was seventeen and it was the first time I had ever done this. For once I didn't want to leave my body. I wanted to inhabit it.

CHRIS WAS THE PERFECT combination of illicit and safe. This was my theory, and I wished I could try it out on Julie. But I couldn't talk about Chris with her. Julie claimed to be happy, but she didn't seem happy, she seemed hurt, and we steered clear of the subject.

Things went faster with a twenty-three-year-old. We had sex in the white-curtained bedroom of his sublet. (*Late teen.*) I went downstairs in a man's shirt on a summer morning and his friend Martin made me eggs. (*Late teen.*) I walked toward him across a lawn, wearing short shorts and cowboy boots, hips swaying. (*Late teen.*) I rode my bike home from Alfalfa's late at night, and he was there, in his car on the corner, playing my favorite song. I got in the passenger seat and at a red light he looked over and told me the restless thing I was doing with my thumbs was a sign of genius. He thought I would be the one in my class to become famous first.

One early evening Chris picked me up for a classical music concert at Chautauqua. A customer at Alfalfa's had given me the tickets. I felt pretty, sun-flushed. I'd gone running before he came, showered; my hair shone. I had on a close-fitting shirt with many tiny buttons.

Julie was also going to a concert that night, at Red Rocks.

"And we were talking," Chris was saying. "And, I'll just ask you this, too: Why do you like going to concerts?"

It took me a second to answer. "I guess I like to see the music being made."

"Exactly!" Chris said. He looked at me as if I had ratified my genius. "Julie said she likes to see what the people look like in real life." I was pleased he liked my answer better than Julie's, though I thought hers was perfectly reasonable, too.

The auditorium at Chautauqua was like an enormous barn. We took our seats amid white-haired couples. The orchestra was tuning. Chris looked at his program, then put his hand on my leg: firm and warm from my run, luxuriant with moisturizer. When he went under my skirt, I felt nervous about the impropriety, but I didn't want him to stop. I gave in to the flurry and closed my eyes. "I'm horny," he whispered, close. It was a word I despised, and the feeling receded in the flood in which it had arrived. Then he tilted his head questioningly, and I followed him up the aisle and out of the auditorium, feeling not desire but embarrassment.

Against a tree we kissed, and I hoarded the feeling so I would not lose it again. Through our closed eyes we saw lightning. We ran across the lawn to the car. The drops fell and we slammed the doors. The weather made it look like the middle of the night. Then Chris was driving up the canyon, parking at a scenic overlook, and we were laughing—we were here, doing this!—and he was unspooling my seat so it reclined, and he was lifting my skirt.

Sometimes I still summoned the first night's easy bliss. But now my enjoyment was inconsistent.

Afterward it seemed like there was evidence, steam. "I wish we had something to drink," I said.

Chris opened the glove compartment and removed a tiny bottle of tequila. "Martin gave it to me when I picked him up at the airport," he said, unscrewing the small cap.

I took a burning sip. "It's illegal to drive with an open container," I said, passing the bottle to Chris.

"Everything in this car is illegal," Chris said. He tipped back the tequila, wiped his mouth. "Even you and me. I'm pretty sure in Colorado it's statutory rape if you're under eighteen." (He was wrong. I was legally of age to consent, and I did so willingly. Our sex was lawful, even if my consumption of the tequila was not.)

"The West is as conservative as the South," I said, which was something I had heard my mother say. Chris replied, but I felt distant. The comment suggested the hazard of our pairing: The older person could not help but take advantage. Chris passed the bottle back to me, and I brushed a strand of hair from my mouth and took another sip.

ONE AFTERNOON ON MY break at Alfalfa's, I went straight to HABA. HABA was the health-and-beauty-aids section. It was run by a golden, breathy woman named Brigitte Mars. Brigitte Mars was one of the most famous people at Alfalfa's. She was often quoted in newspaper articles, advising people to eat raw foods, because they contained the life force, or to prepare millet during times of stress. As a teenager at a New England boarding school, she had begun experimenting with natural remedies. Then she had moved to the Ozarks and lived in a teepee. Through marriage, she acquired her far-out last name. Brigitte Mars was so much of a famous person that when, on another occasion, I'd wandered back to HABA to ask her a question, at first I wasn't sure she realized I was her co-worker. I'd wanted to buy some all-natural sunscreen, but Brigitte had looked maternally at my skin and said, "Love, everything we sell here will make you break out." I was grateful she knew that for a teenage girl, it was better to have chemicals than pimples.

Today I scanned the shelves, wondering if there was an herb known, in the olden days, to cause miscarriages, which now, in modern times, was marketed in a subtle way. I looked for such a product on the shelf with the prenatal vitamins, as if the area were organized like a thesaurus, with space at the end for antonyms.

At seventeen I understood pregnancy in the context of its undoing. I believed in a woman's right to choose. I didn't think of pregnancy in physical terms but in moral and political ones. Some of this had to do with the cultural climate: The early nineties were a time of increasing challenges to Roe. But it also protected me to think of pregnancy as an abstraction now that I feared its reality.

Brigitte Mars was talking to a customer, but when she saw me she squeezed my shoulder hi. I left HABA without asking her anything. I liked the fantasy of receiving aid from the floaty goddess in the gauzy dress, but I needed the solid reality of my mother.

———

SO MANY TIMES I had approached my mother across this yard while she was reading. This bright day, I stepped out of the sliding door onto the patio and crossed the dry, stalky grass.

To the chagrin of our neighbors, my mother had let our backyard return to natural prairie. She thought it was an abomination that Kentucky bluegrass was allowed in our arid state. Though I loved her audacity, I never told her so. Instead, with Betsy—who, at thirteen, was genuinely humiliated by our mother's gesture—I mocked the brown yard. It was like a spell had been cast, rendering me unable to say anything kind or supportive to her.

And now here I was before her, humbled. I needed her, I resented her; I wanted her to help me, I wanted her to look away.

"I'm worried I might be pregnant."

She stared at me for a moment, her book still open in her lap. There was no sympathy. I hadn't anticipated this reaction, but it made sense. My mother gave me a lot of independence because she trusted me—and I appreciated both parts of that. But this was a big fuckup; this was irresponsible.

"How could you be so careless?" she said, tenting the novel on the grass.

My mother had met Chris one time when he dropped me off. They'd talked about books and he'd left with a novel she'd just finished. At the time I had been proud to show him off. But now it was awful that she'd met him, that she could picture us in bed.

I'D THOUGHT MY MOTHER would go to Safeway for a home pregnancy test, but she said the only way to find out for sure was at the gynecologist.

The doctor's office was pink and womanly. I took a clipboard to a chair and filled in a form with a ballpoint pen that wrote dark and retracted with a satisfying click. Behind the receptionist was a framed print of a flower with enormous white petals.

I sat next to my mother until they called my name. In a bath-room, I gave a urine sample. It was embarrassing to hand it to the nurse, the cup still warm.

I waited in the cotton gown on the end of the crisp paper. When the doctor came in, she told me right away: I wasn't pregnant. She would give me a prescription for birth-control pills. She acted bossy, like a cop, and resigned, like she saw my kind of girl all the time. I opened my gown and she palpated my breast for tumors, her fingers grazing a hickey. I felt defiant. I looked right into the doctor's heavy-lidded eyes: *There is somebody who wants me this much.*

They gave you three packets of pills to start. My mother put them in her purse. In the car we were silent. Then I said, "I was worried I wasn't going to be able to go on my outdoor orientation trip."

"That's what you were worried about?" my mother said.

"I'm just trying to be honest," I said.

"Oh, my God, Susan," my mother said.

"I'm not saying it was the whole thing," I said. "It was just this weird small thing that kept coming into my head."

Maybe my mother thought I was trying to provoke her by being vapid. But I was unreadier for any of this than she knew.

AT HOME I PULLED a Jogbra over my breasts. The doctor had given me the birth-control pills because I was sexually active. *Sexually active.* I thought I knew what she pictured by this. Two loose, confident peo-ple, easy in bed, flush with pleasure.

But it wasn't like that. It was like this instead:

Him entering me before the condom was on, the tip of his penis frighteningly wet. Him entering me with the condom, but when I was dry. The regular administration of hickeys. Him going down on me, feeling nothing but licks. And then the taste of myself in his mouth, and the shame that I was interested in him returning to kiss me like this. His enormous penis with a little line from where it was healing: "From your rings the first night," he'd said, and I'd burned with embarrassment. On the night I lost my virginity to him, he'd turned me over and entered me from behind. For an instant I was confused, my face in the pillow. Then I'd thought, *Doggie style.* I'd felt humiliated, and then numb, and then I hadn't liked him at all. He was imagining another girl and didn't want to see my face. Or maybe this was just the way he liked it best. But shouldn't he not be doing this my very first time?

I'D ALWAYS IMAGINED SEX as a way to get as close to someone as you possibly could. But I felt closest to Chris at times that had nothing to do with sex. The fact that I ignored this contradiction is among the reasons I shouldn't have been sleeping with him. I wanted to be ready, but I wasn't. There was little pleasure in it for me, and I didn't know enough to know that this was a problem. But I can't say I'd tell my younger self not to do it; she was going to do it anyway, and there were things in the relationship that were good. There were so many books he wanted me to read and movies he wanted me to see. *Love in the Time of Cholera.* Errol Morris's *The Thin Blue Line.* The Anthony Minghella film with the title he loved, *Truly, Madly, Deeply.* I loved that he loved that title. He expanded the range of what I knew, in both mind and body: He made me aware that I was desirable, that I could be the thing I'd doubted, sexy. He baldly stared as I rounded the corner of the bed, naked: "Oh, God, you're so beautiful." I felt at home in my body then, and in those days that was a rare sensation. Chris was thin, and I was often aware of my flesh in contrast to his boniness. But when he touched me during sex, I didn't feel "fat." Maybe seeing how much he liked my body made me content with it, too—if only temporarily.

One afternoon he called in the midst of a binge, surprising me. I took a shower before going to meet him. Sometimes a shower made me feel better. Surfaces smoothed, buffed. A shower was a do-over, a begin-again.

I sat next to him on the couch.

"You seem sad," he said.

"I am," I said.

"What's wrong?" he said, his hand on my hair.

"I have a problem," I said, "but I can't tell you what it is."

But it didn't work the same way as with Julie. My answer just confused him.

He stroked my hair, trying to make me feel better. Then he lifted my shirt and kissed the mound of my stomach. In me then, terror. I knew my stomach smelled like almond soap—a decoy; but I also thought it must feel hot—a tip. The furnace of my body trying to manage everything with which I'd stoked it. I was so still when he kissed me. It would have read as disengagement. But it was desperation not to be discovered.

I never once imagined telling him. I never for a single instant considered it.

18

LEAVING

A FEW DAYS AFTER CHRIS left to go back to Austin, I went out to dinner with my mother. I wore a scoop-neck top and a khaki skirt. "You should get that skirt in other colors," my mother said. "You look great in it." I was pleased that she said that. I thought I looked good in it, too. For so long I had resisted buying new clothes, admitting to my larger size. But everyone looked better in things that fit.

We were going to a Himalayan restaurant. Our mountain town excelled in the cuisines of high-altitude nations. It was the summer, so it would have been light no matter when we left. But my mother wanted to go early, at six. We drove downtown in what felt like afternoon.

The restaurant was in a basement. It had plush carpet and photographs of Nepal.

"Was it hard to say goodbye to Chris?" my mother asked when we were seated.

"No," I said, dismissive.

My mother looked down and smoothed her napkin in her lap. I pictured her at the dinner table in the Adirondacks with Grack. If she just said the right thing, he wouldn't explode. Later she would repeat this pattern with my father. And now here I was, seemingly having moved into the role of the brusque, angry belittler.

I softened. "I mean, yeah, it was hard," I said.

The waitress came, and my mother ordered off the wine list, naming a varietal like she cared.

"Just water," I said.

The waitress left.

"So, Anna Wood is doing Directed Studies," I said. "Should I have done that?"

Anna was the other girl from my high school who was going to Yale. Directed Studies was the name of a special program you had to apply for, a prescribed course of Western Civ. Until Anna, I hadn't even considered Directed Studies. The whole point of college was that you were supposed to choose.

"The whole point of a place like Yale is that you can choose, follow your passions," my mother said.

I loved my mother the most—loved *both* her and my father the most. It was because of them that in all the essential, best ways, I had come out like I did.

"Okay, yeah, that's exactly what I was thinking," I said.

"I mean, I told you," said my mother. "After I looked at your course book, I had a dream that I was going back to college, that I was going to Yale."

I'd looked at the course book, too. But I was more interested in what life was going to be like at Yale than in the classes I would take there. What absorbed me was the special issue of the *Yale Daily News* that had been sent to all incoming freshmen. I read it over and over in the backyard. The issue was like a guidebook to the school, but it contained more information than anyone could possibly need. I liked how the people who worked on the newspaper took such pleasure in describing their world. I thought they were probably the ones who had once sat in their backyards reading this paper, too.

My mother ordered a second glass of wine, and then a third. She started slurring. It scared me that she was getting like this for no obvious reason. I was being nice now; there wasn't anything stressful here. Why was she was letting it happen?

The waitress came with the check and an offer of ginger tea. I couldn't decide if she had colluded with my mother or if she was on my side, an observer who was also embarrassed to see.

When my mother stood, she was unsteady. I realized then that maybe she had started even before we came.

When we got outside it was still so light. My mother had tried to drink herself under and then she had to come back up and out into this. I felt bad for her, still so many hours to get through. I knew what it was to mess up too early, before you could get under sheets and hide from it.

"Why don't I drive?" I said.

"Okay," she said.

She didn't make an excuse or try to pretend. She handed me the keys and I watched her walk around to the other side of the car.

She hadn't cared enough, or had power enough, to keep it together; she'd made herself weak, incapable; and she'd known she could do it, because I was there to drive. It seemed to mark a new chapter in her drinking. She was no longer hiding from me.

I was sure I would never show her what I did. What I did had to happen in private. It was a total loss of dignity, wild and greedy and fast. If I were observed I would never do it. Was that a way forward? Constant surveillance. Was that a trade I would make? Never eat bad but never be alone again. No, the price of scrutiny was too high.

I drove east, the sun in the rearview. I wondered if her drinking would stop me from eating. Right now I was too upset to eat—but I knew that later I would want to. As rattled as I was right now, this feeling would fade, and hours from now, my need would be as great as hers. I'd be upstairs in my room, seething and edgy, waiting for her to go to bed so that I could take her place in the kitchen.

ON MY LAST NIGHT in Boulder I met Julie Gray on the Hill at Espresso Roma. I was wearing pink pleated shorts I wasn't bringing to college. All the clothes I liked were packed.

The tables were taken, so we sat on the curb. I felt such complete ownership of Boulder then. We belonged here. Knees bent, cars passing; no one would ask us to move. It was like lounging on carpet, I felt so comfortable. We were out in the night with coffee on our land.

"It was hard for me, Sus," Julie said.

We were finally having it, the Chris conversation.

"I'm sorry," I said, not entirely meaning it—maybe because I wasn't sure if it was fair of her to be hurt; maybe because I'd needed him, and I was unwilling to apologize for that.

In the future he was so foreign to me that even looking at his Facebook pictures was startling. What would I do if I encountered him again? With Julie it was different. When I saw her for the first time in almost twenty years, at a high school reunion, I was awash in old feeling. One evening that weekend, we met alone for a glass of wine. We talked about our husbands, our children, our work—in college she'd returned to the violin, and she was now a music teacher—but only touched on Chris. While he mattered enough that we both hesitated to invoke him, he seemed less important at that point—a coda to the main body of our friendship.

I still couldn't tell Julie about what had really been going on for me senior year. "Shame," an old word. "Shamefaced," a bastardization of "shamefast," which describes the way one is held tight by shame. I remained in its grip at thirty-seven.

Now, almost ten years later, I imagine telling Julie about the way I ate and the closeness that this confession might still bring.

That weekend I wound up in the ER with heat exhaustion, and Julie looked out for me.

THE DAY OF MY flight to New Haven, my mother and I left early for the airport. In the morning light, she was vibrant, capable. The one who was ready for the day before anyone else. She'd had her grapefruit and fresh-squeezed juice and sunflower whole wheat toast. Her hair was blow-dried.

At Stapleton we parked on the top floor of the short-term garage. Wind blew and my hair stuck in my lip gloss. From the trunk I removed the large frame pack I would bring on my outdoor orientation trip. When I got to the ticket counter, they put my pack in an enormous clear plastic bag. The pack was heavy, and I was worried that on the trip it would hurt my neck.

This was the kind of thing on my mind, not *I'm going away to college.*

When we got to the gate, Anna Wood was there with her parents. And that was when it occurred to me. This was the moment your story built to as a teenager: the moment you left. This was the end of both the narrative and the developmental sequence. This was when you looked out the window of the station wagon as the scoring music rose. This was the final surge of feeling.

But I was only aware of this because I was watching Anna: Anna standing as the first boarding group was announced, Anna removing her glasses, Anna's mother and father together giving her a hug. This day for me had been just something on the calendar, a scheduled event. But it was supposed to be significant. Suddenly I wanted to do this better. I wanted it to matter. But it was too late to do it like Anna, in part because I could no longer stand in the center of my parents' embrace. My parents' divorce—not college—was my dividing line.

"Call me when you get to New Haven," my mother said. New Haven! Those words I'd heard since childhood. The place where my mother had grown up, where she and my father had met. *New*

Haven. To see the name of this city on the page even now shakes me with feeling. But that morning I was numb to its power. I didn't feel like I was embarking on anything. I felt my body; I felt tired. I felt like I might never feel anything but these feelings, my heft and self-loathing and regret about eating. I could not even contemplate what I felt about leaving home. The only exit I cared about was from the eating. Until I left that, nothing else would matter. I looked at my mother and nodded. Then I boarded the plane.

PART 3

19

KASHA

AS SOON AS I went East, being from the West—my particular West—became a central part of my identity.

Breakfast was served in Commons, a massive college-gothic dining hall. "The granola is stale," I noted one morning, a comment two girls from Princeton High found hilarious. *The granola is stale. The granola is stale! You are so totally from Boulder.*

I was so totally from Boulder, it was true. I knew about soy milk, and silver jewelry, and nuclear-weapons protests. People liked that I was from Boulder, and I started to play this up. I wore thick gray socks and Birkenstocks and a double strand of turquoise. One day I added lipstick, and a boy cocked his head curiously and said, "That's not you." So after that, it wasn't. I was bouncy when I ran into you on Old Campus and half-lidded when I was baked—which was a lot. In high school I'd smoked pot casually, whenever someone had it around. Now I smoked it all the time, because it matched who I was: crunchy but also a little knowing; over alcohol already, onto the next substance. We'd smoke a bowl on a beanbag in someone's room and eventually make our way out for food. My friend Sheva and I would stand before the freezer case at Wawa, and Ben and Jerry would come out and talk to us. We'd go to Yorkside Pizza and watch the mural move as we ate thick, greasy slices. We'd dig our hands into white paper bags of peanut M&M's from the campus candy shop. But no matter how high I was, I was always faking the munchies. Eating was so charged for me that bringing food into any high killed it. Plus, my appetite was so altered by what I'd been doing now for years that pot had no appreciable effect on it. And what I ate with Sheva, or anyone else, was not close to what I needed. This had something to do with the amount and something to do with privacy. I needed more and I needed to do it alone, and right away, I did.

AT YALE IT WAS so much worse than ever. It shook me. I'd hoped so hard that my eating was just habit. That it was connected to my kitchen in Boulder. To *my mother's* kitchen. It turned out, setting meant nothing. Setting meant shit. It didn't even matter that I didn't have a kitchen! Sometimes I found it interesting, how my primitive brain had solved this problem without my even knowing it was doing it.

Almost immediately I not only found food but developed a whole circuit of places I would hit. Wall Food, for plastic-wrapped muffins that were shiny on top when I unwrapped them, as if the plastic still adhered to them. The bagel place, where I always ordered a side of cream cheese, which I didn't even like. David's Cookies, for muffins. Naples Pizza, for muffins. I would get the Naples muffins when everyone else was in the back room waiting for the jukebox to play "New York, New York," the song that closed down the night. I'd creep up to the counter, and the woman with bleached hair in a tight ponytail would say, "What would you like, honey?" and I would ask for two muffins. I'd tell her they were "for breakfast," unless I was getting three or four muffins, in which case I'd switch the story slightly, explaining, "We're leaving early on the bus." Though she never asked where I was going, I was ready to say that I was a member of the environmental coalition and we were traveling to a protest. Claire's, which had vegetarian food and reminded me of Boulder, was different: a place I went to fix everything.

Other places I'd go to begin again: the L&B Room in the library, which had wood paneling and leather chairs in little nooks with arched windows that looked out onto a tranquil courtyard. There I was never eating, just writing, making resolutions. Also, I'd go to the summit of East Rock. I'd run there from campus. People acted like this was a big-deal run, but I still had my high-altitude heart: I was in better shape than anyone. I'd stand atop this ridge that was the closest thing New Haven had to a mountain, and I'd stare out into the water and for an instant be conscious of myself as an American in a country, an American in history. This sounds grandiose but it was actually humbling, a way of being devoid of identity, of being free of my horrible, puny specifics; up here on this outcropping I had—*Thank God, for an instant*—transcended them.

I'd try to hold on to this feeling. I'd run back to campus and shower and dash back out because, after all, it was fall of freshman year, and even to a wrecked girl like me, there was levity. A men's a cappella group stood before more than a thousand of us, singing, *Bright college years, with pleasure rife, the shortest gladdest years of life!* There were moments in which I lived inside their harmonies. A group of us brought our sleeping bags out to Old Campus and spent the night on the lawn. I got a part in a play with the Yale Dramat and a B+ on the first paper I wrote, about *The Odyssey*. The professor commented: *A bit florid—that is to say, overwritten, but clear and elegant.* "Clear and elegant" pleased me so much. The class I liked the best was the History of the American West.

The fear I'd expressed on my orientation trip—*I am scared that I will not have good friends*—had not come to pass. In October, on my eighteenth birthday, I was thrown a surprise party. When I arrived in the room, everyone I knew was gathered around a giant box, and when I opened the flaps, there was a single fat joint at its bottom.

The party was thrown by Sheva, who had become my best friend.

She was raven-haired, stunning; short, curvy, sexy, confident, brilliant. On Halloween we decided to be the sun and the moon; even in costume I was in her orbit. Sheva submitted some cartoons to *The Yale Herald* and they gave her a comic strip. The strip she drew documented the freshman experience of our group. She gave us all other names, but it was clear who was who. William was Russell; Russell's roommate was a lacrosse player named Rick (Rick's lax-playing friends were Matt, Matt, Matt, and Chris); and I was Kasha. Kasha wore Birkenstocks and skirts, made sunnily wise observations, and was often holding a pint of Ben & Jerry's.

When Sheva drew Kasha, she thought she was drawing her new friend Susan, but she was really drawing the person I was pretending to be. My eating disorder was now dictating my self-invention. Kasha was a character who could literally carry my weight. I couldn't be the slender perfectionist I once was, because I was physically not her. I was sturdy and round-faced and there was fat above my knees. I saw no way I could be my old self in that body. But I could be Kasha, this girl I invented to exist as a girl I did not want to be. Kasha could get the munchies. Kasha could shuffle across campus after midnight, in Birkenstocks and a limp knee-length skirt, dreamily spooning ice cream into her mouth like she was stoned under the moon, eating sweets. "Hi, Susan!" someone could say. "Hiiiiii," I could say in a zoned-out way, and someone could make a joke back, and I could tilt my head and look at the joker curiously, kind of cherubic and dazed, exuding a vibe like I was *so* baked, like I was *hella* mellow. But this slowness on the outside was a disguise for something frantic within, for not even being able to wait until I got back to my room, partly because I needed the ice cream, needed it now, and partly because my nerd-homebody roommates would probably be up when I got there. As Kasha I could bobble in and ignore them. As Kasha I could beach myself on my bunk without brushing my teeth under the guise of passing out, a socially acceptable/easily graspable form of excess. I could pretend to be passed out but lie there hating myself and wake in the morning with my gums hurting back by my wisdom teeth and sit up and swear to do everything right, today is the day, never again.

It was like ninth grade all over again, reinventing myself in a place where nobody knew my history, hiding what I didn't want anyone to see. But this time my true self showed in my body, so Kasha wasn't masking who I really was as much as making sense of it.

20

7M

THE FIRST TIME I looked up the eating-disorder books at the terminal in the library, they were all checked out. Because they were all due on the same day, I assumed they were all checked out to the same person. I wondered who she might be. In Commons, the bathrooms off the rotunda were locked at lunchtime. "It's to stop girls from throwing up," everyone said, in the way this comment was always made: those pathetic, gross, superficial girls. But I felt for the girls who couldn't do what they needed to. I felt their fear and desperation, and their anger at the attempt to control them. I didn't think locking these bathrooms would do anything to help. The girls would just stop coming to Commons or would hurry across the plaza to Beinecke. Once, leaving Commons, I tried a bathroom door to see for myself if it was locked. It was. I turned and saw a guard watching me. Was that a smirk? It bothered me then, on behalf of the girls I identified with, and—if it actually was the reason—it bothers me now, the idea you could just lock a door on someone's suffering, increasing her shame.

The day after the eating-disorder books were due back at the library, I took the elevator to the seventh floor of the stacks and then walked up a half flight of metal stairs to 7M. I don't remember whether the books were shelved in this stuffy rear corner or if I brought them with me. What I do remember is that the next day I came back, and then back again.

On 7M I always sat in the same cubicle, one beside an arched window with views all the way to West Rock, an orange-brown ridge jutting up from the mild landscape. (East Rock and West Rock were bookends.) This cubicle became a hideout for me freshman year, and also a sanctuary. High up in this tower I was going to fix this. Fix this, up in the eaves of the library that looked like a church.

I started with the stories. I started with the two eating-disorder memoirs that surfaced in the university's collection. One was a memoir of anorexia by a woman who'd gone to Yale, and the other was a memoir of bulimia by a woman who'd gone to Harvard. Though the anorexic girl had lived in my own dormitory, Silliman, the bulimic at Harvard was the one I related to more. The Yale girl was an ascetic art major. The Harvard girl, Caroline, was an athlete. She jogged along the Charles in icy air, then visited her food places in a ritualistic circuit. She even asked the clerk at Baskin-Robbins for extra spoons. I recognized myself in Caroline.

Were I a freshman now, there would be many more of these memoirs to read, but in 1991, these were among the few that existed. While anorexia and bulimia memoirs can serve a sinister, dual purpose as instruction manuals, inadvertently offering girls tips on how to diet or to purge, it did not occur to me to use the books I read like this. I also wasn't reading to find out how to get better. I was reading for identification. I liked the opening pages of Caroline's memoir best. I wasn't interested in the end, the part where she came out okay. I wanted to stay in the part where she was wrecked. I wanted to feel less alone, because isolation had become the primary consequence of what I did, separating myself from the regular people who lived in the regular way.

———

BECAUSE I WAS OFTEN either fleeing campus in order to fix my eating or going someplace no one would see me in order to binge, I learned New Haven and its surroundings in a way most freshmen didn't. Yale was one of those campuses people never left, a stone island in a struggling city. Only months earlier, a student named Christian Prince had been murdered a block from my dormitory. But I was straying outside the school's gates, furiously shoving food in my face on dark blocks at the seedy edge of downtown. Sometimes I felt eyes on me a second too long. But I felt I gave off a force field, *don't mess with me,* and that I was so odd—hostile, round, neutered—that nobody would have wanted to anyway. I was not engaging with the city in a manner that was meaningful or helpful. I was not a tutor or a volunteer. But roaming the city, even in this limited way, informed my sense of New Haven and Yale's uncomfortable, privileged position in it. On these streets I was a selfish, damaged, needful person— meaning I was just like anyone. I joined, however briefly and superficially, the world we walled ourselves off from, or did good for, or opined on in the *Yale Daily News.*

Other times I'd proceed with more resolve. I'd bike up Whalley Avenue to an organic grocery store called Edge of the Woods, then ride back to campus with familiar brands in my backpack, like a foreign student who'd procured the foods of the old country.

While I joined other freshmen for lunch at Commons, in the evenings I rarely ate in my dormitory dining hall. The gray-haired Catholic-school-office type who manned the desk looked at me hard when I did show up, as if she was trying to figure out why I didn't come more often. Sometimes I was too full to eat there; other times I just wanted real food, not crap spongy bread or baked ziti.

One evening, eating good hard bread and thick lentil soup at Claire's, I ran into a squash player I knew. "I have to eat at weird times because when I finish practice, the dining hall is closed," she said.

"I just don't like the dining hall food," I said.

"You're vegetarian, right?" she said, as if that explained it.

"Yeah," I said, as if it did.

The squash player and I ate our soup and I felt a momentary identification with her. My life, too, was organized around something other than academics. She and I existed outside the world of the standard-experience Yale kids, the ones who dutifully stuck to the schedules, treading the paths from dorm to dining hall to library. But as soon as she stood, zipped her blue team jacket, and left, I felt the chasm between me and who she was, which was also who I used to be. Someone whose body pushed through hard sets, someone who knew what it was like to be sore and spent.

I was not a good enough swimmer or runner to compete at the college level. But I wished I were. I often imagined myself into the bodies of athletes. A swimmer in one of my evening lecture sections would arrive with wet hair. I craved the sensation of being her, of the looseness that follows hours in the water. The surfer boy from Newport Beach, his shirt off on the day of intramural cross-country: I didn't want him; I wanted to *be* him. I wanted to arrow through a hot afternoon.

Far more than I wanted people's bodies next to mine, I wanted them to be mine. Not in a covetous cosmetic way, like, *Oh, I wish I had that supermodel's flat stomach*. I didn't want *parts* of bodies. I looked at other people's bodies and I wanted to inhabit them. I wanted to feel what they did. I wanted to feel the way I once had.

There was a field hockey player from Brookline named Berly Thorne. She was neat and small and beautiful and cold; I was messy and exuberant. No one would ever have thought to categorize us together, but she reminded me of the old me. One day at David's Cookies, ahead of me in line, Berly bought a muffin and left with it in a paper bag. I imagined her walking on the path to the gym, maybe absentmindedly crumbling a couple of bites into her mouth. I knew these muffins, they were dry on the outside, almost crunchy. Mine I was about to devour, my energy would spike and then flatten. While Berly was out on a field in air, I would be dead and crazy, either falling asleep in a dark-green leather chair in the library or writing in my journal, swearing to fix this, swear, swear.

When I heard that Berly Thorne had once been hospitalized for an eating disorder, it only made my identification with her more intense.

BACK UP ON 7M, I turned again to *My Name Is Caroline*.

> I wasn't going to the library; I was going to binge and I had to be alone. The fact that I was bulimic, and had been for more than six years, was my deepest, darkest secret. To the outside world I had it all: good looks, good family, good grades, and athletic ability. But I also had a side that no one knew about. Almost daily I ate vast quantities of food and got rid of it through vomiting, laxatives, diuretics, syrup of ipecac, or compulsive exercising. And as much as I wanted to stop, I couldn't.

In my thirties I read a cultural history of anorexia. It was a serious book by an eminent historian. In the first chapter, she mentioned bulimia and bulimia memoirs, and of them she wrote, "These are among the most disturbing and unhappy documents generated by women in our time." This comment roused something in me. The historian seemed to be falling into a trap she would describe throughout the book: valorizing anorexia simply by deeming it worthy of her study yet distancing herself from bulimia. In that word, "disturbing," I detected the same distaste that characterized my peers' mocking comments about the doors in Commons.

What disturbed the historian? The graphic descriptions of purging or the orgiastic recollections of the binge? Or was it just disturbing to think that a woman's life could be reduced to this? If that was it, my feeling toward the historian softened. It *was* disturbing that a person's life could be reduced to this. I knew from experience.

Of course, I didn't have bulimia. In those years I didn't know what I had. You could have either anorexia or bulimia. Those were the choices. *Well*—hand on my pillowy gut—*at least we can rule out anorexia!* But for bulimia you had to purge. It said this in every text. Usually purging meant vomiting or laxatives, but for some people it was "excessive exercise." I questioned the inclusion of exercise. Often the amounts described did not seem to me to be excessive. I thought the people who put this on the list must have been out of shape or from another time. The Pre-Aerobics Era. (I didn't believe my exercise was excessive; I also didn't see it as compensatory or purgative. Of course it was all these things—but it wasn't only these things. While I thought about burning calories, exercise wasn't primarily a math problem for me. It wasn't subtraction; it was recalibration. It was an attempt to restore a steady state, both physically and emotionally.)

Back then it seemed to me that exercise was fundamentally different from vomiting or laxatives. Exercise was ex post facto. It addressed something finished rather than something still in progress. The other ways were like stomach pumping. The equivalent of rushing yourself to the ER or following instructions from poison control. Like trying to get something out before it could spread through your system. These ways messed with nature and they were dangerous. I had read about the dangers, which were well documented. The experts were so focused on the horrors of purging that they barely acknowledged the horrors of consumption. They seemed more interested in the behavior secondary to the act than in the act itself.

They don't know what they are talking about. Weirdly, not having a name for what I did gave me a kind of power. I believed I knew things the books didn't. I never worried that I didn't have a "real" problem. It was clear to me that I did. In fact, I was often scared that what was wrong with me was freakish. I wondered what it meant that I kept everything in. I didn't purge, there was no outlet, and this was a psychological profile the books I read didn't describe: What kind of mental case never got the food out of her, never released? Someone who was timid, limited. Someone uptight, or scared, or childlike; someone who hid from what she did under covers instead of facing up to it over a toilet.

WHEN I GOOGLED BERLY Thorne years later, I found that she was a nutritionist. It only made my identification with her spike again.

Twenty-five years after *My Name Is Caroline* was published, Caroline Adams Miller wrote a book about her recovery, called *Positively Caroline: How I Beat Bulimia for Good and Found Real Happiness*. Aimee Liu, the author of the anorexia memoir I read on 7M, relapsed in middle age and addressed this experience in *Gaining: The Truth About Life After Eating Disorders*. For both women, adolescent eating disorders became the work of their adult lives.

One part of me sees such trajectories as healthy. These women seem to have confronted their illnesses and then transformed them in outward-reaching ways that might reshape the lives of others, too. But another part argues back that these acts suggest that some of us don't ever get rid of the obsession, that we just redirect it.

I used to have a fantasy that I could restore my original OS. Go back to the brain I had before the disordered eating started, even as I know that in my original factory settings are embedded all the pathways that fostered it. But still! Isn't there some earlier brain, the one I had before I laid down the circuitry all wrong at the critical adolescent moment? The moment that scientists are always telling us about. *Don't let your teenager start vaping; don't let the dentist prescribe opioids after extraction. The developing brain is acutely sensitive, and the patterns established in adolescence will be difficult to change.*

Eating disorders can rewire your brain. I bookmark articles about reward systems and "altered activity" in "corticostriatal processes," and I take note of people who seem not to have performed a master reset. But I am also attuned to stories of those who have. And this is a significant difference between who I am now and who I was back then. Now I am also drawn to the second half of the book, the part where the narrator gets over it. Now I am hungry for the end.

21
BODY IMAGE

ON THE DAY OF the flight home for Christmas break, I waited for a taxi outside Silliman. It was early morning, barely light. I was waiting with a girl named Rachel. While we waited, we mixed Malibu with orange juice in red plastic cups. The taxi wasn't coming and we were maybe going to miss our flight. But it was gray dawn, and we had these drinks that smelled like sunscreen. We sat on our suitcases. We *lounged* on them. It didn't matter if the plane left without us. We were party girls with fun-times plans. When the cab finally came, it, too, was scented like the beach, a paper tree hanging from the rearview. Rachel and I slid into each other on the seatbelt-less vinyl back seat on the way to the airport. On the flight to Chicago, still buzzing hard, I slipped my credit card into the slot of the seatback phone and called my home number, waking up my sister in Mountain time. The buzz wore down as we descended. I had a flat, exhausted feeling in O'Hare, airport of my youth, transfer point between my divorced parents. Rachel went to another gate and I was alone on the flight to Denver. All the alcohol was gone from me now. I was over Kansas, so far from stone and cold and

06520. My face was to the window as the brown land appeared, shockingly leached and open after the cramped, gray, waterwayed Northeast. I was not who I'd wanted to be on this flight—thin, generous, intelligent. I was broad and round and stunted; there would be no way to hide my failings from the friends who would be waiting for me at the gate. I would pretend to still be drunk, pretend to still be altered, as if this whole state, my whole me, was just an effect, just inebriation. The plane landed, and I stumbled down the Jetway, bobbing and dazed and *dude!* when I greeted my friends. And it was hard to relish the affirmation I craved, the whole group of them come to get me. I was so conscious of how I appeared and of what they would say about me after Lisa Tanner dropped me off. I was the one who was supposed to get better in college, the smart girl who would thrive there. I was supposed to come back different, but not in this direction, not in this way.

"IS THAT WHAT YOU look like now?" Betsy had said over the phone just after Thanksgiving. She'd seen a photograph of me that Marcie took on a visit to campus. That day we'd been ferried in a limousine to the Forestry School, where a conservation program was being dedicated in Robert's father's name. I hadn't had the right thing to wear; good clothes no longer fit. It was possible Betsy was commenting primarily on my lank hair, on my not-trying outfit. But she would have also meant my moon face and the space I occupied in the snapshot. Betsy wasn't trying to be mean when she said it. She was confused, like, "That doesn't look like you at all."

When I was a little girl, the movie scene that scared me the most was the one in which a father in a business suit transforms into a sheepdog. I would walk away from the TV when they showed this film, *The Shaggy D.A.* It was scarier to me than things like zombies, or *Jaws,* or Jason. I felt now as if I, too, had been transmuted. But, unlike in the movie, there was no spell to recite to return me to my true form.

In Boulder over winter break, I went up to Fairview and waited for Mr. Rothberg outside his office. He walked right past me when he came out. "Mr. Rothberg," I said. "It's Susan Burton." Maybe he just literally didn't see me—I was against the wall, not immediately visible—but it was hard for me not to interpret the oversight symbolically: I'd longed to be known by him and I no longer was. The reintroduction was crushing. Christmas morning, I opened a package of underwear in a new size, humiliated that my mother had made this selection. A few nights later I made out with a boy I'd dated when I weighed less. As he slid his hands over my hips, I wondered if this was kinky, making out with the same girl in a different body; I wondered if he'd be asked about it by his friends.

If you had tried to engage me in a conversation about body image, I would have looked at you like you were an idiot. "Body image," a meaningless term from a women's magazine. "Body image," a term that made me scream. Body image, body image, what about body facts! Why was everyone trying to tell you this was all in your head? Why did everyone want you to believe you were some occluded, insecure girl who couldn't see what was really in the mirror? Maybe at an earlier point I had thought that I was fat when I wasn't; okay, I could acknowledge that. But this body I had now, this body was objectively different.

By this point I'd gained nearly fifty percent of my body weight; soon, I'd surpass that. I did not feel like me, with that half on me, and I believed I would not feel like myself until that half was off me again.

Looking back now, I recognize the aptness of the term I wanted to reject. My body image was distorted. I was overweight but I was not obese. I was still a woman who could go into a store and find something that fit. My body was larger than it had ever been, but it was also unremarkable, unless you'd known me earlier. But to freshman me that was precisely the issue! All these people in Boulder *had* known me earlier. *I'd* known me earlier, and I was altered now. I didn't understand how people could say you weren't your body, that there was a person "inside." I was my body, lumbering through the world or graceful in it. My body didn't house me; it was me.

SECOND SEMESTER I DECIDED to take an easy schedule of just four classes. Ostensibly this was so that I could devote time to fixing my eating, but my eating was also interfering with my schoolwork. On my geology exam, I'd responded to questions with answers like, *The igneous rocks are not friends with the metamorphic rocks.* I received a D in the class.

I tried out for the Sam Shepard play *True West* and got called back. But on the day of the callback, I couldn't go. I was bursting and stuck. I would not be able to escape myself at the audition. I would be clenched and self-conscious. I could not go to an audition, or anywhere, until the food in me dissolved. The girl who was the director called to see where I was, and I stood over the answering machine. Her voice came out of the little white plastic grid. I listened to her, live, as she was talking, but I didn't pick up, and I didn't call her back, and I never did another play again. I switched permanently to writing. Writing was all mind, no body.

It saddens me now that I abandoned acting so abruptly. But it's true that I lacked an essential skill: *You have trouble physicalizing.* Okay, Rita, you win. Yet it wasn't entirely accurate that I couldn't convey feeling through my body. That's literally what an eating disorder is, the physical manifestation of emotion. I'd always considered myself too inhibited to express myself through my body, and I wonder now whether eating was unconsciously a means of doing so. Certainly later, *not* eating would be: My gaunt body showed my superiority, my self-mastery. The bingeing showed . . . Well, I suppose it showed all I was keeping hidden. My round body showed my desires and the control over them that I lacked.

The thing I could control was writing. I could express emotion with that.

I was doing a lot of writing. For classes, but also for myself. For the first time I was going over the stories of my youth, examining things my father did in Michigan. I was unsettled by what was surfacing. This year I was angry at my father. I was cautious around boys, and I wondered if his volatility was what had made me so fearful and fake. I was angry at my mother, too, though that anger had less charge, because I had already been angry at her. I wrote my parents a joint letter I saved as MOM AND DAD YOU SUCK but never sent. But the anger was also a form of longing: I would run down Whitney Avenue and turn up a side street and stand in front of the white house in which they had met.

Soon I needed to get farther away, and I started taking the train to New York. I was always stuffing something into my mouth on the way to the station; always hot and winter-jacketed and heavy-legged as I navigated crowded, green-ceilinged Grand Central but better once I was on the cold, vaguely menacing streets. I'd walk through Washington Square Park (men murmuring *weed, weed*) and up to a bookstore on Astor Place. My favorite café was in the West Village. I'd sit there in a scrolled-iron chair with my notebook and a pack of cigarettes, and during those hours I was making resolutions to change but also actually thinking about things beyond that. During those hours I was not a girl defined by a problem. I was a freshman who had taken the train to New York City with a Joan Didion paperback and a spiral notebook and a pen.

On the return trip I'd share the train with commuters, khaki-raincoated men out of Cheever stories who came back from the bar car with beer. By the time we reached New Haven, the car would be shuddering and empty. I'd walk in the dark back to Silliman, and even though I was doing it of my own volition, it was like I was being remanded by the authorities. I'd see the big gate and I'd want to make a break for it.

ONE AFTERNOON I WALKED back to Silliman in a good mood. The day had gone well from the start. People in my writing class had liked my essay. After class I'd met Sheva for coffee, and then we'd walked together to a lecture hall and conquered a midterm. And, most important, there had been no stuffing-face episodes—none.

The dorms at Yale were called colleges. Silliman College was arranged around a grassy courtyard, and I lived in the back corner: 1846J, one common room, two bedrooms, four girls. When I opened the door, one of my roommates, Sarah, was there.

"Hi, Susan!" she said, and then she was introducing me to someone, because it wasn't only Sarah in the room; it was a television producer shouldering a large camera and a correspondent holding a notepad.

I had known these people were coming, I had known this was happening today! Why had I come back to the room? It was only because I'd been actually having the good day of a normal person that I'd forgotten about this.

Sarah was being featured in a major news network segment on body image. She had volunteered for the segment at the Women's Center, where she'd gone to attend a meeting of the eating-concerns support group, a group I had been trying to gather the courage to join until I found out that Sarah was a member.

"Hi," I said to everyone. I stood stiffly before the fireplace, which didn't work and in which we kept our newspapers for recycling. Above the mantel hung the obligatory blue-and-white felt banner, FOR GOD FOR COUNTRY AND FOR YALE. I hoped to look as if I were merely annoyed by the disruption of my afternoon, as if there were no conceivable reason a story about "body image," which obviously meant "eating disorders," would raise ten million heart-pounding "issues" for me. "I'm just coming in to change," I told the group. "I'm going running. I'll be out of your way."

"No, that's okay, you can stay," said Sarah.

"Maybe you'd like to join the conversation?" said the reporter.

"Jenny and Mallory are coming," said Sarah, "and Tia and—"

"No, that's okay," I said, cutting her off, and I turned and walked down the hallway to my bedroom and closed the door; and then I just felt such terror, such heated panic, that I put a CD into my compact stereo and turned the music up to a volume that would have been right for industrial, or death metal, but not for the bluegrass sound of the Samples. *So beautiful to be here and a-live!* the band roared now. I knew I was making it impossible for the visitors to film Sarah or even talk to her.

Before the first track even finished, Sarah knocked. "It's okay to have music, but could you turn it down lower so that we can talk?"

I pressed the button and watched the CD spin crazily for a moment before coming to a stop.

"Thank you," Sarah said from the other side of the door.

Who was I, who the fuck was I, that I was in this room, being so rude? Who was I, acting like a girl with a mental problem? *Well, that's exactly who I am, a girl with a mental problem*—a thought that pleased me so much that I not only smiled but also snorted (just like a girl with a mental problem!). Reveling in my derangement made me feel better for a moment, made me feel superior to my roommates, all of whom I was certain lacked experience in such hells as mine, all of whom were clearly living plain, good, orderly lives, just like the kind that I once had.

But any power I felt was fleeting. In the other room, people were coming in. I recognized voices. I put a decisive hand on the back of the walnut desk chair, as if about to act, but really it was a posture of paralysis.

Sarah did have a problem, I knew, because she had reached out to me late one night in the common room. What were her words? I had not been receptive to her confession, because sitting across from her on the couch, I was afraid. Why was she bringing this to me, of all possible girls; why did she think that I would understand? Nobody could know what I did, nobody! Except another girl who did it, too.

But Sarah had turned her problem into a triumph: She was going on national TV. Of course she would be overachieving even in her eating disorder: Sarah, perfect Sarah, valedictorian of her country day school, adored only child of older parents, an architect father and a mother who fund-raised for Democrats. I'd met them in August when they'd moved Sarah in. They drove us to a warehouse on

Dixwell Avenue to buy a rug for the common room. I'd envied Sarah's thinness. I remembered especially an evening in September when she stood on the rug in a wool pencil skirt, completely flat up and down. It was Yom Kippur and she was getting ready to go break the fast at the Hillel. I'd also envied the fast.

But as the fall went on, Sarah's mouth tightened. The seats of her pants strained. After Christmas she'd come back with new clothes.

I wondered if Sarah only ate like me or if she ate and then also threw up. But if she was throwing up, why had she gained so much weight? Maybe she only threw up sometimes.

I released my grip on the chair. I dropped my skirt to the floor and pulled on running tights. (Lycra, still fit.) Then I went through the hall and into the common room, ducking my head, half-raising a hand "bye," and then padding down the steps and bursting out of the gate, straight up onto Hillhouse, pounding in the middle of the street, not caring about cars, imagining Sarah back in that room exposing me. Fuck it, these people, they knew nothing! Sarah knew nothing!

But that wasn't true. What Sarah was experiencing wasn't nothing. The night she had come to me with her confession, I had felt such recognition. Oh, God, this was my subject, this was *me*. Sarah, across the room, saying her thing, then lowering her eyes and pulling fuzz off her sweater. But before I could even decide what to reveal to her, there was a system override; immediately, security protocols were in place. I locked down my own information, my own experience. And even though I could see that Sarah was tormented by her problem, mystified by it, feelings that—oh, God again—I understood, now I simply could not express my compassion. I could no longer even really locate it. I was cold to her, and she probably left that common room humiliated.

Sarah could own up to whatever it was on national TV, but I had to hide, had to keep running, increasing the distance between myself and 1846J, reaching Science Hill and climbing, climbing, doing what protocol dictated, getting away.

22

INDECISION

MIDWAY THROUGH FRESHMAN YEAR we all started to talk about who to room with as sophomores. Sheva and I wanted to room together, but in order to room with her, I had to transfer colleges. This was a big deal, like changing your citizenship. As soon as I'd done it, I regretted it. I wanted to undo the transfer. Or . . . I thought I wanted to. I wasn't sure. Every day I woke up intending to decide, once and for all. As much as I was resolving to quit my bad eating, I was resolving to decide on this.

I wanted to live with Sheva because she was the person who knew me most truly. But I also feared the idea of living with her, maybe for the exact same reason.

I turned this all over in my head one evening as I walked to the gym for lifeguard training. At the pool I stood on the deck, feeling my stomach pressing against my suit. I stood there like a sea lion, like a squat round mammal trying to hold her head high.

Afterward, a friend and I went to David's Cookies. There I had dinner—chili and cornbread and a cookie. When we parted I was set on walking straight to my room, but as I neared Ashley's, the ice-cream place, I thought, *Fuck it,* and the launch sequence was initiated. I went into Ashley's and got a medium hazelnut frozen yogurt with sprinkles and ate it alone at a counter under a wall hung with Frisbees. My hair was still wet beneath my wool hat, and outside it was February and freezing. When I finished, I walked in the dark to Wall Food, and as soon as I was back out the door I stuffed a muffin into my mouth, meanly, like a sock being stuffed into the mouth of someone captured, just balled it in. In my room I tugged open a bag of sesame sticks and tried to eat the little glazed things as slowly as I could, while focusing intently on the course-of-study bulletin so that if a roommate came in she would think I could not be disturbed. And then I finished the sesame sticks, and I knew I was done because I felt so sick. Even though it was not quite eleven, I would have to go to bed, because I would not be able to do anything, even talk, so I climbed up into the top bunk. I lay there, breathing heavily, and then with one last effort I pulled my shirt over my head and threw it on the floor and then unhooked my bra and threw that down, too, and then lay under the sheets, my stomach tight against my waistband.

In the morning I climbed down from the top bunk, my body like a thick trunk. I felt cold and exposed with my shirt off. This was a way a woman's body wasn't supposed to be, a way you never see, a naked bloated torso over green sweatpants.

I took a shower and dried my hair and put on one of the three elastic-waist skirts that fit. I was lower than usual. I was really just going through the motions. Usually I started the day with more hope than this.

I walked to the post office and left with nothing, not even a J. Crew catalog. I wanted a letter from Chris, who'd grown non-communicative except for an occasional postcard signed *C.*

It was only February: I still had time. I still had time to fix this by the summer, when I would see him, and sleep with him, again. I wanted sex now in a way I hadn't in high school. Whether it was age or loosening of inhibition, something had been ignited. Yet I was timid about these feelings. I didn't know what to do with them. I'd read the section of the undergraduate handbook about sex and feel aroused and then ashamed. Sometimes up on 7M when I scrawled lists of food consumed or weight-loss timelines, I'd also doodle penises. It felt demented and base, to be documenting these needs on the same page. I'd raise myself in the chair, imagining the penis inside me.

I continued toward Atticus, the bookstore/café where I was going to have coffee and a scone and make a decision. But as soon as I walked in, I saw my English 129 teacher at the counter. A day earlier I'd cut his class, but the real problem was that at the class before, he'd given us a list of things not to do when we wrote papers, and I'd been crushed and embarrassed because I knew he was about to read a paper in which I had done every single one of them. I couldn't be with him in Atticus, so I looked at my watch and then, in a head-smacking oh-shit way, pushed open the door and headed down Chapel Street, heart racing but feeling free, relieved of the thoughts that near the English teacher were clobbering me.

At Claire's there was a problem, because the only scone they had was cheese. But I didn't know what else to do, so I ordered that and coffee. The scone was the size of a plate. It was like a giant hors d'oeuvre, but I ate the whole thing anyway. And the coffee was watery and now I felt like my morning was so fucked-up because I didn't get to choose in the right way. At Atticus, with strong coffee and a scone that was sweet.

And also I was mad at myself because I was doing the thing I always did, which was tell myself I needed food to make a decision. Even as I knew this made no sense! Eating would not move me forward into action, because eating precluded action. You didn't have to do anything else when you were eating, even think. There was dead pleasure in that offness.

But as soon as there was no longer a bite in your mouth, everything crept back.

I looked down at the empty scone plate. I put my finger on a crumb.

Fuck.

And now, since I'd already fucked up, and since I really, really, really was going to quit today, and, most important, since all my pre-med roommates were at chemistry, I decided to have one final pint of Ben & Jerry's and that would be it, for all time, and then I would decide about everything.

I bought Coffee Heath Bar Crunch at Wall Food, and then in the common room I sat on a corner of the couch and chipped into the unthawed ice cream with a roommate's spoon, and the bite flew up and fell on the floor, and I looked down at it in a dusty corner by the baseboard, not because I was thinking of eating it but because I really didn't want to have to stop and clean it up, I just wanted to finish.

Meanwhile, it was not even ten-thirty A.M. and here I was, still undecided about changing colleges, still with so many hours of the day to get through, hours in which I would be exhausted and useless.

I am scared that I will go crazy.

MY LIFE NO LONGER had structure. I wrecked days with my eating, made them unusable before they even started. I was stuck. My mind corkscrewed. I couldn't tell what I felt, except for terror at how immobile I was, how trapped.

"I think I want to see someone," I told my mother over the phone, tugging the cord. "I'm having trouble with eating again." I closed my eyes for an instant, as if I could blot out the admission. I had never spoken to my mother about the eating. I'd never had the impulse to confess to her or to ask for her assistance. Then I opened my eyes and continued, "And also I can't focus, and also I'm just really depressed," and on and on, so that by the end of the conversation my mother would hopefully not remember the first, most profoundly revealing thing I had maybe ever said. Or that if she did remember she'd think that I was not eating, that I was anorexic again.

My mother consulted my aunt, and the two of them consulted their own therapists, and all the consultations led to a man who was supposedly some leading expert in the field of adolescence.

The psychiatrist was a broad-boned man in corduroys, and his office was in the Yale Child Study Center. The name on the door made me feel overgrown. Or was this where I belonged? On campus I was a woman, but in psychology I was a child.

I found that I could not talk with the psychiatrist about eating, except in the vaguest way possible, like, "Sometimes I eat when I'm not hungry." Instead, I laid out my other problems, which were not inconsequential.

But then one day out of nowhere the psychiatrist said, "How is the eating?" and I said, "Oh, that's not really a problem anymore, that's fine, fine," trying to be calm but all the while experiencing some kind of histamine response, my throat closing up, as if to prevent me from speaking. But it wasn't like my body was running interference, not like my body was getting in the way of my brain; my brain also didn't want to talk about this, and my body was coming to its aid; yes, my body and brain were aligned in an agreement to keep this secret, to never divulge it to the end.

I CAME UP WITH a new plan to fix myself. I would retreat to Florida. I would spend spring break with B.J. and Grack. Two weeks with my grandparents was a mark of my desperation. I'd never been alone with them for so long.

At the airport, my grandparents took me in at the gate—subtly, glancingly—and again, more baldly, as we waited by the baggage claim. We drove to their elegant building on the ocean, me large and silent in the back seat of the yellow Cadillac.

For the next two weeks I felt their scrutiny. My grandparents seemed to be performing their own child study. This granddaughter, why had she become so round and weak and poky, why did she suddenly not know how to dress? The divorce weighed on them.

One night when Grack laid into me about something, B.J. shut him down: "Stop it, Dave. This poor child, she's been through so much already." I felt gratified but then angry: *You don't know the half of it.*

There was another college girl visiting the building. She was taking time off from school. She'd been in a car accident and, B.J. said, she had "brain damage." The girl did seem somehow removed, but I didn't know if this was a symptom or not.

We had nothing in common but we had everything in common, both of us hiding out, both of us damaged.

I understood that what had happened to me was nothing compared to the accident that injured her brain. But the thing was, there was something wrong with my brain, too. Just a different kind of damage. Not the kind where your brain knocks against your head, a mark on the plaster. Mine was different, an electrical fire that starts inside the wall after years of overload and fraying.

WHEN I GOT BACK to Yale I finally made a decision. I asked to undo the transfer. But the master of my college was unwilling to yield. At another moment I might have regarded this as a sign and retreated, but now that I knew what I wanted I was panicked at the prospect of not getting it, and I asked my parents for help. My father called the school, and a few days later the undo was granted. I felt relieved but also exposed, knowing I'd been pegged as an unstable student who was not adjusting.

And my parents: Did they discuss my situation? Did my mother say anything to my father about the ways in which I was struggling? What did he understand of my indecision and anguish? I was embarrassed that my father might have learned there were flaws in me. (Though in quieter moments I'd wonder if it had made him happy to come to my rescue. My mother was always the one I called upon for assistance.)

The psychiatrist and I had talked a lot about the transfer, not so much its pros and cons but my obsession with it. On the afternoon I told him that it had been undone, he suggested that all along I had been trying to "undo the craziness." I was so annoyed when he said this, because he knew nothing of the real craziness. But that was my own fault for not telling him.

AFTER I UNDID THE transfer, things were weird between Sheva and me, and I wanted to explain. On my little Macintosh I would start letters to her. I'd open with an apology and follow with a confession. *It's not bulimia, I don't throw up*. (Making it clear that I didn't throw up was always so important to me. This strikes me now as pathetic. But the fact that I didn't throw up was also critical. It was so hard to explain what I "had.") Some of the books I read used the word "sick" in conjunction with eating disorders, as in, "My daughter got sick when she was only fourteen," but "fucked-up" was my preferred term. Fucked-up was what I felt, a bad-girl state I could claim.

Sometimes I would set the letter in the future. Just a few months ahead. I would open the letter with some funny observations about summer in Boulder and then drop my revelation: *Sheva, I've been attending an eating-disorders group twice a week*. It was always a group I was planning on going to. I thought only other girls would understand.

I would write these letters, but I would never print them out. Telling was something I imagined as much as quitting, but I was nowhere near ready to actually do either of them.

The books I was reading—which, in addition to the ones on 7M, now included several volumes on a shelf I'd sit in front of, cross-legged, at Astor Books in New York City—all said you had to tell. Tell someone, the directive of all of childhood, the raising of the red flag. Tell a grown-up if he's hurting you. Tell a teacher if you're not okay.

Was it seriously possible that this was the only solution?

I wanted to tell someone, but I wanted to control the information. I wanted to be on the other side of the problem when I disclosed it.

I didn't know that decades later I would still be trying to get to the other side, and that the information wouldn't be any easier to deliver.

LOOKING BACK NOW, I sometimes think of what I missed out on, or did not do or experience, during freshman year. But at the time I did not think of it as "missing." What I thought about was "waste." I was wasting time; I was wasting a Yale education. I was wasting money. I was wasting hours, days, years. I was wasting youth, health. I was wasting food by consuming more calories than I needed to function and wasting my body's own energy on digestion. Waste was not honorable! It was my moral obligation to move beyond this.

I also didn't think about it as gluttony. Because it wasn't that—being greedy before a heaving table. By now I was stuck on some setting, some cycle that couldn't be disabled.

23

ADDICTION

N SILLIMAN THERE WAS a boy everyone called Chewie. He was from a rural town and had grown up with only his father. Chewie never drank until he came to college, but once he was there he began drinking heavily. Chewie was the mascot of the football and hockey players he lived with. Their high-proof pet. He had a rocking chair, and he would rock and rock with a bottle of vodka beside him. Finally, during our junior year, it was arranged for Chewie to leave campus and go to treatment. The morning he left was a cool spring Sunday. Outside the dining hall, a blond boy from Savannah said, "Chewie's leaving, do y'all want to come say bye to him?" And I went with my roommates to an enormous wood-paneled common room with a bar. It was the morning after a party, and the floor was sticky and there were still plastic cups strewn around but there wasn't anything in them because Chewie, who was standing in the center of the room, had come in and finished all the ends of punch and beer. Two football boys were talking tenderly to him, and in that instant I felt warmth for these boys I'd dismissed as uncaring and also such profound identification with Chewie. I knew what this was, to swear you're not going to but to be pulled across the courtyard to it anyway, and then just to go all out, because this is the last time, going forward is all new.

CAROLINE, IN HER MEMOIR, talked about needing ice cream now, needing her "fix." To me, "fix" was so affirmative. Caroline understood her eating disorder as an addiction. Everything else I read in those days was about body image, or cultural expectations, or emotional need—and while I recognized all of these as factors in my behavior, by second semester freshman year they barely mattered. Bingeing had become a compulsion.

Today it's not unusual to think of eating disorders as addictive disorders. There's even a questionnaire called the Yale Food Addiction Scale. The scale hadn't been designed when I was at Yale; it was designed later by a group of psychologists, including a professor who became the master of Silliman College my senior year. When I learned about the scale, more than a decade after I graduated, I would think about having stood in the courtyard with this man and how both of us, in different ways, had spent time in the years that followed trying to make sense of similar material. He was overweight, and I wondered whether there was a connection between his size and his research.

The scale measures whether a person's eating behavior meets the criteria for "substance dependence." The grad student who led the development of the scale now runs something called the Food Addiction Science and Treatment Lab. There, among other things, she scans patients' brains for neural markers of food addiction. Once, I considered pitching a magazine piece about this young woman. She was influential in her field and consistently published papers making her case. I was interested in why she was doing this work and also in interrogating the work itself. Sitting at a tiny café table across from an editor, I almost pitched it. But to do the piece right, I would have wanted to get my own brain scanned, which would have involved admitting to my own problems, something I was still not ready to do.

I don't believe there is a solely neurological explanation for my eating disorders; it's one piece of it, not the whole thing. Yet I am curious about the lab with the experts and the equipment. I am greedy for all the information they could put in front of me, to see what regions light up when they put me in the machine. To hold a printout that shows the telltale variation in my reward circuitry.

There's resistance to the idea that food can be addictive. Resistance by some psychiatrists and neuroscientists who argue that the addiction is to a behavior rather than a substance; resistance by laypeople who ask, "Well, if that's the case, then why aren't we all hooked on sugar?" There's also an aesthetic resistance. There is nothing romantic about uncontrolled eating. Other addictions have literary traditions; this one is not known for producing great art. Other addictions whittle; this one makes you thick and plodding. Other addictions are demons, and to overcome them is to triumph; this one is completely pedestrian. Other addictions are not primarily associated with women. Other addictions make you act in a way that is shocking or comic. Nobody ever starts a story with, "I ate a whole cake and you won't believe the crazy shit I did next." Do other addictions make better stories? Their conclusions are clearer: Goodbye forever, alcohol, I will never drink you again. In an eating-disorder story, the protagonist still has to eat. It's a less satisfying end—though also a more interesting one, precisely because of this challenge. There is no clean break. You relinquish the addiction but not the substance. You have to learn to live with it. Maybe you even learn to take pleasure in what you once believed could destroy you.

I've always been drawn to stories of addiction. They compel me, haunt me, pull me in, make me look away. But while they are stories I find myself inside, I also feel they are not entirely mine, and I am uneasy claiming them. I feel as if I exist just outside these stories that seem to explain me. Which is crazy, because I know my own experience. I know my own genetic predisposition to addiction. Yet I've internalized the idea that an eating disorder is not a real addiction, even as I know how destructive one can be.

I was a college freshman pre-Internet, and the range of what I read about my problem then was limited. Some of the material insisted on a chasm between anorexics ("inhibited") and bulimics ("impulsive"). But I knew that I couldn't be the only one with both traits. Today the connection between the two states, limitation and excess, is a given. They coexist or wax and wane. They are really just different expressions of the same thing.

One morning in my thirties I was at the library, doing research in a science-journal database, and it occurred to me: *I bet there is stuff about binge-eating disorder in here.* I entered my search term into the box, and when I got the results I was shocked. It was so different from 1991 on 7M. There was information everywhere. I felt a little frantic. I bookmarked everything. My heart quickened, there was recognition, I *was* this. Yes, to the withdrawal from activities and friends; yes, to the "marked distress" that follows a binge. It was like finding yourself in any text. Except there was an added element of wanting to talk back to the authors, to amplify or dispute some of their conclusions. Or to let them know when they'd really captured something. These clinical papers would mention unintentionally funny things like "The Avoidance of Existential Confrontation Scale" on which those who binge-eat "score unusually high."

I soon found I preferred to read the abstracts than to access the full texts. The abstracts were like teasers. They were so well done, so enticing. They promised explanation. But the papers themselves often disappointed me. I started to wonder about the way the studies were designed. (*Why evaluate in "settings" when behavior is so private?*) I got annoyed at theories about satiety, about the binge-eater lacking the "stop sign" that tells her she is full. This was absurd to me. In binge eating it was clear you were full; you overrode those settings.

The article that explained things best to me that morning was an older one—published in 1991 in *Psychological Bulletin.* It described binge eating in a way that just nailed it, as a "short-term escape from an aversive awareness of self." The authors, who were writing at a time when conclusions were scant, got this whole thing so right it seemed to me they must have had it themselves. It was as if they were beside me in Machine City, "narrowing [their] attention to the immediate stimulus environment and avoiding broadly meaningful thought."

But even these insightful researchers seemed flummoxed: "In short, binge eating is a paradoxical, self-defeating pattern of behavior."

IT WAS NOT JUST *like* an addiction, it *was* an addiction. Every waking moment was about either giving in to it or resolving not to but then succumbing anyway. ("Waking moment"—why that cliché when I know about the sleep, too, how this claims even the unconscious: dreams I had where I was eating loose change.) It was a compulsion I was locked inside. It was physiological dips I had to address with sugar. It was feeling flat and immobile without food. It was feeling I could not lift a limb. It was feeling like thoughts could not even move through my brain without an assist. But it was also eating in an involuntary way that had nothing to do with energy. It was eating *⅓ pint Ben & Jerry's Rainforest Crunch; 2 muffins from Naples; 2 choc chip cookies from Naples; 1 apple* after midnight, then waking up in the morning swearing to quit but immediately eating *waffles w/ syrup & butter from Claire's; 1 chocolate-filled croissant; 1 blueberry muffin; nearly all of a bagel w/ cream cheese* instead, then sitting in a café scribbling nonsense, waiting for it to be noon so that the library would open, feeling sick and thick and hot, feeling like I needed the food to spread through me before I could stand, looking at the two girls at the nearby table drinking coffee and reading the Sunday *Times,* and despairing of ever being a girl at that table again.

24

STOMACHS 2

ONE NIGHT I BROUGHT a whole-wheat raisin scone up to 7M and made the paper bag it came in a plate. I devoured the scone, then balled up the bag with all the crumbs on it.

After the crumpling sound, it was quiet. I felt my heart knocking in my chest. Usually after an episode my heart was wild, but now it was heavy and slow. Now it was stifled, like it wanted to go faster but something was retarding it.

The scone was just the end; I'd eaten a lot before this.

I shifted. I was uncomfortable, my abdomen weirdly taut, as if pumped with air. It was not a sensation I'd ever had before.

I got scared that my stomach would explode.

I bent to put the balled-up bag in my backpack and once I was upright resolved not to move again, because even that small dip felt dangerous. I turned my head slightly to the arched window. Dark New Haven with little lights. Streets through which the ambulance could blare. Could they park outside the library, or was it closed off right there? What would I do, go down to the lobby if it seemed like this was going to happen? It could be hours before this feeling would go away, hours before I'd know if I was safe. I could hardly write anything in my notebook, just crazy-seeming sentences, letters with little curlicues on the ends.

Yet even as I was fearful and desperately sad, at the same time part of me was saying, *That couldn't happen, that can't. Your stomach can't explode. It's not something the human body does. You would throw up first.*

I stayed as still as I could at that desk, as still as I could in that hot, radiator-clanking section of the stacks, until the announcement near midnight saying the library was about to close. Then I rose and took the elevator down to the lobby and showed the contents of my backpack to the guard and walked home carefully over icy flagstone. My roommates were still awake in the common room. Often when I returned to them I was dismissive and angry, but now I was timid and subdued, saying only, "I'm so tired." In my bedroom I dropped my clothes on my desk chair and placed my foot gingerly on the narrow metal bar of the bed and climbed cautiously into the top bunk. Under the covers I did not make resolutions or chastise myself for the waste of my life. I only hoped that in the morning I would wake still whole.

YOUR STOMACH REALLY CAN explode. Or it can get so big that it can cut off your circulation or suffocate your intestines.

The patients who die from this, or nearly die, live in Hungary, Massachusetts, Japan. They are bulimic or anorexic. They are discovered alone in their apartments, or brought to the ER by their parents, or revealed to be hiding the truth from the doctors only when they go into septic shock.

The medical papers that describe these circumstances use dispassionate language, but—and it could just be what I'm bringing to it—I feel like these case reports are tonally off. Like the doctors are all, "Holy shit! Guys, we have to write about this one." Other illnesses are no-fault; not this. This is the annals of freak show. This is directing you to figure 1, where you will see a stomach so big it has ballooned to fill an entire torso.

Was my stomach this way on that night?

It was a watermelon, a beach ball.

Could I have imagined such a stomach on the morning just two and half years earlier, when my mother and I had stood across from each other in our towels?

I'm so thin that my stomach actually goes in.

She's not fat, but she has a little pot belly.

My God, my mother's stomach was nothing, a pincushion.

My stomach was the distended belly of something that washes up on the shore, dead.

THERE WERE NIGHTS LIKE that, when the eating annihilated me. But—and this was a more uncomfortable thing to recognize—there were also times when it raised me up.

One snowy afternoon I sat at a front table in a small, tin-ceilinged café. I had eaten but not a frightening, sick-making amount, just the pillowy calm I needed to start again. I had my notebook open and I was writing well.

I looked out the window and there was my roommate Sarah—Sarah of the body-image news segment. She looked straight at me through the glass. The straps of her backpack were tight over her duffel coat. Of course she would bring a mound of textbooks with her to do this. Studying was probably her means of atonement, just as mine was writing.

I thought I knew what Sarah was doing. I thought it was fair to assume. We were on a far part of Whitney Avenue where I rarely saw another undergraduate. You wouldn't come here unless you were hiding. (Of course, it wasn't "fair to assume" that Sarah had come to this neighborhood in order to binge or to recover from one. She could have been doing an errand, or visiting a professor in an out-of-the-way building. My inference was a measure of my identi-fication with her—not a judgment.)

I looked back at Sarah. Then, at once, as if by mutual agreement, we both looked away. She continued along the sidewalk, and I smiled down at the china plate that had held my muffin, strangely content. I felt such fellowship with Sarah then. I believed she needed to shut me out, to be alone in what she did.

I started to write again but then stopped, because—what was this strange thought? I felt, for the first time, that I would miss this. This day—oh, I was so sure it would be the last, this day of soft snow and good sentences. The wistful feeling left then and gave way to something sharper, more like fear. What would I do without this?

It was the first moment I realized I was getting something from this. That I liked something about this.

I liked the possibility inherent in the act. I liked getting as low as you could and then every day the moment of begin-again. I liked the calm that followed an episode. Something quieted, the need met. Ah, yes, here I am in the place where I make resolutions and start afresh.

But just as much as the loss of calm, I feared the loss of ferocity. I really didn't want to let go of this thing that took me away, made me separate. This thing I lost myself inside for hours at a stretch. This tornado part of the day no one knew about. This furious thing I kept. I didn't want to relinquish that, and I wanted to continue to be alone in it. I wanted to continue not letting anyone in.

I have never for a moment wished to return to those years, years in which I lost access to pleasure, to the ordinary and to joy and to human connection. But it was true that there was something savage I would no longer be able to locate when I left the café and rejoined the world again. And it was true that I would miss the cycle of de-struction and renewal, so regular that it was circadian.

All the books said you ate to stifle feeling or to escape from it. And, yes, this was true. But this wasn't all there was to it. Because this thing that supposedly deadened feeling daily took me deep inside it.

I'D TRANSFERRED SO MUCH feeling to food. That's a thing I haven't kicked. Food remains electric to me.

I do have a perverse nostalgia for that old time. It extends to the foods I binged on, some of which I wish I could eat again: the maple-nut granola my mother bought in bulk at Alfalfa's; low-fat low-sodium smoked Lorraine. Yet there are others I'm grateful I never ate to excess. Certain foods had special protected status, and as low as I went, I would not ruin them.

Sometimes I fantasize about bingeing the way I used to. I imagine myself—my midlife self—into that frenzied state again. Tugging on the freezer drawer in my own grown-up kitchen: That modern-day super-suction would be a problem; I would pull harder, and harder, and break the seal, and later make up a lie to explain. When I imagine the binge, I imagine feeling sick earlier. I imagine feeling scared by all of the food in me. Would my children perceive a difference? They have never known me this way. I imagine feeling I would not be able to cope for the rest of the day and wonder whether I would uphold my responsibilities or (more likely) shirk them. I don't like following the fantasy that far, into consequences, but the opening impulse compels me—raw and giving in.

The fantasy makes me uneasy but also puts me back in a safe and familiar space. The bingeing took place on the sidelines, away. Doing it, I was the shy girl in orthopedic shoes at the edge of the classroom. The girl who wasn't from Michigan, even though she had never lived any other place. The child of troubled parents who knows you will never understand. The observer with her hands behind her back. The second-best friend. The eating (and, later, the not-eating) increased the distance between me and whomever I kept at arm's length and was in the first place probably a reaction to that gap. A way to cope with some discomfort or shyness. But then it protected me from having to ever probe those feelings. I could just stay there, in the place where I was always different. For years, even after my eating was more normalized, I held myself apart. *I will not commit to you. Though I am here, my real life is elsewhere.* It was the only stance I knew how to take.

I spent a lot of time lamenting the consequences of bingeing, but that snowy day in the café was the first time I acknowledged its benefits: the privacy, the hopeful lift, the surge of creative energy. Writing was a necessity, a defense against annihilation. Later, when I stopped bingeing, it was harder to write. Bingeing offered me access to a deep part of myself. But it became the only means of access, and when I gave it up, it took a long time to find another way in.

25

SPRING

NEAR THE END OF freshman year, posters went up for something called the Around the World cocktail party. Because it was in Silliman, there was a good chance the boy I liked would be there. This boy would become my husband, though of course I didn't know this yet. I did know that I'd had a crush on him since the moment we'd met, in September, on a Saturday morning in the dining hall. He was on his way to crew practice and I was on my way to play rehearsal. We sat across from each other in a shaft of dusty light. We were the only people in the whole room, it was so early. Just the two of us, fixed in that beam.

On the day of the party I had an appointment with the psychiatrist. It was cool in his office, but when I came out after the session it was uncomfortably warm. Spring in the East was strange to me after years in the arid West. The air was a mass I had to push through.

Back at Silliman, a stickball game was in progress. Someone pointed in the direction of the beer, and I went into a dark room with a keg, and when I came out everyone was cheering because the boy I liked had just hit the ball over the high gray stone buildings opposite, and this was an unprecedented feat. This was one for the history books, and the boy I liked was grinning beneath a red baseball hat and people were yelling his last name and my insides were swimming; this boy, he was so quietly champion.

I wanted to go talk to him, and I approached, but when I neared, there was a big group, including frat-boy types I knew would look at me strangely if I tried to break in. So I kept walking, over the patchy, dirt-islanded grass, pretending that I'd been heading to my room all along. Once there I put the beer on my desk and decided that since I'd only drunk a little it would be okay to go running, and I changed and snuck out the side.

On the run I thought about the boy—Mike. Two mornings a week we'd leave the Silliman dining hall together and walk to class. On the walks we'd talk: about English vs. American Studies and *The Breakfast Club* vs. *Sixteen Candles;* about our roommates and our professors and about the kids who grew up in New York. Mike was curious about Colorado, but with him I didn't fake it up. I tried to explain to him what it was like to live in that landscape.

A couple of weeks earlier, on a Saturday night, Mike and I had both been dragged by our roommates to a dance club. I saw him near the huge hexagonal bar; he looked as disoriented as I felt. He was wearing a soft, rumpled flannel shirt. We left together and went back to my room. But now (of course) things were weird. Ever since that night I had not been able to be normal. I'd emailed him (email was new, only a few people had it; Rachel across the hall was a computer-science major, and she'd showed me how to sign up for it). I'd visited his room in the evening, usually after drinking, though I played up my drunkenness, made it more than it was, so he could ascribe the visit not to real feeling but to intoxication. One time he was sitting at his computer trying to work and I stood behind him and I knew I was bothering him, but I just wanted to be there. Another time I came over and he was talking to a girl named Scheherazade. Did he like her? Did she like him? I was not the only one who'd responded to his crushworthiness. He was sensitive but not

effete. There was something Sound-of-Silency about him: a rock/
island outsider quality even as he moved through the world with
such ease. Then there was his wholesomeness. He was an archetype
of *boy*. He rode his mountain bike down the stone staircase into the
courtyard. Sometimes he left out of the gate carrying a fishing rod.
He was six feet two and a half inches tall, the same height as Holden
Caulfield.

I came back from my run, and when the party started I went
looking for Mike. Someone said he was playing Twister in entryway
L, and when I opened the door I saw him V'd upside down, his leg
wrapped around the leg of a girl whose father's paintings hung in
the Museum of Modern Art. She was as intimidatingly sophisticated
as her parentage suggests. Several dots behind them was her friend
Emmi, who had a pierced nose (pierced noses: new, like email, and
as intimidating as famous dads). They were not in Silliman; I suspected they'd come here specifically to see Mike. Their heads were
pointed down at the Twister mat and they were laughing, drinks in
a row along the wall beside them.

Everything in me fell. This, too, I'd ruined. I liked Mike, really
liked him. There was something deep there, and I'd lost it, I'd lost
him. Lost him to Emmi.

I left the room. Out in the courtyard, I started acting like I was
in junior high. When people saw me they said, "Schmooze!" greet-
ing me by another name that, like Kasha, wasn't really mine (it's a
long story). But I was not the party Schmooze they were expecting.
When people asked me if I was having fun, I said, "I would be, but
Mike is ignoring me. Just totally avoiding me. He's hanging out
with Emmi—do you know her?"

Once night fell I felt a little better, hidden. Above me, lights spun
in the dining hall's enormous windows. There was a dance party
inside. A little drunk, I sat with my back against a brick wall. Music
pounded upstairs.

Two boys sat down near me. I was not interested in them, but
then I heard one of them mumble, "Susan Burton—you've seen her
in the facebook. But she doesn't look anything like her picture."

(The facebook, not Facebook. It was 1992. The freshman face-book, a bound volume with everyone's picture and the name of their high school and their home address.)

I had an instinct to slip away, to be polite, so that things would not be awkward when the boys noticed I was beside them and had overheard them talking about me. But they knew I was there; that was *why* they were talking about me.

My facebook picture was the kind of picture that boys starred. The kind where they scoped out the girl, tried to meet her. They reserved their harshest judgments for girls who did not live up to their photographs. These were the lamest kind of girls, girls who misrepresented themselves. My photo was my high school senior portrait, and it had been an accurate likeness when I'd submitted it. Yet the boys were right. I no longer looked like the girl in that picture.

The thing was, I hated boys who put asterisks by girls' photographs. I hated how it was like game-hunting, how they fixed girls in their sights and went after them. About this type of boy, I couldn't have cared less. Also, it had been so long since the largest part of my problem was how I looked. Now the behavior was the bigger worry.

But I was devastated by the boy's comment.

I stepped down into the courtyard, and almost as soon as I did I saw Mike.

"Hey, Susan," he said. He always used my real name. "I was looking for you. I heard you were mad at me because you think I'm ignoring you. But I'm not."

My heart was racing. *No, I didn't say that,* was how I wanted to respond, but I couldn't, because I did say it, and I was so humiliated, so caught out in this game.

Instead I just said, "Okay."

He was standing above me, all kindness and curls. I was down on the ground, red-faced, sugar-swollen, looking up at him. At the boy I liked, who was so not like those other boys. Usually I was confident and talkative before him, but now I was quiet and defeated. Ever since we hooked up, I hadn't been myself with him. And that was the miracle of this boy, right? That I was myself with him, even as unlike myself as I believed myself to be. But now all that was over. Because over the past two weeks I'd made a spectacle of myself. Because tonight I'd been catty, attention-seeking. And now I stood beside him in the courtyard, slumping inside, at the end of this year, this year during which I had not comported myself well, this year I had wasted. Above us the lights strobed and there was a whoop as an early-eighties song came on. The music thumped. We stood near the stone wall. I didn't know what to say. I felt certain that after this night he wouldn't like me anymore.

But the miracle of this boy is that he still did.

26

SOPHOMORE SLUMP

JUNE AFTER FRESHMAN YEAR, I was home in Boulder. One afternoon I ate nearly a whole tray of Betsy's homemade
brownies—blacker, fudgier, than those my mother baked. Even before the end I was sickened. I went to my room and as soon as it felt
possible, I left for a run.

The day was an arid one in the nineties, and as I headed out
along the trail, my face prickled with heat. Soon my insides spasmed,
and I wondered if I should turn back. But I had to run. I had to be
moving. I'd planned seven miles. I couldn't just sit with all of this
in me.

Only a mile out, I had to turn around, my feet thumping a circle
on a little wooden bridge. There was no way I was going to be able
to hold this in. I hurried back down the path, praying for safe passage, but then there came an awful sensation, one a person should
have only at home, near one's own bathroom; an outrage foisted
upon you by the universe. But I had done this to myself.

I crouched in the meadow. This was not a meadow on the out-
skirts of nowhere. This was a meadow beside a paved suburban

bike path. Joggers on this path all day. Mothers with children in trailers. Children on their own tiny mountain bikes. On the other side of a diamond-wire fence, golfers. And now me, squatting in thin, dry, patchy yellow stalk grass, losing control of my bowels. It was a moment of total abasement.

THAT SUMMER I WAS trying to be good. I worked at Alfalfa's, picking up so many hours that my supervisor told me to keep better track so that she wouldn't have to pay time-and-a-half; I stayed home, handling artifacts in my room; I ran, swam, biked; and I wrote. I was taking an evening writing workshop at the University of Colorado. I wanted stories to submit to the workshops at Yale, and a class was the only way I would ever get anything done. One story I wrote, "Sunday Morning," was a lightly fictionalized retelling of the weekend in eighth grade when my father had left me alone. *I want it to be 6 o'clock so I can wake up,* was the first line. I now understood that I had entered a new world when I did.

I saw few friends. I was ashamed of my size and felt separate in general. So on the evenings I was not working or in class, I was at home with my mother. We'd sit on the patio, both of us with books in our laps and bottles of Calistoga seltzer at our feet. We didn't talk about what we were trying not to do, and as soon as the other was out of sight, we probably did it anyway. I was so self-involved that I don't remember worrying about her drinking, except for one evening when we went to see an NPR commentator at the Boulder Public Library and I wished I hadn't let her drive. But overall she did not seem as messed up as I was.

"Betsy needed those brownies for swim team," she said on the evening after the incident in the meadow. She had never commented on missing food before. I was sitting at the computer, near the kitchen, where my mother was cleaning up. She paused by the dishwasher, waiting for me to respond. I stared into the lit square of the monitor, my fingers still on the keys. "Okay," I said. Then I saved, quit, shut down, stood, and went upstairs. In my room, I closed my door. I did not know what to do with myself—*sit on floor . . . sit on bed . . . read . . . read what?*—but the most insistent suggestion was to wait for my mother to leave the kitchen and then go downstairs and eat. *No. Why? No. Please. Stop it.*

Another day I received the labs from a yearly physical. For the first time ever, I had results that were *out of range*. That night my mother and I sat cross-legged together on the floor of my room. I cannot remember why I'd given her permission to enter, but I do remember mentioning my high cholesterol: "I mean, I'm kind of worried about it." I looked down, pretending to examine a mole on the inside of my knee.

"You have been eating a lot of fat," my mother said gently.

"Mm-hmm," I said, but in such a way that I strangulated "mm"; "mm" was the affirming sound, and I would not commit to it, would emphasize "hmm," which was neutral, even speculative. I looked back up at my mother.

"Those chips," she added, referring to a day or two earlier when she'd come home and seen me on the floor with my hand in a bag of blue-corn chips. I couldn't tell if she'd mentioned the chips to make the problem seem solvable—*just stop eating sesame blue-corn chips*—to shut down the conversation, or to start one. Whatever she was doing, I would not engage.

One afternoon my mother and I went to see a movie at the Arapahoe Village 4. It was called *Eating*. It wasn't a documentary, but it had the feel of one. Basically, the whole thing was women talking about food—ruefully, seriously, sadly, regretfully, thoughtfully. Acknowledging the space it took up. Their stories were personal and intimate.

After the film, my mother and I walked out into the shopping-plaza parking lot. We'd just missed the daily storm that rolled in from the mountains, and the air smelled of rain. The clouds lingered, low and bruised, and my mother did not need to put on her sunglasses. "That was a really good movie," she said. "A really honest movie."

"I know," I said. "Totally."

And this was as close as we came to a conversation. Other women talking openly about food: It didn't provoke our own discussion, but it stood in for one. We recognized in those women's stories some of our deepest themes. What food was in a family and what it was alone; how food dominated you and how you had to pretend it didn't, even with the people you were closest to. I realized there was no one other than my mother with whom I would have wanted to see the movie. No one else who would have understood exactly why it mattered or where it reached me. Beside her in the car, I felt returned to a stage where food had concerned and even obsessed me but had not yet claimed or ruined me. And maybe, I thought, that was the future, the realistic future. Just as for the women in the movie, food would always take up more space than I wanted it to, but I would also have room for other, richer preoccupations.

WHEN I WATCHED THE movie again, more than twenty-five years later, I found it equally powerful (though also flawed and grating). The setting is Southern California. At a fortieth birthday party, a young French woman is making a documentary film about women and eating. In the opening sequence, she sits alone before her camera and asks herself the question she will pose to all of her subjects: "Tell me, do you have any problem about food?" She confesses that her own eating disorder inspired this project: "And I think that's why I am doing all this stuff, to find out why it happened to me." Later she elaborates, "You know, you can say, 'I'm an alcoholic, or I'm a drug addict,' and that's okay, kind of interesting. But just say, you know, 'Eating disorder, I just want to eat'—that's so unattractive, it's so disturbing, I was just never able to tell that to anyone." But now, at this party, she is able to tell—now all the women are. I was struck, though, that even as the women share their experiences, they seem to remain essentially alone in them. They tell their stories, but they do not seem to connect with the others in doing so, and in the end, the film depicts confession as empty. These women open themselves up but do not receive compassion, understanding, or closeness in the space they have freed. I wonder if this is in part why I didn't tell for so long, because of fear of the hunger that might remain even after disclosure.

BACK AT SCHOOL SOPHOMORE year, I had no visions of a future of any kind. I was firmly in the awful present, where eating felled me daily. That fall there was more frozen yogurt covered in sprinkles that were hard and sugary, like the shredded coating of a pill. One sunny day, I ate three challah bagels inside a dirty repurposed fast-food restaurant on the ground floor of a parking garage and then walked down Orange Street and bought a medium frozen yogurt as soon as the shop opened at noon. But a few minutes later I stopped in my tracks on a brick pedestrian walk, spoon halfway to mouth, stomach cramping. I ate the bite—I always ate the bite—but these were the trail cramps from Boulder again. I was going to be sick. This time I made it back to my room, but I could not make it to my class on the Civil War. Now I was missing things that actually mattered, not just gut classes (gut, ha!) but classes I had come here to take.

I had both less confidence that I could fix the eating and less interest in examining it. I'd moved into a kind of dull acceptance. No longer did I find anything interesting or feral in what I did. It was rote. I still loathed myself. I still swore to change. But there were fewer moments of insight or curiosity. I was still writing but rarely about eating. I avoided looking at it hard, because doing so required me to consider I had become this. The earlier, better girl had been the aberration. This was something I would never look back on but always be in.

I was writing fiction—short stories about teenage girls in Colorado who were distant and obscurely troubled. These girls I invented were always controlled, never wild and scared. The plots were autobiographical; the protagonist who moved through them was a fantasy.

———

I DREAMED THAT I was swimming laps. Doing a flip turn, I hit my head hard on the wall. Things went black, and I was sinking. When I woke I felt as scared as if it had happened. I had a feeling, new to me, of being pulled down to the bottom.

As fall turned to winter, and my knees reddened under my elastic-waist skirts, I started having panic attacks, though in the beginning I didn't know what they were or that they had a name.

The first time I had one, I was at a food superstore called Price Club. I was there with Cilla, the director of the freshman outdoor-orientation-trip program—FOOT. This was the one extracurricular I'd committed to.

I was in charge of food. Of course. The title for the role I filled was "food dude."

I had never been to Price Club before, or to any place like it. The warehouse was brightly lit. Cilla pushed an enormous shopping cart past wooden pallets stacked with packaged food. Everything was a supersize or a multipack, making familiar brands uncanny. It was like the food sold to institutions or entire nations. When I opened the freezer, I saw chicken parts in bags so big you could use them to line your garbage can.

As we moved through the store, I started to feel separate from my surroundings. The sound changed, grew distant. I couldn't get a full breath. I thought I might feel better when we went outside, but I didn't. (A girl with an eating disorder has a panic attack at a food superstore. A girl from the local organic market has a panic attack in the market's antithesis. There could have been a joke in it if I wasn't so scared.)

In Cilla's Wagoneer on the way back to campus, I kept trying for a full breath, but I could not get the air to the bottom of my lungs. Finally, near Silliman, I managed a breath that reached all the way down to the bottom pocket. I could feel it touching, like when you shook the duvet to the corner of the cover.

But the relief was temporary. After the incident at Price Club, the world felt separate from me. I'd become a cartoon superimposed on a realistic backdrop.

I went back to the psychiatrist at the Yale Child Study Center.

"I wonder if it is like a flashback, except from pot," I hazarded.

My real fear was that it was *not* just a flashback. That this was not temporary but permanent. I worried that I had pot in me that I could never get out.

I was increasingly worried about all kinds of contamination. Mainly I was worried I had AIDS. Over the summer I had bled on a twenty-dollar bill, then thrown it away rather than put it into circulation. I was not a coddled rich girl who could blithely toss a twenty. But if I used the bill to pay for something, another person might catch something from my blood. (Yet I also worried that there would be consequences for throwing away U.S. currency. The money would be found in the waste stream and I would be identified.)

The psychiatrist said that what I was having was a panic attack.

Knowing the name for the thing didn't stop it from happening. Over Christmas break I had one at a Boulder housewares store. A few days later I had another one driving Betsy to Denver. I pulled over, made up something about the morning sun. Did Betsy believe me? "It's okay, Sus," she said, comforting me as if she were the older sister.

At home in Boulder I needed my mother, but I did not know how to express this.

"It is really bothering me that, like, a person can never see the world except through their own eyes," I tried one day. This was an odd way of saying what I actually felt, which was that I'd separated from my body. There was a space in me, some kind of gap. I needed a drawstring to pull my skin tight and seal it around me again. I felt this sensation most acutely by my eyes, as if I were too far from the holes through which I viewed the world. I needed to press my head forward, as if against the plastic forehead rest at the ophthalmologist, get back into position.

I had always been so firm that I *was* my body. I mocked the notion that there was a person "inside." But maybe this was the place I had to get to in order to move forward—to shrink away from my own skin. I'd left my body, and the disconnect was so frightening that nothing else mattered. I just wanted to feel whole.

My mother thought I was talking about how a person can never escape her own subjectivity.

But that wasn't it. What it was I couldn't say until one night, lying in bed, I felt myself going under. As in the swimming-pool dream, I was succumbing to a darkness from which I might not return. Inside that darkness, all the details fell away. I was reduced and scared, and in that fear I was the first person I had ever been, the child of my mother. I rose and walked down the hall to her bedroom.

The door was closed; I turned the knob. At night her room had more light than mine. The window was larger and the curtains filmier and they let in the moon.

I looked down at her head on the pillow. She was wearing a long-sleeved nightgown and must have grown hot, because her covers were pushed down and her gown bunched up around her thighs.

I hesitated.

"Mom," I whispered. Then louder, touching her shoulder. "Mom."

She opened her eyes.

"I'm scared," I said.

I don't remember what I said next, whether I said more. I don't think I did. I rounded the bed and lay down next to her.

Long after she fell asleep again, I stayed awake, eyes open. Being next to her did not undo the spell. When I finally fell asleep, it was into that enveloping darkness. But even if I never regained my bearings, I would have her beside me. The one who knew me first and best.

The next day my mother gave me a book of essays by Oliver Sacks. What was happening to me was . . . well, I don't know what it was. Maybe it was connected to the panic attacks or to the secret I was keeping. Maybe it was metabolic, connected to eating. Or maybe it was just a late-adolescent manifestation of torment. Whatever was going on was psychological—different from the neurological injuries Sacks described. But the book comforted me. While the stories Sacks told were painful and sad, through them he revealed the wonder of perceiving the world in ways others did not. I loved that my mother had given me this book. She had not told me that everything would be all right. Instead, she had acknowledged that something might really be wrong. She validated what I was feeling. And she showed me there was beauty in that.

That winter break was a return to her, even if she did not know it. I came back to her that night in her room, three years after the morning we'd faced off in our towels. After years of pushing her away, I needed her to feel like myself again.

PART 4

27

RITUAL PURIFICATION

UNLIKE THE START, WHICH I could peg to one weekend in November 1989, the end is not easy to delineate. There was no date when everything changed. No starred box on the calendar when the binge eating went away. It happened gradually, and once it was no longer a crisis I was so relieved. I didn't even have to decide that this would be a secret I would keep for the rest of my life. It was just obvious that this was a thing I would never say.

By a year out of college, I'd erased all the evidence. The extra half that was still on me at graduation, I got that off. And then even more. I started afresh, on a cellular level. Nothing remained in me from that horrible time. Nothing remained of what I ate. I reduced myself to my essence. Like all anorexics, I was deluded and infuriating. But quitting food seemed to me to be the only solution. I needed to be empty in order to return to the world. And I desperately wanted to return to the world! I didn't want to waste any more time. I was determined, so determined, not to waste time ever again.

———

THE PASSAGE FROM ONE stage to the other was slow and halting, and it started junior year. That fall I came back to school almost as heavy as I'd been the previous spring. Over the summer, my eating had been desperate and unregulated. But I arrived on campus resolving, as always, to be different. The difference was that this time I sort of was. As I settled into the semester, the bingeing dropped from a peak, then held steady in a medium place—not solved, but not an emergency. Each day I swore not to do it, and most days I did it anyway. But turning the dial down to "most" felt remarkable after years of being set to "every." I no longer made ritual rounds of food shops. It no longer felt like a bender. Instead I would run across the street to Wall Food just before it closed at midnight and buy two plastic-wrapped cookies. And then once I'd eaten them I'd be able to sleep. The cookies were soothing, and this was different, too: using food to tamp down or comfort instead of to agitate or stir up.

Because the progress was uneven, it's hard to trace its arc. But there are a few images that stay: like me at a Thai restaurant with Mike and a group of friends on his twentieth birthday—September of junior year. I remember the warmth that bloomed when our eyes met across the table, and the new shirt I wore. I don't remember what I ate or even caring about it. I remember a seminar room that same fall, a class on the Suburbanization of America, with the professor who would become my senior-essay adviser. One afternoon in that room, deeply engaged with the material, a thought flashed: *This is who I could have been in college without the eating.* "Could have been": The tense is telling; somehow I felt it was too late. Even as I changed, I was still defined by "the eating." I remember staying up all night to finish a major paper and the disappointment in the morning that I'd compromised the achievement by stuffing myself as I wrote. I couldn't feel pride, only my thick body and the food I'd eaten. It was the kind of paper you had bound at the copy shop, and when I went in, a beautiful girl in my year was getting her paper bound, too, and she was so thin in her little jeans, and I just knew she hadn't shoved food in her face—frantic, gobbling, but then, *fuck,* renewed.

I resented what was left of the illness. The piece that remained was still in the way. But I was no longer locked up in it, and that was deliverance.

Emotionally I was more stable. I was no longer trying to be someone else. I'd lost the energy for it. I knew how to be alone, and because I now felt confident I could exist without a cohort, I no longer needed to perform for anyone. And I'd never needed to perform for Mike. Sophomore year, he'd become one of my closest friends; by Christmas break junior year, we were skiing together through tree trails, and I was sleeping with his rumpled flannel beside me when he left. No more games in the college courtyard; this was love.

Why had we gotten together at the moment we did? Once I was no longer diverting feeling into food, had I become more available to him, or was it our intimacy that enabled me to move on from eating?

I didn't ask these kinds of questions then. No self-exploration, just discipline. I resisted bingeing with the blind focus of an endurance athlete. *Just don't do it, just don't do it, no, no, no. Keep going, keep going, it's hard now, but once you break through, you can go forever. Willpower willpower head down flip turn again.* I didn't examine what emotions had driven me—were still driving me—to binge. I did even less of this than I'd done previously. I wanted to power it down. I wanted to turn my attention to other things after years of being owned by this.

But at the end of junior year, when I learned that my freshman roommate Sarah was starting a new program for Yale students with eating disorders, I applied to be a counselor. The main part of Sarah's program was a hotline, and in my application I wrote that such a hotline might have changed things for me freshman year. It was the first time I'd disclosed my eating disorder, and I knew I couldn't have done so to anyone but Sarah. She'd opened up to me and, in doing so, had made it possible for me to open up to her. I was proud when she offered me a counselor position.

By the time we came back to school for senior year, I felt totally different. I'd lost confidence. That summer I'd been an intern at a magazine in New York City. I'd lived in a Village sublet with a girl who was anorexic. She had an air popper and jars of Metamucil. Around her I felt my heft. I scorned her, which helped me hate myself less. When I got back to campus and saw Sarah, I felt like a fraud, that I'd claimed to be over eating in a way I was not but also, more urgently, that it had been a huge mistake to reveal myself. What the hell had I been thinking? I didn't want to be identified with this. I told Sarah I couldn't participate. In addition to schoolwork, I was working as a stringer for the magazine and also as a research assistant on a book. All this was true, but still. Sarah seemed annoyed and unsurprised—like, of course I would bail. I thought that to her I was probably still the dismissive, selfish girl she'd known as a freshman. I wanted to tell her that I wasn't that girl anymore, but that was a hard argument to make. After I withdrew, I felt the slightest sag but mainly relief. As if there had been a narrow miss.

Yet now I see this as the single moment of the whole story where things could have gone another way. I wish I'd put myself in proximity to Sarah and to a community of women with their own stories. I might have asked for help; I might have helped others, as well. I didn't. I did the same thing I'd done freshman year. I ran away while Sarah bravely told her own story and encouraged others to do the same. I grew paranoid about that application I'd submitted: Did that essay about my eating exist as part of my permanent record?

Maybe I was in no position to be a counselor on a help line. But, no, I reject this thinking, that someone must be recovered before she can offer wisdom.

FOR MOST OF SENIOR year, the behavior was unbudging—present but subdued.

I grew immersed in research for the senior essay I was writing about *Seventeen*. The magazine had come back into my life junior year, when I'd won a prize in its annual fiction contest. The roommate who delivered this message seemed bemused, and I under-stood that to her, and to others, the worth of the prize was questionable, but the list of previous winners meant something to me. Sylvia Plath had received this prize, and so had Lorrie Moore and Meg Wolitzer. I had not won first prize like they had. I had come in second, which was a distinction that mattered. But still! The fiction editor took me out to lunch and talked to me not as if he was trying to elicit what I wanted to do with my life but as if I was already doing it. (The story I'd written was called "Thanksgiving," and the protagonist was the college-age daughter of divorced parents who seemed like they might be getting back together. This was so far from my own truth that it might as well have been magical realism.)

Winning a prize in the contest made me curious about *Seventeen* again, and I bought an issue on the newsstand. Reading it, I did not have a flood of old feeling. This was a different decade with a different aesthetic. I had a distinct sense of the passage of time. But that passage made me think about what purpose the magazine had served over its history, and when I met with my senior-essay adviser, I said, "It's the fifty-year anniversary of *Seventeen* this year. I think I want to write a history of the magazine."

"I love that idea," he said.

Almost as soon as I started working on the essay, the story of the magazine led me to another story, one about the invention of the teenage girl herself. When I met with my adviser, we'd talk about what was emerging: how in the 1940s, *Seventeen* had been instru-mental in establishing the teenage girl as a cultural type—a capstone to what had been brewing since the turn of the century. I was doing real history, the kind that hadn't been written down anywhere yet, reading primary documents and making connections. I loved it: traveling to a women's library to read the papers of a department-store buyer; scrolling through microfilm at a large, humming ma-chine; visiting *Seventeen*'s offices at 850 Third Avenue, an address I still knew by heart.

I worked on the essay my whole senior year and finished it after an April all-nighter. I called it "Plaid Happy, Jive Jumper, and Soda Fountain Sally: The Invention of the Teenage Girl."

The essay didn't cover my own adolescence. It ended just after World War II. There was not a single I-sentence or little first-person riff about what the magazine had meant to me. The history was what mattered—and so, it turned out, was the experience of doing it. It showed me one thing that being an adult meant. You were no longer limited to observing the world: Now you could join it. Instead of just being a fan of things you loved, you could get inside them. You could make them yourself. I was thrilled to know this. I was twenty-one years old and I was going to move to New York, get a job at a magazine, and become a writer.

BY GRADUATION, I'D LOST a lot of weight. (A metric: I'd put on half my body weight, and I'd lost half of that half.) I honestly didn't really think about how much I weighed. I mean, yes, as always, I was aware of the number, but what the number signified was not a physical transformation but the dissipation of the behavior that had wrecked and shamed me.

Then that summer Mike and I went to Europe with his best friend from high school, Todd. We had Eurail Passes and *Let's Go* guides, and more than once we crossed paths with people we knew. At a nightclub in Spain, we ran into a girl Mike had grown up with in Philadelphia. Serena was delicate and narrow-boned. After we left the disco, Todd had a lot of questions about her. Walking through the late, hot night, across wide stone plazas, I got quiet. Todd's interest in Serena resurrected something dormant. Hey, wait! *I* wanted to be someone who provoked interest that way.

Todd may not have been responding to Serena's thinness, but you can bet that was the aspect of her appearance that I focused on. For the rest of the trip, I drank Evian all day. I would have only a sip of the orxata; just a heel of bread dipped in fondue; one triangle of Toblerone. When we came back and I moved to New York City, my legs looked different, athletic instead of hefty. Serena no longer mattered, but that encounter with her had been an initial spark. It had been so long since size mattered, because it had been so long since I was anywhere near a size I wanted to be. But for the first time in a while, thinness was within reach, and I added it to my list of things that adulthood promised, corrupting a vision that up until now had been so healthy.

THE MAGAZINE I WANTED to work at was the general-interest monthly where I'd interned, which published literary journalism and personal essays and fiction. Now I haunted its offices, doing freelance work, trying to make myself indispensable. When I was at home in my studio apartment, the magazine was the primary subject of my fantasies. I would write EDITORIAL ASSISTANT in letters that mimicked the house font, Goudy Old Style, and then my name underneath, willing myself onto the masthead.

Getting a job there was my total focus. There was no other place I wanted to work; nothing else would satisfy. I was scared I would fall apart without this. But then I was hired, and—oh, the joy! Each morning the elevator doors opened like curtains onto the eleventh floor.

But if I had known exactly how to audition for the part, almost immediately I found it harder to perform. I wasn't exactly sure who to be. I was the youngest staffer, also the least articulate. I was so nervous in editorial meetings that I rarely spoke.

And so I went back to what I did when I was uncertain: I played a role. I couldn't play a teenage girl, but I could play a woman who had recently been a teenage girl. This is a type: the young woman who retains, and then exploits, an affinity for adolescence. To me this choice seemed advantageous. It drew attention to what I believed were my desirable qualities: my energy, my precocity. But what other role could I have played? By now teenage girl was my default. She was a character I hadn't nailed yet, a persona I was still trying to get right. At twenty-two I was finally going to master her.

Clueless was in the theaters and then on pay-per-view. I watched it all the time and talked about how Amy Heckerling was a genius. I wore tiny clothes, because I was thin again. Not underweight— not yet. But thin enough that I fit into children's clothing, which was helpful, because it was cheaper. At Gap Kids, I bought a flannel mini; at a store that sold school uniforms, a plaid skirt.

Staying in character wasn't hard, but it was limiting. It prevented me from addressing whatever I was so scared of: making an argument, or articulating a response. Or facing up to who I was, or all that I wasn't. Instead, I loved it when people would say things like, "How old are you? You look sixteen."

This affinity for youth was my advantage; but it was also odd, this off-note of damage.

ONE EARLY MORNING BEFORE work, when I could stand the wait no longer, I went out to the twenty-four-hour drugstore and bought a pregnancy test. By now it was the summer of 1996 and I was one year out of college. Back up in my studio apartment, the stick showed the line, not the plus, meaning I was not pregnant. I was so relieved, both that I wouldn't have to get an abortion and that I'd be able to have breakfast. If the test had been positive, I would not have deserved to eat. I looked at the stick again, then threw it in the trash.

Mike lived several hours away, in Williamstown, Massachusetts. I had imagined needing to call him, waking him up in his Victorian-house sublet. Now I would let him sleep.

My apartment was dim, but I did not open the blind. I lived across from a YMCA; a row of exercise-bike riders stared straight into my window, and right now I didn't want to be seen. I wanted to be alone with this new information, absorb what the test meant. Not only that I wasn't pregnant but that the reason I hadn't gotten my period for two months was that I was too thin to menstruate. There was a nervous thrill then, a contraction of delight. And also unease, because I knew I wasn't supposed to want this. I hadn't been trying for it. But I could not deny how wonderful it felt. To have shrunk this much. To have started over again, finally gotten all the way back to zero. This systems shutdown was an objective measure of my success.

I'D ALREADY FELT PRETTY happy with my life, but now I was at a new level. Now there were no dips, it was all trapeze, all bursting out into the air and soaring. I loved not having my period. Oh, the ease of moving through the world the same each day with no adjusting. And no discharge, because I was not ovulating. Into the machines in the basement of my apartment building I tossed underwear with pure-white crotches.

I was on some kind of extreme rewind. I was the preteen girl I had never actually been: clear-skinned, flat-chested, buoyant. Rise at dawn, run; walk to work, work; after work, drinks. "Susan can drink!" my colleagues would comment. I could drink, it was true. And it didn't seem to slow me down. Nights I didn't go out, I stayed at the office (I hated being home before ten). I studied the styles of various editors. One composed entire new paragraphs in the margins of the galleys; was it his voice or the writer's? The copy editor, by contrast, seemed to disappear on the page, making the sentences their platonic ideal without getting in the writer's way. I also studied *The New York Times.* I read every word of any given article, training myself to look for the detail that told what the story really was or that suggested a new window into it. I read stacks of books: galleys from the shelf by the mailroom; discounted copies from the Strand; the nineteenth-century William Dean Howells novel revered by our distinguished editor in chief. I stayed up all night with Mary Karr's *The Liars' Club,* brand-new then. Heavy, I'd never wanted to stay awake, extend. Heavy, I'd wanted to burrow into bed and await the next day, the new chance, drag myself out and determinedly emerge again. Now there was nothing to hide from. I could live in all time. Oh, that *Liars' Club* night! Awake in my first apartment with this extraordinary book. At five A.M., finishing, and so exhilarated by the writing that I wanted to be out in the street. On the still-dark sidewalk I felt fiercely alive but also faint. So faint that it made me a little nervous. But only a little. I walked to the one coffee place open early, transported and weak.

One evening, after drinks with co-workers at the polished wood bar that was like our office clubhouse, I walked uptown toward my building in the lovely, hectic, city dark and thought: *My life is just how I want it.* For an instant, there was nothing I would change.

ANOREXIA (SOMETIMES I WOULD permit myself to use this word): It was like pressing Command Z over and over again—undo, undo—until the document was entirely blank. That's what I felt like, all possibility. I was young in New York City and everything was ahead.

Of course, in writing, the blank document represents paralysis. And I wasn't writing, really, except sometimes in my journal. Also, I kept trying to start an essay that began with this sentence: *Even though I am twenty-two years old, I still have fantasies about becoming a child star.*

But it was okay that before the keyboard I was stunted, because I was thin. Thin, I was never derailed. Nothing destroyed me. My life was orderly, and there was no waste. *But I was writing before, and now I am not. So my brain is suffering, yes?* Sometimes such thoughts would surface. I pushed them down. I blamed not writing on the demands of my job. (Which was bullshit. I was too hungry to write and also too clenched. Everything tight and bottled up. The earlier, wilder behavior had devastated me but also broken me open. In that stage I had written fluid sentences. Now I stuttered. Wrote phrases. Typed and erased and typed and erased. Undo, undo. Delete. Shut down. Are you sure? Yes.)

I EXISTED WITH LESS and less. Women's magazines had tips to offer if you wanted to lose weight. Tricks. When I picked one of these magazines up, waiting for a haircut or when taking a plane, I would feel both superior and mystified, reading a list of foods that made you "feel full." As if full was a desirable sensation! The whole point was that I hated feeling full. The whole point was to be empty. "Stave off the hunger": Why? Hunger was what I sought, my steady state. Full was what terrified me.

Multiple times a day I repeated this mantra: *Hunger will set you free.*

Hunger, that was my trick. There was no gum-chewing or fizzy water or fiber. That was the whole thing of my anorexia: Just don't eat.

I was empty. Being empty meant I was always ready, always prepared. Empty for exercise, empty in case of an emergency. I was always ready for surgery, ready to go under, ready for general. Empty enough to go out at night and have room for a Frosty, even though that was not a thing I would ever eat.

Alcoholics had to quit drinking to right themselves. I had to quit food.

I didn't see the illogic of this; I didn't see the peril. I had restored order, and I devoted myself to maintaining it. If the purge that follows a binge is a kind of ritual purification, anorexia was mine. I wouldn't get my period again for another year and a half.

ONCE A MONTH I would buy the new *Gourmet* and *Food & Wine* from a newsstand on Seventh Avenue, then walk a crosstown block to the takeout place I trusted. I'd return to my apartment, and when everything was laid out just right—steaming soup, brown bottle of beer—I'd open a magazine. I read slowly, every word. What I felt was not arousal, but it was on that order. It was so potent that it felt deviant. And it wasn't instead of eating: It enhanced the pleasure to read about food alongside food, the little food that I ate. Maybe the images tricked my starving brain into thinking it was being nourished; maybe the acquisition of the magazines was a kind of "food foraging" undertaken during deprivation. What I knew then was that the experience felt as private as the bingeing. Except you came away exhilarated, still the same size, no crime committed.

I did not see that I was fantasizing about actually satisfying my desires, because I was committed to the opposite. Anorexia protected desire by ensuring it would never be met.

At night in bed, my desire was directed toward the morning, when I could eat. Vanilla yogurt, a spoonful of something sweet. Imagining what I'd have in the morning helped me go to sleep hungry. Overnight I needed to get smaller. To wake up with food still in me—I did not deserve anything then. My stomach was the first thing I checked each day upon waking, whether it was flat or out or in. After that assessment I'd have a careful breakfast. Then I'd eat as little as possible until dinner. Each day I traversed an open prairie sheared of obstacles and threats.

I'd think all day about what I would eat, and then I would sit down to food and think about what I wouldn't eat of it.

28

THE ACCIDENT

ONE MORNING AS I walked to work, a bike messenger ran a red light and hit me in a crosswalk. I blacked out and when I came to, I was lying on Sixth Avenue, a group of bystanders looking down at me. I didn't know how I'd gotten there or what month it was. My memory came back within hours, but they kept me on the neurological ward at St. Vincent's for two nights to be safe. Also, I'd broken my collarbone.

The manager of my office suggested that I take a week off: "After a concussion, sometimes you can be a little addled."

But the idea of being addled worried me, and almost instantly I wished I'd said no to the week off. I wanted to be in the office to prove, if only to myself, that I was alert and oriented. Instead, I was home alone in my tenth-floor studio. It was August and hot. I opened the old casement windows, which beat like butterfly wings against the brick.

Because my collarbone was broken, I couldn't lift my arm over my head to put on shirts. My mother FedExed me blouses with buttons. They were her own blouses and they smelled like her floral perfume. In them I felt sophisticated but also withered, because they were too big.

In the midst of that empty week, I had a visitor.

"Yes?" I said into the plastic grate over the buzzer.

"Your father is here," announced the doorman, Gene, and I swelled with pride that sleepy Gene had seen my handsome father.

Though my building had a doorman, it was not fancy. The taps spat brown water; there were bugs. I lived there because they would rent to anyone, even without a tri-state guarantor. There were a lot of Japanese kids with pink hair, studying at the Fashion Institute.

A few minutes later, the bell rang. My father stood in the fluorescent-lit hall. He was wearing a suit and a red-and-navy-striped tie. Since graduation, I'd seen him frequently. He had regular business in Stamford, and he'd take the train to Grand Central and we'd meet for dinner.

Once, over a drink at the polished wood bar, the magazine's silver-haired editor in chief had asked if I was close to my father. He had children my age and sometimes he used me as a metric. I said, "Yes," definitively, meaning it.

I did feel close to my father. I was like him in ways that were easy to tick off on a list: both American Studies majors; both runners; both savers. We were also alike in ways that were more subterranean. We seemed like we fit in, looked like we fit in, but we didn't. We had trouble staying, belonging. We had . . . well, fits, of different natures, and removed ourselves. (Now, years later, I see in my bingeing echoes of my father's anger and impulsiveness; in my anorexia, his need for discipline; and in both of them, an attraction to compulsion and self-punishment.)

My father stood in the center of my studio apartment. It felt small with him inside. I was newly aware that my TV and boombox were on the floor instead of atop furniture. He hung his suit jacket over the back of a flimsy, glossy, plastic folding chair. I sat on the edge of the futon. I felt a wave of gratitude that a parent was checking on me. I hadn't realized I'd wanted this. I imagined him calling my mother and giving a report, even though they would never voluntarily get on the phone and speak.

The anger I'd felt at my father early in college had dissipated. I was back to empathy. After writing the short story about the weekend he'd left me alone, I'd gone back and, for another class, written an alternate version of the same story, this one from his point of view. In my story, he was a typical Raymond Carver protagonist—inarticulate, regretful, impulsive—but also recognizably Robert Mason Burton.

"Just one room," my father marveled. We'd always met at restaurants and he'd never been inside my apartment.

I'd always thought of my parents as knowing the most about the East, the most about New York, but I'd become the one who was the expert on the city, I realized now, as my father peered into the tiny dark closet that made the kitchen.

He walked over to the open casement window. On the old brick building across the street, a stack of letters like giant alphabet blocks spelled YMCA.

"That's *the* YMCA," I told him. "The one in the song."

We stared out at the exercise-bike riders. Some of them were lazy. Others furiously pedaled with their heads down, then jerked up, exhaled, and bent forward again. Down, up, down, up, down again.

Then my father turned to me and said, "You know, it's good to be thin, but not too thin."

I looked down at the little pearlescent buttons on the front of the blouse my mother had sent.

"I know," I said.

But my heart was racing. My father had never said anything about my weight. How to respond to him? If my mother had called me out on my thinness, I would have flared in anger. This very thing had happened only weeks earlier. She was now dating a man who lived in Manhattan, and on a visit we had gone shopping. In a tiny department-store dressing room, she had seen the bones in my back.

"Susan, you're too thin," she'd said. I had been angry—she was ruining the shopping; or had this been the point of the excursion, a trick to get me to disrobe so that I could be inspected? I would not fall for it. Instead, I had looked baldly at what I perceived as her dimpled, heavy legs, her sagging arms. My gaze saying what I did not: She in her elephantine body could not touch me. My visible bones were an exoskeleton that made me impenetrable.

But now, here in my apartment, my father's words found a way in. There was some part of me that heard him and thought, *He is right.* But I didn't want him to be right, and by later that night, unbuttoning my mother's blouse and stepping feetfirst into a nightgown, I had filed my father's comment in *bike accident and related materials.* He wasn't really worried that I was thin; he was just worried because I'd been in an accident.

In the morning my father had a few hours before he had to return to Stamford. We walked down West 23rd Street, and from a sidewalk vendor he bought an old coin. "I will always remember buying this coin with you," he said, and I felt so glad that I'd been able to take days off from work and be with him. Whenever I walk on that block now, I see us under the white sky of that August morning and I think, *This is where my father bought the coin.* It is like a memory we own together. I have the tails side of it, and he the heads.

AFTER MY FATHER LEFT, I still had time to kill before I was scheduled to return to work. Outside alone, I felt tentative. When people neared me on sidewalks, I seized up, protective of my injury.

I started to make notes on the accident for a personal essay. But I didn't finish the essay, like I didn't finish anything, because I wrote the same three sentences again and again, making them hard, polished, and senseless. Also, I didn't know what the point of the essay would be. *Initiation into the city,* I noted, but that felt dull and straining. As always, the real meaning of the accident lay in things I would not say.

———

I'D BROKEN THE COLLARBONE, the clavicle, one of the most commonly broken bones in the human body. So breaking a bone had nothing to do with being anorexic. Right? Part of me worried that my bones were crumbling. Yet another part of me liked the idea that I had turned fragile. Like the cessation of menstruation, weakened bones were hard evidence of achievement. More physical proof, ticking off symptoms listed in the textbook.

Still, after the accident, anything milk-based I ate was promoted to myself as "building bone," like I was a member of the dairy lobby. I imagined frozen yogurt going straight into the marrow. The brand of vanilla frozen yogurt I liked best had a plastic safety seal over the top. Sometimes it stuck so hard it was difficult to peel off. I loved that it was affixed so securely.

My fears of contamination were back. This was comfortable, a return to first principles. But as a child my fears had not been so literal. These days I would clip things from newspapers, a wire story about a recall of Minute Maid fruit punch tainted by cleaning fluid. That went onto my bulletin board at work, along with a magazine photograph of Japanese children wearing surgical masks in their school cafeteria. I wanted to be in that cafeteria. Once, when I got sick, I knew—knew!—it was because the cashier at the grocery across the street from the office had gripped the head of my spoon between her fingers.

One day at lunch I walked to my favorite café and bought a muffin. A few bites of muffin was a typical lunch. But this muffin was bran, or something with fiber. In the office all afternoon it felt like the muffin was up to my neck. It felt like a stopper. I was supposed to go to a play with a friend that night, but I didn't. I couldn't go out until the muffin was out. In my apartment, I lay on the futon under a Pendleton blanket. I wouldn't move until I was rid of this.

The curtain was closed to the YMCA cyclists. I squinted over a book in the light from the cheap halogen lamp. I'd wanted to return to the world, but I'd shut myself in again. Not eating was supposed to release me, but it hadn't.

Not eating was the same as binge eating: Both made food the primary determinant of feeling; both ways, I was controlled by it. Hunger was no different from excess. But if you'd tried this interpretation out on me then, it would have sounded like the biggest made-up bullshit.

I remember that night as a shift. Not a transformation, which would have meant both recognizing that anorexia was as limiting as bingeing and vowing to do something about it. My solution was deprivation. My solution was to never eat one of those muffins again.

For hours I stayed on the futon under that blanket. It was like waiting for rocks to dissolve.

A FALL MORNING. THE office manager touched my hip bone through my flannel mini and said, "Are you okay?"

The weirdness of that touch—she was British, did that explain it? But also my pride. Nobody else's hip bones were visible through their skirt.

I felt limber, agile, even though I was inflexible in every way.

29

THE END OF SOMETHING

M IKE GOT A JOB in book publishing and moved to the city. In the weeks before he came, it felt like a dream coming true. Now I had the job I loved and the person, too. But once he arrived, I understood that his presence would also be stifling, because I was so reliant on my rituals.

At a rooftop party one night, a friend pulled Mike aside.

"Eli said his girlfriend was anorexic," Mike told me the next morning.

I ignored the implication.

"His new girlfriend?"

"No," Mike said. "One earlier."

"I'm not anorexic," I said. "Not like a girl in *People* magazine." What I meant was that I didn't belong in a sensationalist cover story. I did not think I was in imminent danger. It was like high school: Only a handful of pounds, not dozens, separated me from menstruation. I identified with a woman on TV, Calista Flockhart, who played a young lawyer named Ally McBeal. Calista Flockhart was startlingly thin but—as I saw it—not direly emaciated. I didn't look at her and think, *That girl should not be walking around.* Every article ever written about Calista Flockhart asked whether she was anorexic, and though she said she wasn't, duh, yes, clearly she was, but in the same way as me. Anorexic, but not really. This was what I believed.

"Eli came up to me because he noticed you," Mike persisted. I felt uncomfortable. This was hard for him to talk about.

I knew that what Eli would have noticed wasn't just my size but my aspect. Clenched alone at the edge of the roof, both because I was freezing cold (always) and because every part of me was elsewhere.

Mike and I were sitting beside each other on the edge of his unmade bed. The bed was below a high window in his fifth-floor walk-up: on its scuffed floorboards were stacks of books, a fly rod in a long metal tube, a dove-colored bike. He'd bought the bike to make it easier to get to my apartment. Between Chelsea and the East Village there were no good trains. He was wearing boxers and a white T-shirt, but I was already dressed. As always I'd been awake for hours. I'd wandered through the littered streets, waiting for the café I trusted to open.

"You need to eat," Mike said. Then he set his coffee on the bedside table and stared into the corner where his odd-shaped apartment narrowed to a point.

"Okay," I said.

"Susan, I am really worried about you," he said.

This was not how a relationship between twentysomethings was supposed to work. I was like a child or an old woman, someone tantrumy or crotchety, someone clinging to systems, someone who pushes everyone away. Before this, sex had been a source of pleasure for us. But now I was indifferent. Sex was not something I needed anymore. Nothing thrilled me.

My focus was now on keeping the outside from getting in. It was the most interior state imaginable. I was not suited for a sexual relationship, or any other kind.

Mike stood, walked to the refrigerator, lifted the lid of his paper takeout cup, poured in half-and-half.

"You wanted cream?" I said.

Mike didn't answer.

DESPITE MY CONVICTION THAT I did not look like someone with a problem, strangers started to notice. Boys on the street: "Hey, white chick. Do you eat?" Girls on the street: "Excuse me, are you in ballet?" Collapsing in giggles. The endocrinologist, the flat out: "What do you eat?" I was there for a thyroid referral, but it was so clear to her I had another problem.

But doctors were strange in their responses. One suggested I eat tapioca pudding to gain weight. Did tapioca pudding even still exist? The endocrinologist asked for my typical daily menu, took notes, and then said, "Except for a little butter on your bagel, you're hardly getting any fat." As if it were that simple. As if by adding fat I would accumulate it. As if it were a single ingredient I was missing instead of thousands of calories.

My grandfather assumed the same thing. For Thanksgiving I flew down to Florida. In the small galley kitchen where five years earlier on freshman spring break I had been feral, grabbing fistfuls of oyster crackers and dense, frozen slices of key lime pie, I was serene and bony. He said he'd make me a grilled cheese but then slathered both sides of the bread with butter. I tensed up. He was doing this purposely. "Don't do that, Dave, she won't eat it," warned B.J. The sandwich was in the pan, sizzling, my grandfather standing over it. Emboldened, I echoed, "I won't eat it."

My grandfather was just worried about me, just trying to help. Now I feel sadness about rejecting that sandwich. But that afternoon I felt such relief in being back to who I'd been in my family, Susan who did not like foods, who would not eat.

I saw Sheva, from college, on a visit to New York (she was now living in California). It was a party on a raw, sleeting night. What had I been doing before this, she asked. I'd gone running. Her mouth screwed up. "Why would a person go running in this weather?" And then later, after drinking: "I guess I just have to accept that this is the way you look now."

But this was the way I'd always looked! The way I was meant to look. Just not when you knew me. Kasha was not me. *This* was me. At my essence. Controlled and thinnest.

Betsy, who'd seen me on a visit to our father's, sent an email to my mother that my mother forwarded to me. *I am really worried about Susan,* she wrote, and guessed at my weight.

I was not worried. I believed that someday there would be a study showing that not menstruating helped you live longer. I possessed information about the human body that others were not equipped to understand.

My theories were grandiose—which is one reason anorexia is so grave. It took me a disturbingly long time to recognize the seriousness of the illness. When, at thirty, I got pregnant, my new endocrinologist asked how long I'd gone without menstruating.

"A year and a half," I said.

"You're lucky, you know." She seemed angry. "You're really lucky you were even able to get pregnant."

"I know," I said, and got a little scared, that something bad could still happen.

"A lot of people can't after that."

Why was she belaboring it? If I'd told her about the bingeing, there would have been sympathy, maybe, or confusion about whether it was relevant, but not anger.

The bingeing was still so charged for me. Sometimes I felt as if my whole life had been lived in reaction to it. Anorexia, that hadn't been my principal problem! It existed only because of bingeing. Bingeing was the primary site, anorexia the metastasis.

I was wrong, of course, about all of this. Psychologically, anorexia and bingeing are equivalent; physiologically, they are radically different. Binge eating is nowhere near as risky as anorexia. For many, that story has the most final of all ends, and the endocrinologist was right: I am lucky.

———

THE SUMMER I WAS twenty-three—by this time, it had been a year since I'd menstruated—I went to Aspen during a week off from the magazine. The prop plane flew low over the rumpled peaks, then dropped fast into the narrow valley. I walked down the steps and across the tarmac to Marcie, who stood, disapproving, inside the terminal.

"I was hoping you wouldn't look like this anymore, but you still do," she said in the car. We'd gone through town, passing little Victorian bungalows and the Hotel Jerome, and now we were driving up the mountain where she and Robert lived. I looked out the window at the cottonwoods. I remembered this same drive, the summer after my senior year of high school, and telling Marcie, "I'm going to lose the freshman fifteen instead of gain them." The memory of the giant, scared girl I had been on that ride made me cringe. I thought, *I would rather be who I am now than who I was then.*

But my thoughts raised the ghost of the other girl. She was with us now in the car. Marcie seemed to see her, too. "You've always had trouble with food," she said.

I stayed still.

Marcie hadn't fallen for the story my body was telling, which was also the story I was telling myself, that the girl in college had been the anomaly. That the girl now was me and the other girl wasn't. Marcie alone saw that they were the same person. Or she was the only one who would say it.

We pulled up to the house. Usually I would have been exclaiming, "Everything looks so great, I'm so glad to be here," but as I opened the car door, I was silent. I had been exposed, which wasn't supposed to happen. Anorexia was an act of cleansing, but it was also a method of concealment. Encapsulating the secret, stowing it in an unlikely case.

———

WHILE I WAS IN Aspen, Marcie made me see her doctor for a bone-density scan. In those days, bone-density scans were new. I was worried it had chemicals. Even when there was nothing to swallow, no shot, I still didn't believe, lying on the table, that something wasn't getting in me.

Weeks later, back in my apartment, I opened the envelope from the doctor on West Main Street. *Susan has frank evidence of osteoporosis in her wrist and . . .* I folded the sheets and put them back inside the envelope. My heart was wild in me; there was something about that stern, objective sentence. I'd been putting frozen yogurt in my bones, yet they had holes in them.

At the same time, I still didn't trust the machine. There was no baseline measurement. Maybe my wrists had always looked like this. But even if I accepted the machine's conclusions—wasn't it worth it, to have holes in my bones, to be back to me? And for the first time, my answer to this question was uncertain.

The medical evaluation mattered. It spoke directly to my long-standing fears about my body—and undid most of my disturbing superiority about health. The conversation with Marcie mattered just as much. She had made a brutal and startling observation rather than an entreaty: *You've always had trouble with food.* (Later, she and my uncle Robert would be the ones to get my mother into rehab. They were doers, fixers, solvers, and Marcie especially said the things the rest of us avoided.) For the first time I saw that the anorexia was not a corrective to the bingeing but a substitution for it. It would be years before I knew what to do with this knowledge, but it did begin to settle in me.

But most of all I changed because of Mike. I loved him. I wanted to be the open and generous girl he'd fallen for, not the rigid mess. With him I had the intimacy I craved. He was the person I wanted to be with more than any other, and there was nothing more important than being that person for him.

Slowly, I started eating again. Half of the tortilla in foil that came with my takeout soup. The thick, hearty black bean soup instead of the thin, watery tomato corn. A cookie with lunch from the little sandwich place in Soho where everyone got lunch. A *sandwich* from the little sandwich place in Soho.

SIX MONTHS LATER, ON the last day to send packages for delivery by Christmas, I came up the steps of the post office shouldering gift-wrapped books in two heavy tote bags and waited in a snaking line. Outside again, unburdened, the bags now holding only tracking labels, I stood on the steps, surveying the wet gray streets. The post office was a grand structure, one fixed in the promise of another time. Block-long marble steps leading up to the Beaux Arts building, words carved around it like Latin on a college, except in sunny American English: NEITHER SNOW NOR RAIN NOR HEAT NOR GLOOM OF NIGHT . . .

And then I felt something. And I knew, just as I'd known on the beanbag in the classroom at ten.

The fullness, that old dull ache: I had my period again.

All romance deflated. The sensation shifted my focus, turned me away from the world and back in. That ache in my middle made me hate myself. What had I been eating, that it had come to this? Who had I become? It was a sign of unhappiness. If I were happy, I would not need to eat.

I wanted to get away from this. I was supposed to go to my office, but my strongest urge was to go home and change and go running. I walked down the steps and went to a drugstore to buy tampons. Here was another thing to deplete the budget.

A softer part of me recognized this as a sign of renewal. A mature part of me had sought this change. But I also had the feeling of being at the end of something. At the end of an era. At the end of refusal. At the end of *hunger will set you free.* At the end of shopping in the children's section, both proud and ashamed that I fit into size ten. At the end of being exceptional in an instantly legible way.

———

THE HARDEST MONTHS WERE the ones right after, feeling things again. Bodily sensations, like cramps and ovulating, but emotion, too. All the focus on eating, or not eating, had limited the variety of what I felt. I knew extreme emotions—euphoria, self-loathing—but I had less experience with moderate ones.

I remember in particular one completely ordinary afternoon, a Sunday in Brooklyn. Mike and I had just moved in together, to a top-floor brownstone apartment in Park Slope. It was small and pretty, with marble mantelpieces and an alcove for our bed. Through its back windows we could see the Twin Towers. A girl from my office was having a party and I did not want to go. My mood was silent/gray Sunday. Still, it would have been easy to get on the subway and deal; also easy to see her at the office on Monday and make an excuse. But I was in a torment. I sat in the dark middle room before the hard-candy-green Macintosh, clicking around. It was a simple feeling—I did not want to go to a party—but I didn't know how to handle it. I ascribed not wanting to go to having eaten too much bread at lunchtime. Though other reasons could have easily explained my reluctance—fatigue or social insecurity—I barely considered them, instead attributing the problem to my bad eating, as if that could be the only reason for any feeling. Food still determined the cadences of my days, and I could not yet conceive of experiencing emotion apart from it.

After the end of the most extreme bingeing, I'd felt gratitude. After the most severe anorexia ended, I was full of resentment. It was hard to accept that this was better. Everything in me went against it. A sense of failure persisted, and at times I was just as stony as I'd been at my thinnest.

Eventually the clock made the decision for me. Once it was officially too late to make it to the party, I could move forward again. Still at the computer, I opened my journal. Eating had been at the center of my existence since I was fifteen. Now I was twenty-four. In a Lois Duncan sci-fi novel I'd read as a young girl, the protagonist fell into a years-long coma and when she returned she had to catch up. I felt like I'd been in a coma, not to the culture but to myself. I'd disrupted the process of becoming.

Years would pass before I realized that the eating disorders hadn't delayed me; they'd defined me, and they continued to limit me, because I was still too ashamed to talk to anyone about them.

EPILOGUE
TELLING

IN MY EARLY THIRTIES, an acquaintance came up to me at a party and said she was gathering essays for an anorexia anthology. "And I'm trying to find people, just through word of mouth or mentions in their work, and I hope you won't take this the wrong way, but if you would be interested in writing something . . ."

"Sure," I said. "Sure, I'd love to."

I said yes because that's who I tried to be: smiling, agreeable, no problem, totally! But almost immediately I knew I would not do it. I didn't think I could write something smart enough. Or honest enough. My anorexia was no secret—people had seen it. But I couldn't tell that story without telling about the bingeing, and long ago I had locked that in as something I would never say. I'd sealed around that experience, and holding it in had become a condition of selfhood. I didn't reevaluate.

And then, unexpectedly, I did.

The first time I told the secret, I was thirty-six. It was to a woman I'd literally just met. She was a book editor. She'd heard a radio story I'd done, and we were talking about ideas for books I could write. We were in upholstered chairs in a coffee shop on a spring evening in the neighborhood where we both lived. I liked her; she was smart and warm and interested in me. I had a little list of ideas. Working through them, I said something vague about an eating disorder in my teens. She went straight for it: "Were you not eating, or were you eating and throwing up?"

And then, for some reason, I explained.

Afterward, I walked home along an avenue lined with prewar buildings and flowering trees. It was my own, safe street, a pretty pink night. But I felt dislocation and fear. Who was I, if I was no longer holding this in? What mattered, if not this secret I'd sworn to protect? Also, now I could clearly never work on a book with this woman. Even on the street I would have to pretend I didn't see her; there was no way I could ever be normal around her again.

In the weeks that followed, I held the secret tighter than ever. But now I had tested saying. And the result of the test was that I began to consider not only what the consequences of the eating had been but the price of the secret itself.

NEUROSCIENTISTS SAY THAT AGE twenty-four is the end of adolescence, as did that psychologist who basically invented adolescence as a life stage. (G. Stanley Hall, who loved the idea of life stages: His work also led to the development of gerontology.) His foundational rubric was age ten to twenty-four. These ages could seem arbitrary, yet for me they are symbolic. I got my period when I was ten and I got it again at twenty-four. The first time, I entered adolescence, and the second time, I left it. Adulthood started then. In the years that followed, I got married and had children. I got a new job—in radio, like my father. I watched my mother get sober, which is one of the most extraordinary transformations I have witnessed. I watched my father's moods steady and his relationship deepen with Donna. I watched Betsy become a mother. I watched my own children grow, and then one day the first child was a teenager himself.

Getting my period again at twenty-four marked the end of my

extremes. I've never been so rigid or powerless again. But this was the end of a chapter, not a real and final end. I'm healthier than I was as a young woman, but "recovered"? No. I want to be clear about where I am. It's not widely understood just how enduring eating disorders can be. For most of my adulthood I perceived my own problem as both intractable and illegitimate. And while I might have felt differently if more people talked about how tenacious this stuff is, what's more important is that I might have felt differently if I had ever talked about it.

"You wrote a whole book about this and you've never talked about it with anyone."

On a winter morning, I was in a psychoanalyst's office. "Yes" was the answer. The "whole book" wasn't a published book. It was a draft of this one.

What she'd said wasn't really a question but a restatement, one that underlined how deeply I'd remained both invested in and detached from my eating disorders. It was frightening, when she laid it out so plainly. I liked her immediately.

Four years earlier I'd made that visit to the psychiatrist during which I had not been able to get the words out. But in this room with J., I could. The difference was that I was ready now and that she was the right person.

IN THE YEARS SINCE my adolescence ended, I've gone through stages with food. For a while I thought of these stages as echoes of the disorders, but that was my own convenient fiction: These weren't mere traces of the disorders but continued manifestations of them. There was that dull low after my period returned. Then maybe a year of feeling things again; of taking the F train to work and looking out over industrial Brooklyn and experiencing a swell of joy; of being alive without being empty. At twenty-five I fell back into the bingeing. It was both better and worse this time: better because I was an adult with a job that prevented me from making rounds of food stores; worse because I was an adult with a job and the eating interfered with my work and my desire to do well at it. I could continue with every different iteration, but honestly it would read just like this, like a list, because what's happened in the years since is stuff I've barely begun to examine. I rebuilt bone after that grim scan in my twenties and am now in the normal range for a woman my age; sexual desire returned; I had healthy pregnancies. But I've also been consistently inflexible, paranoid, and self-loathing about food.

For most of the past two decades, I've lived just over the anorexia borderline. When I first took up residence here, I saw it as kind of a demilitarized zone: Here I could be thin enough to keep myself psychologically safe but healthy enough to protect myself from physical destruction. I now recognize this as a ludicrous treaty, one that I am trying to pull out of after years of entrenchment.

During all this time, I knew that my remaining "preoccupation" with food was not normal. I tried to fix it, and I couldn't. At the same time, I believed someday I would fix it and that fixing it would *fix everything,* would be the transformation that would lead to all other transformations, to wisdom, generosity, maturity. That's what I thought even through the writing of this book. That's what I thought until I met J.

One morning I was telling her the metaphor I had for the eating stuff, which was something from sound editing: The eating stuff was a track that ran in my brain under all the other tracks. Sometimes it would get so loud it would drown out all the other tracks; sometimes I could lower the volume, but I was never able to remove the track from the session. Deleting the track was the wrong idea, J. said; lowering the volume was good, but the main thing was to boost the other tracks. *Boost the other tracks.* Develop other strengths and ways to cope; raise the signal on all I'd neglected. This had seriously not occurred to me. In a way I was still in the same mode as I'd been when I thought I could fix the bingeing with anorexia, when I thought I could fix everything by being empty. But it wasn't subtraction that I needed; it was addition.

How would I raise the signal on the other tracks?

"Who's the engineer?" J. said. It was just the right question.

———

I USED TO FANTASIZE about telling as much as about "quitting." Yet as soon as I did stop bingeing, the telling fantasy went away and stayed dormant for a long time.

The book I originally set out to write, the one that would intertwine the story of my adolescence with a cultural history of teenage girlhood, seemed when I started it in my late thirties like one I'd been meant to write my whole life. It would even have shared a title with my senior essay, "The Invention of the Teenage Girl." The eating disorders would have occupied a chapter or two. They would have been contained in accordance with the most rigorous safety objectives. But then there were containment problems—a meltdown, release into the atmosphere—which was truer to my experience of the eating disorders and also truer to any story I could tell about my own invention.

This book is a confession, and in that sense it's the substance of a wish; but it also gives form to my fears that I'm telling too much or telling the wrong way. The prose is controlled, but the project feels dysregulated. It proceeds out of a conviction that the only way forward is extreme. I tell myself that I "had" to write about this, but no one ever "has" to write anything.

Writing was the coda to every binge. So this book itself is a symptom: a purge, a purification, a ritualistic act. As I wrote, I worried about finishing, which I eventually recognized as a symptom, too. Writing was a release but also a retreat. It was a way of not giving the illness up—of keeping it alive; of remaining alone with it; of not letting anyone in. Who would I be without this secret? I wondered. Without this thing that kept me separate? It was almost identical to the exchange I'd had with myself about the loss of bingeing. Twenty-seven years later, the exact same Q&A.

By writing this book, I've moved not from illness to recovery but from secrecy to telling. I am in a liminal stage. This is a vulnerable position to write from, because I know there's a lot I still can't see.

But it's an honest account written from where I am. Telling my story hasn't solved these problems, but it has set me on my way.

Right now, "telling" this story mostly means that I have laid it out on paper and told it to myself. I understand now that it was the step I had to take before telling it to another, and also that "telling" is not the right word for what I wanted. This isn't a message book, partly because I don't know that I have the authority to offer a message from where I sit, and that's not really my style anyway. But I will claim what authority I do have to say something I have learned to understand with J.: Eating disorders are so profoundly a coping mechanism for failures in human relationships that to get over one it's essential to strengthen the capacity to relate to another, which is a lot of what happens in therapy. Underneath my desire to tell was a desire to connect. Maybe the most important thing writing did was get me to start talking.

"FIX"–*FIX EVERYTHING, FIX MYSELF, fix my eating*—that's another word that feels odd to me now, too, with its implication of brokenness or damage.

How about "empty"?

Empty, what does that word evoke? Shall I free-associate? Hollow, bereft, going clear. Empty is vapid, zero, of no interest. Empty is absence. So different than the valence the word carried for me! Empty was promise. Empty was power. Empty was the ultimate security. Me the empty safe. Try me, spin the dial, every combination: You won't get in. Empty: Its meaning evolved. At first it just meant room. Room for a Frosty on a Saturday night in a Wagoneer. And maybe empty was the wrong word—an ill-considered, adolescent choice. But the unconscious choice matters. And the language stuck. I never thought of it as empty-headed. If anything, the reverse. I thought of it like the protagonist of Jean Stafford's *The Mountain Lion* thought of it. This is a mid-century coming-of-age novel about a girl in Boulder (!). Molly hates the word "body," and she wants to be "a long wooden box with a mind inside." I associated being empty with the life force, but a long wooden box is a coffin; Molly was more clear-eyed about where empty ends. But at the beginning, empty allowed me to take everything in. At the start, empty meant receptivity and only later meant rejection. Empty—for years I still loved it. I found hollowness extremely satisfying. Like a straw, something you could blow through. That was some of the most relief I could get in life, was being empty. That was a way I knew I could be open to sensation, when I was diminished, slim. And when I was: It was a gliding feeling. I could do a bridge; I could do a backbend. I could straddle you. I could leave for the airport and just get on a flight. There was no problem with anything. There was no reason not to get dressed. I recognize that I am still attached to the word; my impulse is to defend it. Emptiness is possibility. Empty is the moment before the future gets filled in. But it's a state of impoverishment, not sustenance, and my unwillingness to accept this has been my great mistake. Empty amounts to nothing. If I wasn't empty, then almost any other version was a failure. *Already ruined, already wrecked.* Writing about my eating disorders is in a way a renunciation of empty. A forsaking of empty; a salvo against it. Because I'll fill the blank white pages, I'll fill the emptiness in; and inevitably I will get it wrong, it will not be perfect, I'll feel somehow as if I've ruined it, as if I've wrecked it; and I will have to live with that. I will have to learn to live with something other than blankness and the possibility of a future in which everything is exactly right. I will have to learn that I can feel regret, disappointment, discomfort; that I can have those feelings, any feeling, and still be okay. And maybe, finally, I will learn to feel full.

J. SPECIALIZES IN EATING disorders and addictions. Initially I was reluctant to see a therapist with such a focus. It was one thing to recognize eating as the defining experience of my adolescence, but as a woman in my forties I hesitated to name it as the central aspect of my identity. And I understood that seeing such a specialist wouldn't necessarily make it so, but I also worried it would, kind of? The stories we tell about ourselves—whether for forty-five minutes at a stretch or over hundreds of pages—shape our self-inventions. What I have come to realize is that if an eating disorder is at the core of my identity, it's because I've allowed it to roost there. And that the purpose of therapy isn't to ratify this identity but to redefine it.

The story I am figuring out with J. differs from the one in these pages. I fear that I might look back at this book and think: *That's all wrong. Holy shit, that's so offensive! That's blind, naïve, strange. You only scratched the surface. You left the most important part out.* I mean, I *know* that will happen, and that knowledge is tormenting. But if you wait until you understand everything, you never say anything at all. You step down from the stage and spend the next thirty years wondering what would have happened if you'd revealed yourself. I am learning, gradually, to do so, both in the room with J. and elsewhere.

Those sensations I always craved, light, relieved, unburdened: These are associated with the telling of secrets. But I am finding more sustenance in other sensations: transparency, alertness, generosity, and an interest in what else might be possible.

For years I came up with excuses about why therapy wouldn't be right—e.g., I didn't want someone else's language. I didn't want a psychological vocabulary replacing the words I might find to understand my experience. But, also, the illness kept me from it. The same old story: It was a risk to let anything, or anyone, in. It might contaminate me. It might compromise my integrity. But what, after all, was really compromising my integrity? The illness I tried to contain in just the right prose remained in control of me.

I was still determined to go away and address this on my own without anyone knowing. I wanted to solve it in the notebook I wrote in by a little arched window and come down from the tower graceful and renewed. I wanted to finish what I'd started up on 7M. But now that I have finished this book, I see that I have not ended the story so much as claimed it.

FOR SO LONG I was scared to write about my eating disorders. Once I did, I imagined who might read what I wrote. I imagined adolescent girls who had eating disorders, also people I was close to, and scientists. But because it felt arrogant to imagine that what I wrote might offer solace to adolescent girls, and uncomfortable to imagine the people I was close to, I focused on the scientists.

Science! Yes, here was a way I could make something of this experience. Here was a way I could redeem the waste. So many articles I read said that binge eating was "poorly understood." Well, I could help them understand! Not because I was special but because I was typical. I could help them with their research. I knew it wasn't perfect, because they couldn't study me in the moment, but maybe they could interview me for a longitudinal study, an outcomes study; I had the data. I had mounds of it. Everyone with an eating disorder record-keeps. I have inventories of what I ate and charts of my weight, both historical and projected, and how much I exercised, down to the exact meters of my swims. I have real-time logs of the changes in my emotional state in the hours following a binge. Or I could help someone doing something more narrative. They could fit my experience into their matrix. I could add to or upend their theories.

So I hoped that scientists would find my writing. But I also hoped that they would find *me*. They would find me and say, We read your paper. A copy of it is with our panel for peer review. We have a good sense of your methods and your materials. But we noticed your discussion section never really arrives at a conclusion. A conclusion will be required for publication, but don't worry. We are scientists. We have already drafted a conclusion based on the evidence you provided. We think you will be pleased with our analysis. We think it will be the paragraph that makes sense of this for you.

ACKNOWLEDGMENTS

THIS BOOK IS MAINLY the product of memory, not of research, but like any book it is also the product of *reading*. In addition to the books and articles I mention in the text, there are other sources I do not cite, or to which I only vaguely allude:

In the prologue, the epidemiological context for BED comes from Tomoko Udo, a professor at the University at Albany's School of Public Health. She is the lead author of the most recent comprehensive study of the prevalence of eating disorders in the United States, "Prevalence and Correlates of DSM-5–Defined Eating Disorders in a Nationally Representative Sample of U.S. Adults," published in 2018 in *Biological Psychiatry*.

In "Artifacts," my ideas about middle age and evolving representations of our adolescent selves were stirred by Patricia Meyer Spacks's *The Adolescent Idea: Myths of Youth and the Adult Imagination*.

In "Secrets," I came across "unfit persons" in Peter Stoneley's *Consumerism and American Girls' Literature, 1860–1940*. Stoneley is citing G. Stanley Hall's *Adolescence,* published in 1904. Hall, in turn, seems to be nodding to Henry Maudsley's *The Pathology of Mind,* published in 1879.

Also in "Secrets," the history of the adolescent female body is *The Body Project: An Intimate History of American Girls,* by Joan Jacobs Brumberg.

In "The Obsession," the "exceptional girl" essay is "Carson McCullers and the Female Wunderkind," by Constance M. Perry, published in 1986 in *The Southern Literary Journal.*

In "7M," the anorexia memoir is *Solitaire,* by Aimee Liu, who is named later in the chapter. The anorexia history is Brumberg again: *Fasting Girls: The History of Anorexia Nervosa.*

In "Addiction," the 1991 *Psychological Bulletin* article that spoke to me is "Binge Eating as Escape from Self-Awareness," and its authors are Todd F. Heatherton and Roy F. Baumeister.

And now looping back, as one does, to "The Obsession": *The Obsession*—whose title I name in recounting my reading of it as a high school senior, but whose author I do not—is by Kim Chernin. I went back to Chernin's book only after I'd finished writing this one—had finished the manuscript, the epilogue, the copyedits, everything but these notes. I was stunned by the resonance of Chernin's foreword. She describes her position on the eve of her book's publication in a way that is uncannily similar to mine. I found myself in her words all over again, and I began highlighting, this time dragging my finger over a touchpad:

> I was then forty years old. Forty and obsessed with a strange suffering that had begun when I was seventeen; forty and by no means an expert in anything, although I had spent the previous twenty-some years trying to puzzle out the reasons for this preoccupation that at times took over my life and threatened to make everything else in it (marriage, motherhood, divorce, study, writing) irrelevant. Should I have solved the problem before I dared to write of it? Could the writing become part of the struggle for a solution?

The writing has become part of the solution for me, but only because of those who've supported me in it.

Hilary Redmon saw what I needed to write and encouraged me to do so, thereby transforming both story and teller. She is an ideal editor. Sarah Burnes is responsible for the invention of this book. She believed in it, and me, through almost a decade of iterations.

Many thanks also to Hilary Elkins, for checking facts; to my *This American Life* colleagues Julie Snyder—for assigning stories that laid the groundwork; for reading an early draft; and, most of all, for friendship—and Ira Glass, who's taught me so much of what I know about telling stories, and who gave me the time I needed to write this one; to Kendra Harpster and Andy Ward, who nurtured the book through its early childhood and adolescence; to the MacDowell Colony; and to J., who is helping me write the next chapter.

My sister, Betsy Goldin, moved me with her immediate support and understanding. My parents, Nancy Burton and Bob Burton, made me a reader and a writer. My mother introduced me to books that would become my touchstones: among them, *Anywhere But Here, This Boy's Life, The Liars' Club*. When she said, "Write anything you need to about me," she offered both freedom and security. Her grandmothering made it possible for me to finish. My aunt and uncle, Marcie and Robert Musser, are models of living without secrets.

Mike Agger: I love you and it is the great gift of my life that one morning in 1991 we sat across from each other in the dining hall, and now, in the next century, sit at our own table with Nick and Will. One evening as I was hunched at my desk, staring into my laptop, Will asked, "Mom, when will access to you be unlocked?" It was a funny and also profound question. I hope that what I have come to understand through the writing of this book makes me even more available to you, Will and Nick. (Just don't read it until you're older!)

ABOUT THE AUTHOR

Susan Burton is an editor of *This American Life*. Her stories have aired on that show, and she has written for the *New York Times Magazine, Slate, The New Yorker, New York* magazine, and others. She began her career as an editor at *Harper's*. The film *Unaccompanied Minors* is based on one of her radio essays. She lives in Brooklyn with her husband and their two sons.

ABOUT THE TYPE

This book was set in Granjon, a modern recutting of a typeface produced under the direction of George W. Jones (1860–1942), who based Granjon's design upon the letterforms of Claude Garamond (1480–1561). The name was given to the typeface as a tribute to the typographic designer Robert Granjon (1513–89).